DISABILITY, CULTU…

Alfredo J. Artiles and Elizabeth B. Kozleski, ***Series***

Transition by Design:
Improving Equity and Outcomes for Adolescents with Disabilities
AUDREY A. TRAINOR

After the "At-Risk" Label: Reorienting Educational Policy and Practice
KEFFRELYN D. BROWN

DisCrit—Disability Studies and Critical Race Theory in Education
DAVID J. CONNOR, BETH A. FERRI, & SUBINI A. ANNAMMA, EDS.

Closing the School Discipline Gap:
Equitable Remedies for Excessive Exclusion
DANIEL J. LOSEN, ED.

(Un)Learning Disability:
Recognizing and Changing Restrictive Views of Student Ability
ANNMARIE D. BAINES

Ability, Equity, and Culture:
Sustaining Inclusive Urban Education Reform
ELIZABETH B. KOZLESKI & KATHLEEN KING THORIUS, EDS.

Condition Critical—Key Principles for Equitable and Inclusive Education
DIANA LAWRENCE-BROWN & MARA SAPON-SHEVIN

Transition by Design

Improving Equity and Outcomes for Adolescents with Disabilities

Audrey A. Trainor

Foreword by David J. Connor

TEACHERS COLLEGE PRESS
TEACHERS COLLEGE | COLUMBIA UNIVERSITY
NEW YORK AND LONDON

Published by Teachers College Press, 1234 Amsterdam Avenue, New York, NY 10027

Cover photo by Mo Elnad / Getty Images

Library of Congress Cataloging-in-Publication Data is available at loc.gov

ISBN 978-0-8077-5840-3 (paper)
ISBN 978-0-8077-5841-0 (hardcover)
ISBN 978-0-8077-7576-9 (ebook)

Printed on acid-free paper
Manufactured in the United States of America

24 23 22 21 20 19 18 17 8 7 6 5 4 3 2 1

Contents

Foreword

Twenty-five years ago, as a high school teacher in New York City, I was designated to be the transitional linkage coordinator (TLC) in the department of special education. This position translated to reassigned time from teaching one self-contained class in order to organize ways in which the entire department could best prepare students labeled with various disabilities for life after high school. The role was presented to me as an institutional response to the challenge of better helping students with disabilities succeed in the world at large. I endeavored to educate my colleagues of the need to meet their student advisees, provide various interest inventories, draft plans based upon student desires, and make sure that required areas were documented within their Individualized Education Plans (IEPs). In addition, I attended monthly meetings at the regional Superintendent's Office where we were provided updates, ideas, and information to help us facilitate visits with students to potential employers such as retailers. Students were also provided with information about the state agency charged with helping them find employment. However, despite my efforts to have them register with the state agency, students resisted vigorously, because they did not wish to explicitly acknowledge (or arguably, accept?) their status as disabled citizens. Ironically, although self-determination was a central component of their IEP Transition Plans, I had not foreseen that it would be enacted this way. That said, I could see students' points of view, a desire to shed a disability label bestowed upon them by our educational system. At the same time, I was aware that 12th-grade self-contained classes had half the number of students as 9th-grade classes. It struck me that the very structure of high school itself created a sifting process wherein students self-elected to leave or were forced out, depending on how one perceives the situation. I was equally troubled by the lack of options for those who had "dropped out" of school, along with those who would graduate.

In my next position as a professional development specialist within the Office of the Superintendent of Manhattan High Schools, I collaborated with a colleague who served to coordinate all TLCs in forty schools. Although she was well intentioned, I felt her vision of transition to be simplistic, resting on unquestioned middle-class values that caused cultural conflicts pertaining to "work readiness." I recall one occasion when she coordinated a transition-focused conference for high school students at the prestigious Metropolitan

Museum of Art. My colleague had provided instructions to all teachers that their students had to dress as if they were attending job interviews, including the need for all males to wear a tie. There would be no exceptions. I remember being at the registration area and seeing a teacher arrive with a dozen or so students, including some males who did not wear a tie. My colleague grew angry, noticeable by her flushed face and stern tone of voice. She would not let the tie-less students enter. In return, the teacher's response was elegantly restrained anger, realizing her efforts to bring students were in vain. I found myself analyzing what I had witnessed in terms of a racial and social class. Over a lack of a few ties, a white, middle class authority figure denied an African-American teacher and her entire class of all African-American and Latino students access to information about options for their futures because they did not wear an item of clothing symbolic of white collar work. I realized the intended lesson that was supposed to be learned ("dress for the part"), but what of unintentional lessons learned? My heart went out to the teacher who had mobilized her students to be on time and travel across town together for the event, only to find an inflexible situation. Likewise, I wondered about students who may not have had access to a tie for a number of legitimate reasons or simply felt very uncomfortable–physically or psychologically–wearing one. The incident has always stayed with me, an example of clashing cultural values and students losing out.

Fast forward to more recent times when I have been working with Dr. Wendy Cavendish at the University of Miami in researching how three urban high schools prepare students for their transition to post-school possibilities. Although the focus is on Transition, now a long-established staple of the special education landscape, our findings have been noticeably mixed, ranging from educators providing little preparation for students in regard to planning their own futures (Cavendish & Connor, in press) to teachers who create rigorous student-centered plans grounded in self-advocacy (Cavendish, Connor, & Rediker, 2016).

When reading this book, these and other memories–both old and new–bubbled to the surface of my thoughts. Transition is a worthwhile if challenging concept, a legally mandated component of planning that seeks to organize and operationalize services, while simultaneously engaging students as individuals. It is often understood in schools primarily in terms of compliance, and is summarily executed in a pro-forma manner. However, Transition encompasses a constellation of areas that constitute a life experience including self-determination realized through employment, leisure, community integration, housing, and so on. The experiences related to these areas are deeply humanizing, all forged via social interactions, with the quality of them contingent upon the context of the community. As Artiles (2003) has argued, culture is central to our understanding of any phenomena within education, including special education, as culture is inextricably linked to the racialization of ability (Artiles, 2011).

In many ways, *Transition by Design* is a long overdue book. Emphasizing culture, diversity, and equity within special education's sub-field of Transition, Audrey Trainor calls attention to ways in which the field must broaden its current limited approaches to how the Transition process is conceptualized and operationalized–so it is actualized within diverse cultural contexts, with the intent to help students ground themselves in who they currently are and how they envision their future. In foregrounding intersectional issues of race, ethnicity, dis/ability, social class, and gender (along with other markers of identity), Trainor considers histories, contexts, processes, and procedures that either enable or disable students in their quest to complete high school and forge a strong sense of direction in their young adult lives and beyond. With great care Trainor foregrounds the actual contexts from which students must learn to transition, to those into which they aspire, illuminating the limitations of traditional research in its sometimes willful neglect of social, cultural, and historical considerations. As we come to see, special education's failure to contextualize Transition as a larger cultural practice has resulted in its continued narrow perception of what actually constitutes disability, the proliferation of deficit-based paradigms of human difference, misplaced overemphasis on "scientifically proven" interventions, and holistically speaking, a lack of explicit focus on social and emotional wellbeing of students.

This book respectfully challenges the field of special education for its noticeable failure to contextualize culture and community within the overwhelming majority of existing transition studies. Trainor does this by deftly analyzing social processes that create reality–informed by sociocultural framings culled from Bourdieu (1986), Bronfenbrenner (1979), Rogoff (2003), and Cole (2010)–highlighting ways in which the Transition process can stunt or cultivate growth of students, depending upon an array of considerations and influences. Importantly, Trainor considers Transition in relation to pressing areas that have not been fully considered to date for its implications, including the School-to-Prison-Pipeline (STPP), self-determination and health care, inclusive post-school successes, and creating and sustaining equal opportunities for fulfilling adulthoods. By bringing this much-needed sociocultural lens, she provides a means by which familiar issues about Transition can be re-viewed and rethought in meaningful, *useful* ways for educators and the students that they serve.

It is by considering Trainor's astute observations and helpful suggestions that we can grow as advocates for changing both school practices and priorities in Transition research. As my own past and present experiences with Transition suggest, the time is ripe to carefully rethink ways in which we can better understand and support marginalized students who have historically struggled in schools. Considering culture and equity within Transition research and school-based practices is a crucial step in the right direction. This book will greatly help us along that path.

—David J. Connor

REFERENCES

Artiles, A. J. (2003). Special education's changing identity: Paradoxes and dilemmas in views of culture and space. *Harvard Educational Review, 73,* 164–247.

Artiles, A. J. (2011). Toward an interdisciplinary understanding of educational equity and difference: The case of racialization of ability. *Educational Researcher, 40,* 431–445.

Bourdieu, P. (1986). The forms of capital. In J. G. Richardson (Ed.), *Handbook of theory and research for the sociology of education* (pp. 241–258). New York: Greenwood Press.

Bronfenbrenner, U. (1979). *The ecology of human development: Experiments by nature and design.* Cambridge, MA: Harvard University Press.

Cavendish, W., Connor, D. J., & Rediker, E. (2016). Strategies for engaging students and parents in transition focused IEPs. *Intervention in School & Clinic.* DOI: 10.1177/1053451216659469

Cavendish, W. & Connor, D. J. (2017). Toward authentic IEPs and transition plans: Student, parent, and teacher perspectives. *Learning Disability Quarterly.*

Cole, M. (2010). What's culture got to do with it? Educational research as a necessarily interdisciplinary enterprise. *Educational Researcher, 39*(6), 461–470.

Rogoff, B. (2003). *The cultural nature of human development.* New York, NY: Oxford University Press.

Acknowledgments

I dedicate this book in gratitude to all the people of color, people with disabilities, and those marginalized in any way who have generously and patiently guided and educated me. They pulled back the curtain, letting the light shine through to expose some of the most beautiful rays of diversity in all its dimensions, and some of the most insidious and detrimental affronts to equity. As a White person without a disability, the learning curve has been steep at times. My friends, colleagues, and mentors have pushed me forward and pulled me up when I have fallen, leaving me with a library of personal experiences that is as informative and impactful as the scholarship I consume and store in my desktop database. I also dedicate this book to family and friends whose privileges are similar to mine, but who are willing to accompany me in a search for equity, not just in education, but in all aspects of our everyday lives.

Chapter One

Two Constants in a Sea of Change

Improving Outcomes and Increasing Equity

The transition from adolescence to adulthood is a period of time pregnant with paradoxes. It can be both a time of joyful learning and excitement, and a time of painful lessons that may have powerful consequences. It can be a time full of hope and a time when dreams seem out of reach. It can be a time when the possibilities are promising and endless, and one of overwhelming choices that dauntingly demand decisions. For adolescents, transitioning to adulthood is a time for acquiring freedom and responsibility in the very same breath, and for learning how to balance these unwieldy conjoined twins. For the adults who are chaperoning, coaching, mentoring, teaching, and guiding adolescents, gifting a young person with freedom and responsibility may also be rife with contradictions. Adults may not be ready to part with the gift, wanting more time to coach and be needed. Adults may also feel as though they are foisting the gift on an unsuspecting, unenthusiastic recipient. Processes, rather than discrete points in time, mark the landscape of transition, bringing to mind a phrase often attributed to American poet Ralph Waldo Emerson, "Life is a journey, not a destination." In the context of diversity–of perceived and actual abilities; of the lived experiences of racial and ethnic groups; of languages; of homes, schools, and communities; of the continuum of sex and gender identity; of socioeconomic background and status; of religion or the absence thereof; and so forth–precious few universal truths exist, except, perhaps, these two: transition is messy with paradoxes, and it is a process of continuous action and, thus, effort.

On one hand, a universal truth can be attractive, especially when one is treading unfamiliar waters (as is the case when transitioning to the future, whatever that might represent). It might be comforting for adults in the lives of children with disabilities, or for individuals with disabilities themselves, to think that all adolescents are gradually moving toward adulthood and facing the same life choices. Planning for the future means that unknowns abound, regardless of disability labels and identities. On the other hand, "universal truths" can be elusive and even false. Individuals with disabilities and their families may develop a different pace or path than their peers without disabilities, ringing truth to them and others who experience disability. Similarly, our many identities wax and wane as we make choices and decisions; some trajectories into the future may prove to have kernels of universal truths while simultaneously separating us from our local or immediate in-group experiences. The landscape of our social, political, cultural and even geographical lives is also ever-shifting. A decision to marry seems normative enough, particularly given the 2015 U.S. Supreme Court decision upholding marriage rights for same-sex couples, but a decision to marry between two consenting individuals with intellectual disabilities may introduce additional unknowns and/or elicit biases and opinions about disability, independence, parenting, and so on.

DISABILITY, DIVERSITY, AND EQUITY IN THE TRANSITION TO ADULTHOOD

Diversity is not solely about pattern and variation. Normed experiences and expectations are, by definition, dominant and instantiated with power. Future planning itself, particularly as envisioned in the Individuals with Disabilities Education Improvement Act (IDEA; 2004), is a construct that employs Western notions of will and control over fate and destiny, and American ideals of individualism and choice (Kalyanpur & Harry, 1999). The metaphor of a journey is both staid and prominent in special education transition. Students with disabilities are on a "journey toward achieving their academic and career goals" (Stein, 2012, p. 175) and are pursuing "personal journeys" to "achieve their dreams" (Schuh, Sundar, & Hanger, 2015, p. 154), and "individual student journeys" to adulthood are shaped in high school (Eisenman, 2001, p. 14). Similarly, Emerson's snippet of wisdom depicting life as a journey of sorts is laden with the beliefs and values of American Romanticism and 19th-century Christianity, with philosophical underpinnings of freedom and learning through experience.

These dominant beliefs are often also associated with the White race; however, race is a socially constructed category for identifying people and, as such, it is rife with inconsistencies and deeply buried meanings that serve to oppress people by creating false and indefensible renderings of what it means to be deserving of privilege and power (Leonardo & Broderick, 2011). In this exploration of disability, diversity, and equity, both the use of racial/ethnic categories (e.g., White, Black, Native American, Asian) and the signifier of the oppression of these categories (i.e., Whiteness) are both used as conceptual tools.

Further, like other cultural artifacts, the Emerson quote itself has morphed over time, constantly being shaped by new influences and being attributed more recently to religious texts, modern philosophers, and even rock bands. According to O'Toole (2012), the actual citation may have originated in an essay Emerson wrote in 1844, "To finish the moment, to find the journey's end in every step of the road, to live the greatest number of good hours, is wisdom," (p. 63). The original is more complex and thus subject to further interpretation. The point is that transitioning to adulthood is a socially constructed process that changes; the outcomes associated with successful transitions are valued differently over time and place, by different groups of people, with further variation among individual members. Moreover, prioritizing and valuing outcomes is not neutral, with the identification of desirable outcomes being a first step in pinpointing resources necessary for goal attainment.

Illustrating this point is the current push to make college enrollment a goal for all high school students as articulated by the U.S. Department of Education under the Obama administration (U.S. Department of Education & Office of Planning, 2010) and in the most recent reauthorization of the Elementary and Secondary Education Act of 1965, known as the Every Student Succeeds Act of 2015. One manifestation of this goal is learning standards that target the outcome of college readiness for all students, including those with disabilities. The shift toward college enrollment as a powerful and normed outcome of high school represents a shift from dichotomous foci on either employment (frequently a goal for students who struggle in high school, many of whom are identified as having disabilities) or college enrollment (a goal often reserved for students who succeed in school, many of whom are not identified with disabilities). In the past, U.S. high schools hosted a range of vocational programs that prepared students for initial employment in careers that typically did not require college degrees or postsecondary training, such as manufacturing, construction, agriculture, and retail. In today's world, high school curricula rarely encompass such vocational programming (Levesque et al., 1995). Many argue that the job market of today demands some postsecondary education or training–even for entry-level jobs.

For adolescents with disabilities, the societal shift toward college for all has many implications. For some students with disabilities for whom college has always been a dream, increased preparedness and more opportunities may surface. For students with disabilities for whom prolonging classroom- and program-based learning experiences is too demanding, too expensive, or too open ended, opportunities for transitioning to postschool employment may exist. On the other hand, some would argue that the sociopolitical climate and changing world demands of postsecondary education makes the college/employment dichotomy of past generations obsolete and no longer representative of U.S. career trajectories. Further, proponents of college as a normative postschool experience assert that young adults with disabilities who do not seek postsecondary education credentials are susceptible to low-income, low-status jobs without opportunities for growth and the acquisition of both material benefits and intangible status indicators (Madaus, Grigal, & Hughes, 2014). This assertion is supported by patterns of underemployment and high poverty among people with disabilities documented in the U.S. Census and other datasets and discussed more fully in subsequent chapters in this book.

More important, the historical postsecondary employment/education dichotomy has been criticized for being a thinly veiled mechanism for tracking, which disproportionately affects high numbers of Black and Brown adolescents, as well as adolescents across races/ethnicities who experience poverty in their everyday lives (Lewis & Cheng, 2006). So while it is important to consider disability and how individuals and others perceive these students' futures based on their strengths, needs, and preferences relative to disability-related challenges (e.g., academic difficulty leading to a decision not to enroll in college), it is equally important to consider the effects of historical marginalization associated with race/ethnicity, gender, home language, immigration, and so forth, and the systemic challenges associated with both general and special education systems that are the brick and mortar of walls that can block education opportunities. These challenges include, but are not limited to, consistent patterns of inaccurate or imprecise disability identification, stigmatization of people with disabilities (resulting in, among other attitudes, low expectations and deficit orientations), and diminished access to effective educational practices and resource-rich educational settings. All of these challenges are more likely to affect African American, Latino, Native American, multiracial, and bilingual youth, and adolescents from across groups from low socioeconomic backgrounds, than their dominant-group peers (i.e., White, and/or from middle- and upper-class backgrounds across racial/ethnic groups).

Returning to the central theme of this book series, *Disability, Equity and Culture,* it is necessary to contextualize this discussion of transition by exploring what is valued, by whom, and to what end so that we can understand how related resources are pooled, distributed, accessed, and used by all involved participants. It is especially important to understand how privilege and power during transition processes advantage or disadvantage groups of adolescents with disabilities, as well as how individual and collective agency are enacted to circumvent obstacles to goal attainment in postsecondary transition. First, to understand the urgency and scope of the problem, we must examine current trends in postschool outcomes.

HIDDEN VIEWS AND SHIFTING CONCLUSIONS ON POSTSCHOOL DISPARITIES

As the field of transition has grown from its formal inception in the late 1970s, it has become more conceptually robust as a field of study and more complex as a field of practice. Studies of the postschool outcomes of young adults with disabilities have consistently shown both improvement over time and persistent pockets of trouble and concern. Unfortunately, most patterns have revealed that adolescents and young adults who are also members of historically marginalized groups (e.g., individuals with disabilities who are also people of color, whose home language is other than English, who experience poverty at home, who attend under-resourced schools, and who live in low-income communities) often struggle in school and into early adulthood. This struggle is typically measured by rates of high school completion, employment, college and other postsecondary education enrollment and degree completion, and financial independence. Whether the comparison group is comprised of dominant-group peers who also have disabilities (e.g., European American, English-dominant or monolingual, from middle- or high-socioeconomic backgrounds) or peers without disabilities from across racial/ethnic groups, dually marginalized adolescents and young adults often fare worse after high school.

The scope of this problem is challenging to define. Reports from the second National Longitudinal Transition Study (NLTS2–see text box) revealed steady improvement for all adolescents and young adults with disabilities. For example, the high school completion rate across disabilities improved an average of 17% between the first and second NLTS studies (Wagner, Newman, Cameto, & Levine, 2005). Moreover, some of the biggest gains reported were for young people from historically marginalized groups; school completion rates of African American students with disabilities improved 22% and completion rates for the poorest students with disabilities improved 19% (Wagner, Newman, Cameto, & Levine, 2005). However, outcome data from the NLTS2 are interesting and deserve further examination because they do not consistently align with outcomes for young adults who are from historically marginalized groups who do not have disabilities (Kim, 2013; Maynard, Salas-Wright, & Vaughn, 2015). Further, these results do not consistently reflect evidence from small-scale studies of youth with disabilities who are also from historically marginalized groups (Gil-Kashiwabara, Hogansen, Geenen, Powers, & Powers, 2007; Povenmire-Kirk, Lindstrom, & Bullis, 2010; Trainor, 2005, 2007). According to the 2013 *Condition of Education* report, the average high school graduation rates for African Americans (66%), Latinos (71%), and Native Americans (69%) without disabilities were lower than the average rate for both European Americans (83%) and Asians (93%) without disabilities. These calculations do not take into consideration socioeconomic backgrounds, and therefore the intersection of race/ethnicity and economic status is not reflected. African American (39%), Latino (34%), and Native American (36%) school-aged youth, however, do experience familial poverty at greater rates than both European American and Asian youth, for whom the poverty rate of both is 13% (Aud et al., 2013), potentially fueling larger gaps.

In the single NLTS2 report dedicated solely to high school completion of students with disabilities, statistically significant differences across racial/ethnic groups were not detected, yet differences across disability categories and socioeconomic backgrounds were noted (NLTS2, 2005). For example, adolescents with disabilities from families with annual incomes over $50,000 were significantly more likely to graduate high school than were their peers from families with annual incomes between $25,000 and $50,000, and those from families with annual incomes under $25,000. Further, students with emotional and behavioral disabilities (EBD; 56%) are significantly less likely to complete high school. For groups who are likely to be overrepresented in both low socioeconomic and EBD disability groups (e.g., African Americans and Native Americans), an examination of the intersection of race/ethnicity, socioeconomic backgrounds, and disability at the national level is warranted. An examination of intersections might reveal larger gaps and/or places where efforts are

The NLTS studies comprise the largest, most comprehensive data on the high school experiences and transition outcomes of students with disabilities and are referenced heavily throughout this book. There have been three longitudinal, nationally representative studies of the secondary experiences and transition outcomes of students with disabilities commissioned by the U.S. Department of Education's Institute of Education Sciences (IES). The first two studies were implemented by SRI International and began in 1980 and 2000, respectively. These are known as the first and second National Longitudinal Transition Study (NLTS and NLTS2). Detailed descriptions of the studies and the resulting datasets for both studies are publicly available at nlts2.org.

Each study included a nationally representative sample of students with disabilities as a whole and in each federal special education disability category individually. The more recent NLTS2, which included more than 11,000 adolescents and young adults with disabilities, was conducted from 2000-2010. Participants were ages 13 to 16 when the study began. The sample was stratified by region, school size, and disability classification. Data collection, which occurred in 5 waves, included parent and youth surveys and interviews, school characteristic, school program, and teacher surveys, direct assessment of students' academic achievement, and high school transcript reviews. Response rates for specific types of data collection ranged from 36% (the general education teacher survey in Wave 2) to 82% (Wave 1, the parent/youth survey). The sample obtained for each data collection source was weighted so that it represented the universe of students, defined by age and disability category, from which the NTLS2 sample was selected, independent of response rate. School and program surveys were discontinued after Wave 2, when a portion of the NTLS2 sample were no longer in high school.

Results, reports, and secondary analyses of the NLTS2 continue to be widely disseminated in the field of transition. In addition to the more than 30 descriptive reports and briefs produced by SRI, IES has also funded secondary analyses of the NLTS2 dataset. More than 60 scholarly papers based on secondary analyses of the NLTS2 have been published in multiple peer-reviewed journals in special education and related fields.

Phase 1 of the third study, the NLTS 2012, was implemented by Mathematica, and related publications are forthcoming. Phase 2 of NLTS 2012 currently is being conducted by RTI International and SRI International. Information about the NLTS 2012 can be found at http://ies.ed.gov/ncee/nlts/.

especially needed to improve our understanding of both learning opportunities and postschool outcomes.

Defining the parameters of high school outcomes and measuring success indicators such as high school completion is challenging when responding to questions about diversity and equity across groups of U.S. public school students. The NLTS2 school completion report (2005) focuses on the improvement over time for youth from historically marginalized groups in drawing conclusions such as the following: "However, the lowest and middle income group shows significant increases over time in their school completion rates (19 and 26 percentage points, respectively), an increase not shared by the highest income group" (NLTS2, 2005, p. 3).

The focus in the NLTS2 on the lack of statistically significant differences without respect to the intersection of multiple sociodemographic variables for this indicator (i.e., high school completion) and others, potentially allows researchers and other stakeholders to misunderstand the scope of problematic outcomes for young adults with disabilities who are also from other historically marginalized groups. Important to note, the NLTS2, the only nationally representative, longitudinal dataset that includes extensive transition variables and postschool outcomes for adolescents and young adults with disabilities, is a prominent source in the established knowledge base, upon which research, policy, and practice are based. This work has resulted in over 30 fact sheets, data briefs, and full reports detailing primary, descriptive analyses. Additionally, transition researchers have used the dataset in secondary analyses, publishing over 60 studies that employ descriptive, correlational, and experimental (e.g., propensity matching) methods between 2003 and 2016. Although exceptions do exist (see Trainor's 2016 transition and postschool outcomes study of bilingual students identified with disabilities), much of this work focuses analysis on subsamples based on disability (see Chiang et al.'s 2012 study of postsecondary education and students with autism). When individual characteristics such as gender are considered, few studies examine intersections of other diversity indicators such as race and class simultaneously, presumably because the sample sizes of the more limited categories are not sufficient for some types of statistical analyses. Moreover, when conclusions are drawn from comparative, statistical analyses with limited attention to intersectionality, conclusions such as this one from Wagner, Newman, Cameto, Garza, & Levine (2005) can flummox the field of transition:

> There are no differences across racial/ethnic groups in the likelihood of being engaged in school, work, or preparation for work shortly after high school; enrolling in college or a vocational, business, or technical school; living independently, having active friendships; having had or fathered a child; or ever having been arrested. However, independent of other differences between them, African-American youth with disabilities are at a 16-percentage-point disadvantage relative to white youth in their rate of current employment. Also, white youth with disabilities are more likely than others to have driving privileges and a personal checking account. (p. ES-10)

Initial descriptive results from the NLTS2 were published in multiple reports on postschool outcomes for young adults with disabilities, up to four years after high school (Newman, Wagner, Cameto, & Knokey, 2009), six years after high school (Sanford, Newman, Wagner, Knokey, & Shaver, 2011), and eight years after high school (Newman, Wagner, Knokey, et al., 2011). This set of publications makes an important contribution to the knowledge base because—as most adults can relate—opportunities and outcomes change as one ages. Yet, similar to the school completion report (NLTS2, 2005), the four-year postschool report (Newman et al., 2009) referenced differences in post-high school employment and markers of independent living across racial groups while making the following claim:

> Similarities and differences also were apparent for youth with different racial/ethnic backgrounds. There were no significant differences across racial/ethnic groups in the likelihood of being engaged in school, work, or preparation for work; in postsecondary school enrollment; in social or community involvement; in parenting status; and in involvement in violence-related activities or with the criminal justice system. (p. xxii)

In the eight-year postschool report, the authors again note, "no significant differences across racial/ethnic groups in the likelihood of being engaged in school, work, or preparation for work; in postsecondary school enrollment or completion . . . and in involvement in violence-related activities or with the criminal justice system" were identified (Newman, Wagner, Knokey, et al., 2011, p. xxv). The reports, however, also identified outcomes for which significant differences were noted. For example, adolescents who were identified in high school as having EBD and intellectual and developmental disabilities (ID; the disability category formerly known as mental retardation) fared worse on most outcome measures than their peers with other disabilities. Racial/ethnic comparisons were made across three groups: White, African American, and Hispanic (Newman, Wagner, Knokey, et al., 2011), and some statistically significant differences surfaced. African Americans (45%) were significantly more likely to have fathered a child than European Americans (26%); they were less likely to be married (17% as compared to 4%, respectively); and European Americans were more likely than African Americans to have checking accounts, credit cards, and driver's licenses, all potential signifiers of financial literacy, if not financial independence (Newman, Wagner, Knokey, et al., 2011).

Examining employment outcomes reveals further challenges to understanding the scope of the problem specific to young adults with disabilities who are also from historically marginalized groups. The U.S. Census Community Survey data from 2009–2013 illustrated the following unemployment rates by racial/ethnic group irrespective of disability status: 8.4% for European Americans, 17% for African Americans, 16% for Native Americans, 8% for Asian Americans, and 12% for Latinos (factfinder.census.gov). Outcome data from the NLTS2 eight-year postschool report also revealed gaps in rates of employment since high school; differences based on race/ethnicity were not found to be statistically significant while differences based on socioeconomic background were found to be significant (Newman, Wagner, Knokey et al., 2011). Whereas 94% of European Americans with disabilities have been employed at any point since high school, the same was true for 86% of their African American peers and 85% of their Latino peers. Similar differences are evidenced across socioeconomic backgrounds; 95% of young adults with disabilities from the highest income bracket (over $50,000 annually) have been employed at any point since high school, but the same is true for only 85% of youth from the lowest income bracket (Newman, Wagner, Knokey, et al., 2011).

Again, this NLTS2 report did not examine the intersection of disability, race/ethnicity, gender, socioeconomic background, or other variables such as home language. Further, the racial/ethnic groups established in these reports for purposes of comparison do not include analyses of young adults with disabilities from Native American, Asian, or multiracial backgrounds. Hence, our understanding as a field is limited when it comes to issues of diversity and equity associated with transition. For these reasons, chapters in this book will focus on examining equity and diversity during the transition to adulthood with a critical perspective toward the ways knowledge is constructed and the conclusions that can be drawn about the scope of the problem. First, however, it is helpful to understand how the field itself has developed over time so that we understand how the knowledge base, including studies such as the NLTS2, creates and is created by research, policy, and practice.

To better understand the scope and complexity of disparate secondary and postschool outcomes related to transition, the impact of these disparities on education equality in the United States, and, most importantly, how to effectively problem solve, we need to operationalize what we mean by *culture* to better grasp its interface with transition education.

OPERATIONALIZING CULTURE IN THE CONTEXT OF TRANSITION

Education anthropologists, sociologists, cultural psychologists, and other scholars have long been working on the question, What does culture have to do with education? (Cole, 2010). Understanding the relationship between individual characteristics and group membership as drivers of thought and behavior has historically been the focus of research, but key limitations of this conceptual relationship have also long been identified (Rogoff, 2003). Identities of individuals and groups are overlapping, fluid, dynamic, and instantiated with social, historical, and political experiences. Further, processes and practices shape and are shaped by individuals living in society, at times conveying dominance and, at other times, indicating marginalization. These complexities make culture, and hence its diverse manifestations, difficult to study, its importance difficult to measure, and conclusions challenging to interpret. Of the multiple theories of the role of culture in human development and education that have been developed across the social sciences, this discussion of transition will draw heavily upon two of these theories, with an emphasis on the second theory.

First, transition will be analyzed as a set of developmental processes that are a result of sociocultural activity. Barbara Rogoff and Michael Cole, contemporary American scholars of cultural psychology, have made strides, along with many others, to bring sociocultural theory to bear on education. Rogoff (2003) explained that human development (i.e., becoming/being considered an adult) is a cultural process that involves practices requiring the use of tools and strategies inherited from group members. Moreover, when individuals engage in these practices they simultaneously change them. As such, "culture is not an entity that influences individuals. Instead, people contribute to the creation of cultural processes and cultural processes contribute to the creation of people" (Rogoff, 2003, p. 51). Here, the focus is on the cultural practice of transition research and education.

Second, transition and transition education will be analyzed as a cultural practice that both requires and conveys power to and from its key stakeholders, including educators and other community members, in addition to adolescents with disabilities and their families. Pierre Bourdieu, a French sociologist whose career spanned decades beginning in the late 1950s, brought a poststructuralist view of power and agency to the study of education. Bourdieu (1974) explained that education is constituted of capital in multiple forms, including economic, cultural, and social capital. Bourdieu's development of capital theory in education is also useful because he explained how cultural practices, education and otherwise, are often hidden and invoke rules and a field of practice that may not be completely visible or obvious to either the insiders or to those outsiders who study the insiders and their practices. This work also draws from other scholars' Bourdieu-influenced scholarship. Bourdieu's concepts of social reproduction, agency, and capital theory upon which I draw most heavily, deserve explication, as their application can vary from scholar to scholar (Winkle-Wagner, 2010).

Applying Bourdieu's Sociocultural Theories and Concepts in Transition

Bourdieu was a prolific scholar whose work evolved and influenced many other scholars across disciplines and interests in education. I focus here on some key concepts, originally introduced by Bourdieu and his colleagues, that I argue are particularly salient to transition education. In particular, I focus on field, capital, habitus, and the tension between social reproduction and agency embedded in these concepts.

Field: Locations and metaphorical spaces where transition happens. Researchers, educators, families, and individuals with disabilities generally agree that transition education matters. Successful transitions to adulthood require planning and concerted effort to prepare adolescents to pursue their preferences, capitalize on their strengths, and address their needs with the assistance of others. Among the predictors of successful postschool outcomes, Test, Mazzotti, and colleagues (2009) and Mazzotti et al. (2015) identified both services and the settings in which they occur that have evidentiary support. Educational settings can be likened to Bourdieu's construct of field. The field is a place (either actual or metaphorical) where key players interact, forming perceptions, taking action, and so forth resulting in life experiences (Bourdieu, 1990). According to Bourdieu, field is centrally important to understanding sociocultural phenomena such as transitions to adulthood, because field functions as "a critical mediation between the practices of those who partake of it and the surrounding social and economic conditions" (Bourdieu & Wacquant, 1992, p. 105).

Bourdieu's work theorizing field, and later that of his protégés (e.g., Passeron, Wacquant) as well as those who have extended his work to other disciplines and questions in the social sciences (e.g., Emirbayer, Grenfell, Harker, Lareau, Webb, Winkle-Wagner), is not unrelated to Bronfenbrenner's conceptualization of ecological systems (1979, 2005). Bronfenbrenner and colleagues provided a way to understand the field as an interrelated system of permeable and amorphously bounded settings and contexts that embed human development and social interaction. Bourdieu and colleagues' work embraced an examination of power and agency within settings and contexts. Both theoretical positions and the empirical work that has served to explicate and expound Bronfenbrenner's and Bourdieu's initial work are particularly useful to research and practice in transition because they serve to move us beyond transition education as a set of interventions aimed at individuals with disabilities. Expanding our unit of analysis is essential to generating new knowledge that addresses affronts to equity affecting adolescents with disabilities, particularly for those who are from other historically marginalized groups.

Capital: Types, sources, and functions. There are three major types of capital: economic, cultural, social (Bourdieu, 1986). All three can take on material and/or symbolic forms. For example, it is generally understood that retaining legal representation in cases of special education disputes requires economic capital. When parents bring a lawyer to a special education Individualized Education Program (IEP) meeting, they demonstrate the financial means necessary to hire professional advocacy. Beyond the material wealth conveyed, however, the money spent to hire a lawyer may represent or be interpreted as the parents' devotion to the well-being of their child, their willingness to fight for what they believe is right, their underlying knowledge of due process, and other inferences. Capital leverages power during interactions that demand participation in a culture of practice (e.g., special education) encompassing knowledge and skills such as reading forms and communicating in legalese, using special education jargon, and adhering to foundational assumptions about disability, independence, compulsory schooling, and so on.

Capital in one form is also potentially generative of capital in other forms. Economic capital can be exchanged for information and skill development. For a fee, the lawyer at the special education meeting conveys information about rights and responsibilities to parents. This information can be technical, beyond what parents access in the handbooks that schools are required to give guardians of students who receive special education. Thus, economic capital is exchanged for cultural capital. Similarly, parents might develop their knowledge of special education processes by attending a community-based or school-based workshop about special education. The understanding of special education processes, policies, and other information (i.e., the culture of practices) that adolescents and their parents gather exemplifies cultural capital. Parents without time for a course or a meeting might seek informal opportunities to gain the same through their contacts with friends and acquaintances, asking questions about special education processes. In this situation, social capital is forwarding cultural capital. The process of using capital to get capital can be difficult to track as it bubbles up or mushrooms.

Moreover, the value of capital varies. In school meetings where local education agency representatives have power over meeting proceedings, a lawyer's interpretation of special education regulations or knowledge of legal precedence may prevail. Alternatively, in an informal conversation between parents of children with disabilities, knowledge generated from the lived experiences might be more highly valued by participants.

In addition to the nonlinearity and messiness of amassing capital, the process is not unidirectional. Students and parents, in their interactions with school administrators, educators, and other institutional representatives, share their knowledge, expectations, and practices as well. Not only are they exposing and sharing capital resources, they are exerting power on processes. For example, in New York City and other urban areas, parents whose children have experienced exclusionary discipline have come together with legal advocates from the American Civil Liberties Union to address, with some success, punitive responses that disproportionately affect children with disabilities, particularly those from other historically marginalized groups (New York Civil Liberties Union, 2015). In response to these concerns, the City of New York, under the leadership of Mayor Bill de Blasio, and the NYC Department of Education has amended suspension and expulsion policies to address the problem (de Blasio, 2015).

Studies that have used Bourdieuian capital theory in education have focused on caches of capital and how these function in home–school interactions. All three forms of capital are implicated in the distance with which parents and teachers work together toward common goals for students' academic achievement and socio-emotional well-being, with socioeconomic background as a driving factor in the expectations and actions of all parties (Lareau, 1989). Social networks connected to professionals and other sources of cultural capital advantage families in home–school interactions (Horvat, Weininger, & Lareau, 2003). Time used to engage at school on behalf of one's child is a type of cultural capital, and having time for home–school meetings (e.g., hiring professionals to do other chores, working at home and caring for one's children, etc.) is often associated with economic capital.

Further, capital exchanges require that all parties accept the capital in play. Gender, race/ethnicity, and socioeconomic background intersect. Child rearing and education responsibilities are often associated with mothers, a group who faces marginalization associated with sexism. The labor of mothers, particularly single mothers who also are likely to work outside the home, is undervalued, which contributes to disadvantage when interactions with school processes and teachers require presence and attention from parents (Reay, 1998). Similarly, parents of color who have experienced marginalization in schools or immigrant parents who have not experienced the U.S. educational system as students themselves may identify sources of capital that are not valued or recognized by school personnel (Harry & Klingner, 2006). Further, teachers may employ deficit views of parents who have less time for advocacy and interactions at school (Trainor, 2010b). Despite the acknowledgement that cultural capital, both material and symbolic (e.g., disability labels, referrals for services, disciplinary proceedings, and other processes) is salient to special education interactions in particular, marginalization can minimize its availability, use, and efficacy (Lareau & Horvat, 1999; Trainor, 2010a).

Capital theory is particularly useful for understanding how ableism, racism, sexism, classism, English-language dominance, and other forms of discrimination, coupled with poverty and other disadvantage, can lead to poor postschool outcomes (Swartz, 1997). Understanding marginalization, biases, and efforts, intentional or not, of dominant group members to remain powerful and control education resources, is necessary for avoiding simplistic, deficit-oriented, and unproductive applications of capital theory. Critical perspectives of capital theory have also identified forms of capital that are associated with community strength, advocacy, and the collective resistance to marginalization (Winkle-Wagner, 2010; Yosso, 2005). The underlying conceptualization of disability, the expectations of key stakeholders, and the information they use during interactions are all types of cultural capital. Scrutinizing cultural capital, both symbolic and material, exposes cultural ways of knowing and doing (Bourdieu, 1986; Bourdieu & Wacquant, 2013). The rules that guide how capital functions in a given context are part of another of Bourdieu's concepts, *habitus.*

Habitus: Bourdieu's meaning and use of disposition. Dispositions are internalized ways of knowing, being, and acting that function, often in subconscious ways, as we go about our daily life. Following such guidelines may or may not be in the consciousness of the actors and these guidelines may be taken up, variably, by both individuals and groups. This constitutes *habitus* (Bourdieu, 1990). In other words, habitus is a set of "principles which generate and organize practices and representations that can objectively be adapted to their outcomes without presupposing conscious gaming at the ends or express mastery of operations necessary in order to obtain them" (p. 53). Put into plain language, habitus, not unlike habit, is a way of operating without full awareness of how one's actions are filtering certain outcomes and results (Webb, Schirato, & Danaher,

2002). Yet habitus exceeds habit; such routinized action is not only tacit, it motivates actors by rewarding actions that follow established rules (Bourdieu, 1990). Bourdieu's understanding of capital and its relationship to power exposes both reproduction of inequality and opportunity for agency.

Habitus explains the relationship between cultural capital (i.e., what one knows and values) and dispositions that drive, or do not drive, one's agency. Habitus is not unidimensional; it is a system of dispositions that function "as principles which generate and organize practices and representations that can be objectively adapted to their outcomes without presupposing conscious aiming at ends or an express mastery of the operations necessary in order to attain them" (Bourdieu, 1990, p. 53). Habitus evokes the automaticity of both subconscious thought and habitual behavior, of both verbal and nonverbal language, supported and developed by amassing cultural capital (material, symbolic, embedded) particular to a given field. Habitus is cumulative and provides a set of options for what constitutes appropriate action based on the value of capital, as interpreted using a set of rules that are context specific (Winkle-Wagner, 2010).

For example, the knowledge that a teacher prefers students who raise their hands and wait to be called on prior to speaking is a type of capital that can be used to guide behavior to both reach an immediate goal (e.g., get called on to join a classroom discussion) and to generate more capital (e.g., curry favor with the teacher). Given a field change and entry to another teacher's classroom, perhaps a teacher who uses Socratic seminar methods, raising one's hand is no longer necessary for goal attainment. Knowledge of this rule, whether stated or part of the hidden curriculum, is additional cultural capital that may drive a student's participation.

Importantly, Bourdieu's capital theory is one in a family of conflict theories in the Marxian tradition (Webb et al., 2002; Winkle-Wagner, 2010). He was most interested in social reproduction and the roles of power and privilege in education (Bourdieu, 1974). Habitus was Bourdieu's theoretical tool for explaining that, although education was a major conduit for increasing the capital necessary for agency, such dispositions are internalized and durable, infrequently affording opportunities to challenge existing inequity and agentive change (Webb et al., 2002). Despite scholarly criticism to the contrary, Bourdieu also asserted that social fields reflect the push and pull of nondominant groups and that power and status are not immutable.

> I do not see how relation of domination, whether material or symbolic, could possibly operate without implying, activating resistance. The dominated in any social universe can always exert a certain force, inasmuch as belonging to field means by definition one is capable of producing effects (if only to elicit reactions of exclusion on the part of those who occupy its dominant positions). . . . there is no denying that there exist dispositions to resist and one of the tasks of sociology is precisely to examine under what conditions these decisions are socially constituted, effectively triggered, and rendered politically efficient. (Bourdieu & Wacquant, 1992, pp. 80–81)

To continue with the above example, if a student with multiple physical and communication disabilities is included in a Socratic seminar, she may understand how to participate but she will need the cooperation of the teacher to facilitate her use of an augmentative/alternative communication (AAC) device. She will also need the teacher and the other students to develop habitus that prioritizes inclusion, requiring an understanding of disability as difference rather than deficit, so that her participation is seen as value-added despite that AAC communication is atypical, computerized, staccato-sounding, and slower than typical speech. The individual student's understanding of the rules of this classroom (i.e., cultural capital in a given field) may support her disposition (i.e., habitus) to participate in class, and is necessary, but not sufficient, for inclusion in the Socratic seminar.

Winkle-Wagner (2010) conducted a comprehensive review of education research that employed Bourdieuian theory. Her study included 105 studies that spanned K–12 education and higher education. She found that most researchers isolated cultural capital as an object of examination without consideration of other key components of Bourdieu's full theoretical position. This isolation can be considered a maladaptation of theory, or one that has introduced limitations that are relevant to the sociocultural examination of agency, using Bourdieu's capital theory (Winkle-Wagner, 2010). First, if cultural capital is seen as a part of an economy in education, one where simple acquisition is the focus, educators might wrongly assume that helping students build caches of capital and exchanging this capital for goal attainment is the key to their success. This conceptualization relies upon the underlying ontologies of individualism and rationalism where the value of capital, which is symbolic and context specific, is knowable and its exchange intentional. So, as with the hypothetical student using AAC, the student must be motivated to use her cultural capital to reach her goals. The extent to which these align with teachers' and parents' goals for her, or peers' goals for the class, is another matter. However, habitus suggests a less deliberate and unplanned use of capital. If this same student has internalized the habitus of the larger group, that the efficiency and flow of communication is more important than what she has to say, perhaps her knowledge of the seminar participation will not be exchanged as a means to meet her goal to be a part of the discussion. Winkle-Wagner (2010) argues that when cultural capital is understood in relation to habitus, which incorporates the social and communal aspect of values and norms, a complexity is afforded to the theory.

Second, cultural capital is symbolic and often embedded. The economic metaphor is too reliant upon cultural capital as material, a thing that can be identified, counted, and exchanged in a marketplace (Winkle-Wagner, 2010). Some researchers have documented how groups of people who have been marginalized (immigrant groups who face racial/ethnic and linguistic prejudices) do amass cultural and social capital, but that this capital is not valued or recognized in the larger, dominant society (Stanton-Salazar, 2001; Stanton-Salazar & Dornbusch, 1995). Conceptualizations of collective and resistance cultural capital have emerged from within critical studies of education, diversity, and equity (Winkle-Wagner, 2010). These concepts push Bourdieu's definitions of capital to include shared knowledge and values that sustain group success in the face of aggression through dominance. Other scholars have pushed further by critiquing contemporary interpretations of Bourdieu, asserting that scholars have used an acritical and instrumentalized view of cultural and social capital as some *thing* that minority populations do not have but need to acquire to escape poverty and marginalization (Yosso, 2005; Yosso & García, 2007).

Drawing from critical race theory and the concept of funds of knowledge, Yosso and colleagues explain that communities of color have developed and shared a range of cultural capital, deeply embedded in intergenerational, historical, and political experiences, that has served to fortify resistance. This type of capital, although undervalued or not well understood by the dominant group, is powerful and representative of agentive change and disruption to social hierarchies (Yosso & García, 2007). Further, these scholars argue that the deficit lenses that White scholars have brought to the interpretation of Bourdieu overemphasize the reproductive nature of his theoretical position. Rather, they return to Bourdieu as a primary source and focus on his assertion that dominant groups' control of and access to power is neither strictly material nor impermeable to change. In their view, resistance and collective capital interrupts dominance.

Returning to the illustration herein, how about the AAC user's identity as an adolescent? How might this present as resistance capital in the accumulation of resources for interpreting the rules of the field? How is her desire to fit in and befriend classmates, a desire that is often unfulfilled for students with disabilities, a factor in both this student's habitus and the habitus she shares with her classmates? Despite being one of the most prolific and influential sociologists (Swartz, 1997; Webb et al., 2002), Bourdieu did not address disability directly in any major work. At the same time, his theory of habitus is appealing to scholars in disability studies because it explains how the societal interactions influence, often subconsciously, the way people carry themselves and embody insider status that confers power and privilege (Edwards & Imrie, 2003).

Living with Terms and Categories

When studying inequity, we often rely on snapshots and patterns of unequal outcomes. Throughout this book, I use racial and ethnic categories as descriptors in understanding the state of transition research and practice in relation to issues of equity. In part, I do so in an effort to speak directly to my special education colleagues and audience, using constructs that are in the vernacular to my in-group and thus provide common understanding. In special education scholarship, disability, racial/ethnic, and other categories are most often considered to be sociodemographic characteristics that are stable and associated with individuals. Race/ethnicity continues to be conflated with culture in some disseminated research, and the field has been slow to incorporate critical or conflict theories into its repertoire of tools for both research and practice. Similarly, awareness of power and privilege associated with identity constructs and sociocultural phenomena are infrequently invoked. I also use categorical terms to provide comparative analyses. The danger in using these categories is that I risk "reification and legitimation of the naturalness and neutrality of the bureaucratic system of special education as a whole and, by extension, of the deficit-driven and psychological understanding of 'ability' and 'disability' within which it is grounded" (Leonardo & Broderick, 2011, p. 2208). To counteract this limitation, I make concerted efforts to destabilize the categories themselves using several strategies.

First, I use multiple, acceptable terms for racial/ethnic groups with discretion. For example, I use *White* and *European American* to describe the same group of people. I do not use the term *Caucasian*, however, because of its connection to historical scientific racism (McDermott & Samson, 2005). I also do not use the term *Anglo*, indicating its lack of popularity or perhaps nothing more than my own preference and identity as a White person. Nevertheless, all racial and ethnic categories, and thus related terminology, are problematic, including both terms I chose to use for White, my own racial group. White is associated with the contemporary history of Jim Crow and racism, and European American is flawed for its impreciseness; not all descendants of Europeans are considered racially White, and neither is power and privilege associated with Whiteness conferred to all European Americans or Whites. Other racial/ethnic group terms are also interchanged throughout the book (e.g., Black and African American). In this way, I am acknowledging complexity and I am also rejecting the notion that any racial and ethnic categorizations or schemata are legitimate or true.

Second, in discussions where I invoke the rhetoric of categories of people and the statistical methods and measures used to answer questions about disproportionality and transition outcomes, I attempt to draw from Crenshaw's (1991) conceptualization of intersectionality, pointing out whenever possible how race/ethnicity, gender, class, home language, immigration status, sex, and gender identity intersect with disability to create both advantage and disadvantage in access to education opportunities. Often, descriptive statistical measures are not available to examine intersectionality. In special education, the default has been to focus on disability characteristics, deemphasizing or omitting details such as racial/ethnic and linguistic backgrounds (Artiles, Bal, & Thorius, 2010; Artiles, Trent, & Kuan, 1997). Also problematic, large-scale and nationally representative datasets may have too few participants of color to examine the intersections of disability and race/ethnicity and/or sex.

Third, I use the term and concept of Whiteness, borrowing from Leonardo and Broderick's (2011) elucidation in the context of (dis)ability, throughout this book to point out instances in which an ideology of racial/ethnic stratification serves as a tool of oppression. I agree that all disability terminology is imperfect and provides limited information. Disproportionality, by race/ethnicity, language, socioeconomic background, sex, and other factors, frames the discussion of transition herein. Some youth, particularly those of color, are identified with disabilities, separately served, and disciplined at higher rates than White peers and this surely affects postschool outcomes. My work is tethered to precedent work on racial/ethnic disproportionality, which is a part of a larger body of research outside of special education. I do not go so far as to renounce "smartness," which invokes a parallel critique of ability-based stratification (Leonardo & Broderick, 2011). Such a denouncement is not unpalatable to me; however, this book is grounded in special education, a system in which I am a member, having invested great personal effort and other resources to build and to improve it. I do not think it realistic or desirable to dissolve in the current special education system and I am not confident that the larger education system has students with disabilities in its best interests. Having been a classroom teacher for nearly a decade prior to engaging in research in higher education, I am hard pressed to imagine schools without mechanisms for supporting students who struggle, no matter how flawed those are. I am willing to entertain the idea and to engage in scholarship that attempts to answer related questions. Here, though, I do not go that far.

Categories beyond disability, race/ethnicity, and sex are also equally problematic and simultaneously impossible to escape in this discussion. I use the word *sex* in male/female binary comparisons associated with large-scale dataset. I attempt to use *gender* as a way to distinguish biology from expression, although most studies of sex and gender in special education transition do not make this distinction clear. Because this book is about equity, *sexual orientation* and *sexual identity* as they pertain to the marginalization of the lesbian, gay, bisexual, and transgender (LGBT) communities also come into play. Whenever possible, I use terms that are specific (e.g., ethnicity of participants) and gleaned through self-identification of participants in the original studies.

Returning to transition research and practice as the context for this examination of diversity and equity, it is helpful to view the field of practice, beginning with a broad historical overview.

A GLIMPSE OF HISTORICAL INFLUENCES

In the context of U.S. education, transition is often associated with the education of students with disabilities. Although life transitions are numerous, even in the relatively short lives of young people, the term most often refers to the movement from adolescence into early adulthood in which noticeable changes are anticipated–changes in human development, activities, roles, and responsibilities. The U.S. public education system, with processes that reflect broader cultural movements, has invested heavily in the importance of planning for change. A widely accepted conclusion is that an individual can control or better steer the direction of his or her future trajectory if they plan for life's transitions. Planning, however, requires know-how; *transition planning* in special education has morphed over time into *transition education* to address knowledge and skill development. Understanding how the field of practice, including research, policy-making, and teaching, has developed over time is instructive in understanding broader issues of equity in special education, particularly those pertaining to postschool outcomes.

In the United States, education has long been prized as a way to combat marginalization. Individuals often see education attainment as a step toward economic, social, intellectual, and other personal betterment. Collectively, education attainment is often considered to be a key to equal opportunity–in employment, housing, financial independence, and so on. Not all attempts to use education as a tool for improvement, however, have focused on or resulted in equalizing power and privilege across individuals or groups. For example, GI Bills that have postsecondary tuition benefits for U.S. veterans–many of whom are members of historical minority groups, have experienced economic disadvantage, and/or are individuals with disabilities acquired during military service–have been criticized for their limited capacity to fully support the education-related needs and preferences of veterans (Ottley, 2014; Smith-Osborne, 2009). Despite imperfect outcomes, education attainment remains a stated goal, articulated by many: parents who experience limited incomes associated with entry-level and low-wage jobs; immigrant parents, who come to the United States hoping for education opportunities and an improved standard of living for their children; and parents who have experienced low-quality and under-resourced schools without much personal success in schooling. Similarly, many educators and policymakers express the hope that children will transcend economic poverty through educational attainment. Nevertheless, some would argue that the formal U.S. education system functions more like a floodgate, opening for some and closing for others. As such, social reproduction theorists argue that education systems reinforce power and privilege already in play in the larger society. Others would argue that access to education opportunities have improved over time, particularly for people from historically marginalized groups, and that social reproduction theories do not sufficiently account for individual and group agency. The historical development of special education, and specifically the subfield of transition, illustrates both views.

The contemporary wave of the disability rights movement, focusing on transition-related issues such as independence, began on the heels of the federally mandated racial desegregation of U.S. schools as a result of the U.S. Supreme Court's 1954 decision in *Brown v. Board of Education* and the civil rights movement (Wehmeyer, 2013). Disability rights activists, many of whom were White parents, emboldened with privilege and power associated with Whiteness, demanded education opportunities for individuals with disabilities and planted the seeds of inclusive education, requiring educators to develop practices for teaching and learning to meet a wide range of student ability. Much like legal precedents that initially destabilized racial/ethnic segregation, special education legislation has inarguably resulted in changes in education opportunities and settings for students with disabilities who are served by the U.S. public school system in increasing numbers each year. Also similar to desegregation efforts, resistance from the dominant group, federal and state government disharmony, and limited federal funding mar the implementation of inclusion. As such, policies around both issues have generated mixed results. Despite the federal government's original promise in 1975, as part of the ratification of the first iteration of IDEA, to fund 40% of the costs of the average per pupil expenditures associated with IDEA, this promise has never been fulfilled (Council for Exceptional Children [CEC], 2015). Clearly, innumerable individuals with disabilities and people from other historically marginalized groups have achieved impressive educational goals and have experienced life success, financially and otherwise, but improvement in opportunity has not been experienced to scale.

Special education transition also has historical roots in the fields of vocational education, career development, and rehabilitation psychology, employing the frameworks of economic theories of capitalism and medical models of disability. An early cultural artifact of the dominant view that work provides purpose and value to the human experience can be seen at least as far back as in the vocational curricula implemented in 19th-century residential schools for the deaf (Van Cleve, 2007) and schools for the blind (American Action Fund for Blind Children and Adults, 2016). Another indicator of this connection is legislative mandates in Section 504 of the Rehabilitation Act of 1973 and the first iteration of IDEA (Public Law [PL] 94-142, the Education for All Handicapped Children Act of 1975), both of which specify an imperative for individuals with disabilities to have access to vocational training and career development. As early as 1976, employers engaging in federally contracted work were required to develop and support employment for people with disabilities and, in 1977, states were required to spend a portion of their federal vocational education monies on vocational opportunities for people with disabilities (Razeghi & Davis, 1979).

Undoubtedly, families and individuals with disabilities, scholars and teachers, and others in the field of special education have been powerful change agents throughout the history of the U.S. public school system before and after the passage of key legislation. Disability awareness and equitable opportunities to learn, become employed, and live independently in the community have improved for many individuals with disabilities during the past century and into this current one.

At the same time, obstacles to equity for all people with disabilities, particularly those who experience exclusion associated with racism, ethnocentrism, classism, sexism, xenophobia, and homophobia through hegemonic and biased attitudes and discriminatory actions, have endured over decades. Results from the original NLTS revealed that disability, gender, and racial/ethnic group differences interacted, and that patterns of employability for young adults with learning disabilities (LD) who were from middle and upper socioeconomic brackets, those who were male, and those who were White exceeded employment patterns for young adults with disabilities who were from other backgrounds. These findings drew attention to inequity in postschool outcomes (Blackorby

& Wagner, 1996). In fact, more directly than in the recent NLTS2, analysis of the earlier NLTS data revealed that "minority status may present further obstacles to successful transitions beyond those that youth experience because of disability alone" (Blackorby & Wagner, 1996, p. 410). Patterns of outcomes, however, were, and remain, only one of several competing drivers of practice (i.e., research, policy, and teaching) in the field's development. Important to note is that transition is a relatively young field of practice.

Driving Forces of Special Education Transition

In 1983, Madeleine Will, a parent of a child with a disability and then assistant secretary of education for the Office of Special Education and Rehabilitative Services for the U.S. Department of Education under the Reagan administration, introduced a model for transition for adolescents with disabilities that deliberately created a bridge from school to work, and this became known as transition planning. Transition planning then became one of the disability-related services focused on in the 1990 iteration of IDEA (PL 101-476, Education for All Handicapped Children Amendments of 1990 [EAHCA]) and became a formal, mandated component of U.S. public school special education services focusing on employment. Hence, less than two decades after the special education services were first defined and states had clear mandates to serve children with disabilities, the impact of special education services on the lives of individuals with disabilities begged to be measured, as some of the first cohort of youth covered by EAHCA completed high school. Unfortunately, some of the earliest postschool outcomes studies of adolescents with disabilities depicted patterns of poor postschool outcomes. Young adults with disabilities were not faring well by standard measures of adulthood such as obtaining competitive employment, enrolling in college, and maintaining independent residences from their families, all dominant group views of successful adulthood. Further, patterns of success and failure to achieve these normalized outcomes varied according to disability category, race/ethnicity, and other sociodemographic variables.

Employment and postsecondary education outcomes. Results from the NLTS painted a general picture of unimpressive postschool outcomes of adolescents with disabilities. Across the then-recognized 11 disability categories, within the first three years since high school, 55% of young adults with disabilities had competitive employment, 28% were living independently, and few, 17% and 15%, respectively, had enrolled in postsecondary academic and vocational programs (Wagner, Blackorby, Cameto, & Newman, 1993). Attaining both employment and postsecondary education, particularly for those with LD, ID, and EBD, presented challenges with some notable exceptions hinting at success. For example, young adults with LD had an employment rate of 63%, mirroring the rate of their peers without disabilities, yet their enrollment in college or other academic postsecondary education settings was significantly lower than young adults with speech and language impairments, and those who were deaf or blind (Wagner, Blackorby, Cameto, et al., 1993). For young adults with ID and EBD, employment outcomes, as well as postsecondary enrollment in either academic or vocational education, were noticeably worse. For example, young adults with EBD and those with ID were 11% and 8% less likely, respectively, than young adults with LD to be employed (Wagner, Blackorby, Cameto, et al., 1993). Although these differences were not statistically significant, total wages earned by individuals with EBD and ID were significantly lower.

Results of the first NLTS demarcated other patterns of outcomes. Gender differences surfaced. Although males with disabilities garnered significantly higher total earnings, females with disabilities were more likely to be living independently and more likely to be married (Wagner, Blackorby, Cameto, et al., 1993). Additionally, patterns of outcomes based on racial/ethnic group comparisons from this same dataset illustrated that African Americans with disabilities were significantly less likely to be employed after high school, and that their total wages were significantly less than those of European Americans with disabilities (Wagner, Blackorby, Cameto, et al., 1993). Results of comparisons between Latinos and European Americans showed smaller disparities in a time in history when the U.S. Latino population was much smaller. No overall difference in employment was significant; however, enrollment in postschool vocational education was significantly greater (11%) for Latinos. The first NLTS was groundbreaking in the scope and breadth of data collected and descriptively analyzed, painting the first comprehensive picture of what adult life entailed for individuals with disabilities and the extent to which newly-found educational rights were of benefit for this population.

These first attempts to capture complete pictures of the results of special education in the form of student outcomes, however, were not designed to address the emergent issue of disproportionality. As research and legal precedence on inaccuracies in the identification of Black, Brown, and bilingual children as disabled moved into the focus of the broader field of special education research and other related fields, transition research and the use of this nationally representative, longitudinal data did not fully take into account the potential instabilities in disability categories. Further, intersectionality, the study of dimensions of identity and structural barriers (Crenshaw, 1991), was not well understood, having only begun to take form in the field of law, and later in critical race theory.

Expanding the domains of adulthood. In its nascent stages of development, transition primarily addressed employment as an outcome of secondary education, but not long after its establishment as a field of practice and related research, the interconnectedness between having paid work and other aspects of adulthood were evident. The multidirectional ways in which employment connected to other postschool outcomes such as achieving a high school diploma, enrolling in and completing postsecondary education, and living independently surfaced the need to further expand models for transition education. Will's

(1984) early conceptualization of transition as a bridge from school to work had contributed to a narrow employment focus in policy (Halpern, 1991). In an effort to explain why transition planning was not resulting in markedly improved postschool outcomes, Halpern (1985, 1994) cogently argued that adult life was about far more than employment, and that satisfying adult lives are about community belonging and engagement. As a result, subsequent to the reauthorization of IDEA in 1990 (PL 101-476), and through the most recent in 2004, have increasingly broadened transition planning and instruction for adolescents with disabilities beyond employment to include postsecondary education and independent living. Developing a more comprehensive view of transition circled back, at least in part, to early concerns regarding limited postschool outcomes. Consistently low rates of full-time employment and postsecondary education degree attainment, as well as limited independence and community participation, continued to plague many young adults with disabilities, despite concerted effort to bridge adolescents from high school to employment. Transition education needed to be more conceptually holistic, capturing aspects of adult life engagement that may be connected to, rather than defined by, work.

The domains of adult life are expansive, as any adult understands. Participating in community, interacting with family and friends, pursuing further education and skill development, partaking in civic responsibilities, maintaining a household, and working to support oneself are only a few of the activities that contribute, with great variability, to adult life engagement. This expansiveness is evident in the field of transition: As both practitioners and researchers have responded to transition mandates, primarily those included in IDEA, the conceptual parameters of transition have expanded beyond education, employment, and independence, and have shifted to include various components of or requisites for attaining these outcomes after high school. This conceptual expansion is not uniform across the field, and it has included personal development domains such as self-determination, social-emotional well-being, and life satisfaction, as well as the development of practical skill sets such as using public transportation and other services, disability awareness, self-care, and so on. For example, in 1993, Ysseldyke, Thurlow, and Gilman identified the following domains: presence and participation in the community, physical health, responsibility and independence, contribution and citizenship, academic and functional literacy, personal and social adjustment, and satisfaction (as cited in Wagner, Blackorby, Cameto, et al., 1993). Most recently, Patton and Clark (2014) expanded their list of 9 transition domains originally included in the Transition Planning Inventory (Clark & Patton, 1997) to the following 11: career choice and planning, employment knowledge and skills, further education/training, functional communication, self-determination, independent living, personal money management, community involvement and usage, leisure activities, health, and interpersonal relationships. At a minimum, IDEA requires the domains of employment, education, independent living, and community participation to be addressed on students' individualized education programs

(IEPs). Hence transition has primarily been evidenced through postschool goals included on students' IEPs; however, as changes to its definition in each successive iteration of IDEA reveal, planning requires education and instruction.

Moving from transition planning to transition education. In the policy language of IDEA 2004, subtle changes in the definition of transition illustrate the further expansion, not only in domain requirements, but also in the area of transition instruction and services. The current IDEA 2004 definition states that transition is

> a coordinated set of activities for a child with a disability that–(A) is designed to be within a results-oriented process, that is focused on improving the academic and functional achievement of the child with a disability to facilitate the child's movement from school to post-school activities, including post-secondary education, vocational education, integrated employment (including supported employment), continuing and adult education, adult services, independent living, or community participation; (B) is based on the individual child's needs, taking into account the child's strengths, preferences, and interests; and (C) includes instruction, related services, community experiences, the development of employment and other post-school adult living objectives, and, when appropriate, acquisition of daily living skills and functional vocational evaluation. [(20 USC 1401 § SEC. 602. DEFINITIONS. (34)]

This definition reflects key policy mandates that transition is not merely an annual planning activity but is representative of multiple efforts (e.g., a set of coordinated activities) that are organized around a group of domains (i.e., postsecondary, vocational, and adult continuing education and services; employment, independent living, or community participation) for the purpose of achieving specific academic and functional outcomes (e.g., results; how a person with a disability fares after high school). In the further enumeration of transition requirements, the language in IDEA 2004 again stresses a process approach, by requiring that individualized transition goals be "based upon age appropriate transition assessments related to training, education, employment, and, where appropriate, independent living skills" [IDEA, 2004, Section 614, (d) (I) (A) (i) (VII)].

Thus, the field of transition education, in both practice and research, has been made more expansive in terms of what needs should be addressed and how it is to be done. Beneath the surface of policy wording, however, perspectives of what it means to have a good life after high school drive transition planning efforts in special education practice and research. The heart of this question is inextricably related to worldview and experience, and thus, culture. For some, going to college is a clear path to being fulfilled and it marks a lifelong dream. For others, achieving a high school diploma represents the same dream. At the same time, what these diverse dreams represent in contemporary U.S. society differs. A college degree often, but not always, translates into more capital (e.g., economic, cultural, and social) and additional opportunities for agency. In the current era, educators are held accountable to prepare U.S. school children to be college and career ready, and this sometimes represents a tension between the macro-cultural ideals and policies and the micro-cultural lived experiences of adolescents with disabilities and their families. In transition, this tension has often been taken up as a school–home conflict with roots in cultural mismatch theories.

Another tension, one that is less often researched, has surfaced, exposing the challenges to developing curricula and instructional practices that address how best to plan and support individualized goal attainment. Emphasis on instructional methods in transition and the field's embrace of intervention terminology such as *evidence-based educational decision-making* are reflective of a larger movement in education first articulated by Slavin (2002, 2003) and then taken up in the broader field of special education in discussions of rigorous special education research and practice (Cook, Tankersley, & Landrum, 2009). Three prominent reviews of transition research reflect the paradigmatic assumptions of intervention research and practice, using definitions of evidence that aligned with random control trials (RCT) and quasi-experimental methods to identify promising transition practices and practices that predict postschool outcomes (Mazzotti, et al., 2015; Test, Fowler, et al., 2009; Test, Mazzotti, et al., 2009). The prominence of intervention marks a turn in the field.

Transition Research: A Search for Solutions Through Intervention

The contemporary research on intervention has centered the construction of the transition knowledge base on research about students and student development. Test, Mazzotti, and colleagues' work (Test, Fowler, et al. 2009; Test, Mazzotti, et al. 2009; Mazzotti et al., 2015) illustrates the point that correlational and causational intervention studies are highly valued, and the bulk of these types of transition studies have targeted student development and individuals with disabilities as the recipients of interventions. Intervention research, and a focus on the scientism of special education, requires samples that are accurately defined. This is in some ways at odds with practice in classrooms. The inclusive education movement has made the heterogeneous grouping of students, and the range of general and special education classroom settings, more common than in previous decades where separate settings were the norm. Simultaneously, changes in the growth of the LD category and the challenges with disproportionate disability identification and service delivery across disabilities disrupt confidence in the establishment of homogeneous research samples nested in educational environments, especially for students who are also members of historically marginalized groups. Therefore, the connection between transition intervention and student development, reflective of the synergism between research and practice, may be only loosely connected. This shakes up the search for solutions through intervention, a problem underscored by outcome data illustrating continued unequal education opportunities.

Research and Practice with an Eye Toward Diversity and Equity

The development of the field of transition highlights societal, dominant-group values about what it means to be an adult with a disability and achieve success after high school, as well as what obstacles or problems need to be solved in order to achieve this success. The concerted focus on self-determination as a strand of transition research provides a clear illustration of this point. In the 1990s, the U.S. Department of Education invested heavily in research targeting the development of self-determination. In brief, transition researchers effectively argued that transition planning required students with disabilities to have knowledge of self and disability, and the skills to identify strengths and needs, articulate goals, self-assess progress, and adjust goals based on experiences and outcomes. Relatedly, federally funded, field-initiated research flourished during this time and it remains an important prong of transition education in both practice and research today. Both researchers and practitioners, most of whom are members of the dominant racial/ethnic and socioeconomic groups with common education backgrounds, established definitions of expansive concepts such as "disability," "adulthood," and "success," leading to hegemonic views of self-determination specifically, and transition education more broadly.

Research involving both researchers and participants from outside the dominant group, however, began to challenge and engage in a scholarly dialogue that questioned dominant values and the construction of the problems facing the field. Cultural mismatch theories supported by empirical evidence were among the first to illuminate the limitations of having a narrow and dominant view represent the field of transition. For instance, Rueda, Monzo, Shapiro, Gomez, & Blacher (2005) presented interviews from Latina mothers of children with disabilities that demonstrated perspectives of independent living that did not align with the dominant, legalistic view that children become adults and gain independence at the legal age of majority, based on U.S. policy and law. The study of parent involvement emerged across special education procedures, including transition, and in concert with research questions about diversity and equity (see, for example, García, Perez, & Ortiz, 2000; García, 2002; Harry, 1992a, 1996; Harry, Kalyanpur, & Day, 1999; Harry & Klingner, 2006; Voltz, 1994; Zionts, Zionts, Harrison, & Bellinger, 2003). Together, results from these studies generated questions about equity and diversity in transition education, many of which remain unanswered.

RESPONDING TO RENEWED CHALLENGES: ELEVATING EQUITY WITHIN THE CONTEXT OF HISTORY

Despite growth in the knowledge base, the challenges of improving postschool outcomes for all students, including those with disabilities who are also from other historically marginalized groups, have not been sufficiently addressed to warrant complacency or even a sense of security that we are on the right track. The purpose of this book is to synthesize transition education around questions of diversity and equity and clear a path forward. In Chapter 2, I examine transition as a cultural practice, tracing the ways in which the models we have employed have privileged dominant views of what it means to be a successful adult and how this is observed and measured in research. Explored chronologically, this synthesis helps to explain how the targets of transition research and practice have been too narrowly focused either on a particular outcome such as employment, or often by default, on a particular population such as adolescents with a single disability classification. I conclude the chapter by identifying opportunities for expanding the extant scholarship, using a wide angle lens from which to view successful postschool life and connecting to a larger range of diverse transition perspectives and experiences.

In subsequent chapters, I explore two contemporary problems that have consistently interrupted equal opportunities in education for adolescents with disabilities, especially those who also experience discrimination based on race/ethnicity, immigration and language, sex and gender identity, and socioeconomic background and status. In Chapter 3, I draw on interdisciplinary scholarship to explain how exclusionary discipline has far-reaching consequences for adolescents who are transitioning into adulthood. I draw upon the small body of work in special education transition that addresses related transition needs, adding traction to this subfield by merging it with scholarship from fields such as law, education policy, and critical theory. My purpose here is to identify specific steps for deconstructing the barriers that discriminatory punishment and separation introduce in the lives of adolescents with disabilities, particularly for those who are also from historically marginalized groups.

In Chapter 4, I focus on the important role that health and self-determination play in the lives of adolescents with disabilities by increasing the possibilities for physical and socio-emotional well-being, social engagement, and financial stability. I highlight relevant research in the fields of medicine, psychology, and health policy, bridging to the limited but related body of work in special education transition. This chapter serves to underscore the interrelatedness of transition with other fields of study. My purpose here is to illustrate how the culture of the practice of transition should cover a broad landscape, depicting trajectories into adulthood situated, not only within the walls of the school, but also in families and communities in order to address equity for a diverse student population, many of whom regularly experience marginalization and/or occupy spaces where the effects of historical marginalization influence everyday existence.

In the final chapter, Chapter 5, I present a set of recommendations for research and practice, establishing equity as a key goal of transition education. Informed by my use, throughout the book, of theoretical and empirical sociocultural studies, I spotlight three strategies for harnessing the strengths of diversity and meeting the demands of equity. These are: Expanding our paradigms, and hence the methodologies used to study and teach transition; joining special education scholarship with relevant work in other fields of study; and, balancing the individual with the social, cultural, historical, and political contexts and groups to which they belong. It is my hope that these recommendations open the doors to the development of specific strategies for making the culture of practice in transition education more effective and just.

At least three specific sociocultural theoretical frameworks are visible in this work: Bourdieu's capital theory, Bronfenbrenner's ecological theory, and Rogoff and Cole's shared conceptualization of cultural human development. Many mentor texts and theoretical frameworks, from special education, disability studies, anthropology, and so on, influence my analyses of the extant special education transition scholarship–so many that it would be impossible to trace the lineage of my thinking in a completely transparent way. Therefore, I identify these as major players in my work, but they do not represent an exhaustive list of the foundations upon which my thinking has developed. Using sociocultural tools, I want to see how culture, diversity, and equity get operationalized in transition research and practice.

Chapter Two

Transition Education as a Cultural Practice

What does it mean to experience a successful transition into adulthood? If life is indeed a journey, which paths and destinations sustain and motivate travel, making the effort worthwhile and fulfilling? As the brief introduction to the field in Chapter 1 illustrated, transition practice and research has expanded from earlier emphases on employment and vocational training to broad domains of adult living that include career development, postsecondary education, self-determination, and community participation, as well as other related specific domains such as financial literacy, transportation, and social relationships. Postschool outcomes studies frequently document significantly lower rates of high school graduation, college enrollment, college degree attainment, and financial independence for young adults with disabilities who face or have faced additional marginalization as a result of racial/ethnic, linguistic, gender, and class biases as well as other forms of discrimination.

People who have experienced a convergence of multiple types of marginalization or disadvantage may not have had sufficient opportunities to meet important milestones and/or successful trajectories to adulthood when compared to dominant group peers. Explaining disparities as individual deficits might be tempting because it takes the onus off systems, schools, teachers, and the higher education faculty who prepare them. These explanations, however, provide little leverage in changing the trajectories of adolescents from historically marginalized backgrounds. As the identification of 32 evidence-based transition practices (Test, Fowler, et al., 2009) demonstrates, however, researchers and practitioners have devoted time and other resources to the construction and implementation of transition education, ameliorating, treating, or developing knowledge and skill deficits associated with disability.

Reframing the question from its current perspective (i.e., How do we intervene and address perceived/identified student weaknesses?) is essential to increasing our capacity to address postschool outcomes disparities and improving transition outcomes more generally. Understanding individual challenges and barriers associated with the manifestation of disability is important, but this knowledge is more powerful if we also understand the culture of our practice. From this perspective we might ask, Are the paths leading to successful adulthood (e.g., leaving high school with a diploma, developing a career through postsecondary education and employment experiences, maintaining financial independence) clearly marked? Are universally understood guides, maps, and other tools available for the routes? Do these roads have turn lanes and entrance/exit ramps that are accessible? Are there many modes of transportation and paths to destinations that symbolize success, allowing for diversity in travel itineraries?

Examining and producing a knowledge bank about the other elements of the journey, beyond our focus on the individual with a disability and his family, is critical in a landscape of rich diversity represented by school-aged youth in the United States. In doing so, it is possible to embrace transition education, including research, as a constellation of practices in which individuals and their families, as well as educators and service providers, are situated to act with agency. Arzubiaga, Artiles, King, and Harris-Murri (2008) underscore the importance of this shift in the perspectives of education researchers, stating,

> The traditional response to this challenge has been to conduct research on cultural minorities. However, . . . this practice is fraught with theoretical and methodological limitations. Instead of focusing on culture as the exclusive possession of certain groups in society, we propose a view of culture that defines the human experience; thus, culture is ubiquitous, dynamic, and has historical roots. (p. 312)

Promoting equity in postschool transition outcomes for young adults with disabilities across all strata of ability, race/ethnicity, sex, and gender identities, languages, socioeconomic backgrounds, and so on, begs the use of expanded lenses for examining the complex intersection of culture and transition. Invisible practices become visible, assumptions about universal experiences are challenged, and differences can be reimagined, not as individuals' deficits, but as opportunities to change the culture of a field. Using the lenses of sociocultural and capital theories will augment current approaches to transition research and practice by exposing gaps in our knowledge base, by expanding our tools for inquiry and practice, and by evolving our understanding of culture to a practice in which we are all agentive participants. Our first step is to examine transition itself, as both an object of research and a school-based practice, through these analytic lenses.

TRANSITION MODELS SEEN THROUGH LENSES OF CULTURAL THEORIES

Numerous transition models have been employed by researchers and practitioners since the inception of the field in the mid-1970s when career development for individuals with disabilities was established within special education (Brolin, 1983; Brolin & D'Alonzo, 1979). Models are visual representations of theories and concepts that underlie both research and practice and reflect the ways of thinking in a field of study (Ougaard, 2013). Examining these models is an exercise in reflexivity–the act of looking at the tools we use to analyze as representations or reflections of how we as social scientists and educators see, make sense of, and make claims about the field (Bourdieu, 2004). Reflexively examining the models provides insight into a field's *culture of practice*, and as Arzubiaga and colleagues (2008) note, this illuminates the types of research questions asked, the methodological decisions made to answer those questions, the results, and the conclusions drawn from them. This reflection is a necessary step in addressing inequity, revealing assumptions and hegemonic thinking, knowledge gaps, and pointing to opportunities for new frameworks, tools, and strategies.

In the field of transition, models address the process of moving from adolescence to select domains of adulthood. As the following examples illustrate, conceptualizations of this process, however, have often leaned toward a school-based view of activity and outcome. The focus on school experiences and outcomes can be traced to the field's development as a subfield of special education, largely a study of disability in school contexts. Additionally, formal transition planning is a regulated process; federal education policies such as IDEA 2004 have operationalized planning and enumerated compliance requirements. The heavy focus on transition as a process that can be implemented and measured in school contexts is central to the field, in the Bourdieuian sense of the word. Bourdieu's meaning of *field* includes places, structures, and mechanisms in which people live, learn, and work, with an understanding that people are simultaneously producing and being produced by the values and practices that constitute the rules of the field (Webb et al., 2002).

Early models of transition reflect the location of school as institution, governed by federal and state policies and regulations that address transition. Federal policies initially identified employment as the most important measurable outcome of schooling for students with disabilities and one that must be addressed on IEPs. The field is not only comprised of visible and discernible structures and regulations, nor is it entirely "a product of deliberate creation" (Bourdieu & Wacquant, 1992, p. 98). In this way, the extent to which insiders take up or reject its values, practices, and outcomes also shapes the field. Moreover, fields overlap, the passage of time occurs, the structures within the field evolve, and the people who populate the field change its landscape. Following early models' focus on employment, newer transition models expanded to include postsecondary education. These models reflect the demands of a larger field, including the national economy and a societal trend whereby a high school diploma is considered an intermediate outcome and a conduit to continued education at postsecondary institutions and programs. The iterative nature of the field's evolution is not, of course, on autopilot, happening without human agency. Bourdieu and Wacquant (1992) also explained that players or actors in a field can and do work to change its values, rules of operation, and structures. Individuals with disabilities and parents of adolescents with disabilities, as well as transition scholars, have argued for and supported the expansion of targeted outcomes to include postsecondary education. As the following chronological study of transition models demonstrates, conceptualizations of transition have become increasingly broader over time.

FROM A CULTURE OF PAID EMPLOYMENT TO LIFE SATISFACTION

Arranging major transition models in historical sequence shows that, rather than competing with one another, the models have lineage and become increasingly complex, to a point, over time. Employment has always been a prominent component of transition planning and education. Since the field's origins, employment was considered a cornerstone in one's value as a community member and key to independence. Using a sociocultural lens highlights the relevant underlying assumptions about human development. Developmental stages and the expectations of learners at each stage are defined both by the activities themselves and group members' participation in those activities (Rogoff, 2003). As we expect adolescents to accept the role of adult through work experiences, we also shape the experience of working adults. To follow Rogoff's theory of culture and human development, working has been defined as a transition process by which individuals become increasingly independent (financial and otherwise), indicating a transformation from child to adult. Early transition research reflected this. "As for other Americans, a major prerequisite to economic self-sufficiency for individuals with disabilities is a job. Employment is an essential key to successful integration into community life and is associated with greater independence, productivity, social status, and financial security" (Weicker, 1987, p. 7).

Illustrating Rogoff's (2003) point that culture and people are mutually constitutive, sequencing the models also shows that over time researchers and educators, with input and urging from families and individuals with disabilities, have become increasingly aware that the transition to adulthood involves more than getting a job. Nevertheless, the models have reinforced the importance of employment, postsecondary education, and independence over time. The predominance of employment and the macroculture values it represents, however, is coupled with initial de-emphasis on transition domains that are central to a robust vision of life after high school. Employment in these models reflects the logic and chronology of U.S. policies, and the values that undergird them, relative to general and vocational education and to the overarching values associated with individualism and capitalism. Competitive employment, necessary for independence as represented by choices in housing, food, and other material needs and wants, is a defensible cornerstone in transition research and practice. Additionally, employment leading to self-sufficiency is considered a normalizing experience.

Yet one could also point out that social and emotional (or socio-emotional) well-being, absent from most models, is a necessary foundation for being able to secure and sustain employment, shedding light on a gap or hole in transition models. For some people, social and emotional well-being, as both a domain in transition education and as an outcome, is equal in value to employment. For example, *bien educado* is associated with Mexican education values and traditions that stress the importance of social competencies such as respect and care for one's elders as an indicator of one's educational success (Valenzuela, 1999). The point here is not to stereotype; culture is fluid and multifaceted, interactional and associated with systems and institutions, as well as with people. Prioritizing the transition to independent worker over the transition to respectful adult creates a tension, illustrating an example of cultural dominance–seeing adults as employees, or people with disabilities as human capital–that perhaps does not resonate with all members of American society. Having a sociocultural lens is useful for expanding conceptualizations of what transition is and can be, and thus, for expanding transition education and opportunities to successfully move into adulthood. In fact, early transition models did eventually morph, implicitly addressing social and emotional well-being, as represented in transition assessments by socio-emotional indicators; however, the extent to which this was done in response to a changing, more racially/ethnically and linguistically diverse population that included a wider range of definitions of adulthood and values is not well documented.

Expanding the models is not just potentially more culturally responsive. The importance of relationships and social networks, conceivably reliant upon a person's social and emotional well-being, gained attention in vocational rehabilitation (Winch, 2000); social networks are associated with wages for employees with disabilities (Phillips, Robison, & Kosciulek, 2014), and with access to community-based transition resources (Williams & Le Menestrel, 2013). Social capital, a related concept also addressed in more recent transition research, has introduced a discussion of power and dominance, critically questioning the transition opportunities of adolescents with disabilities who are separated from their peers without disabilities (Vorhies, Davis, Frounfelker, & Kaiser, 2012; Williams & Le Menestrel, 2013). While there are many definitions and a constellation of related concepts, none are really represented fully in current or past transition models. Not only does this illuminate a limitation in the current knowledge base, but it also shows an opportunity to expand the models to be more culturally responsive.

EARLY MODELS OF THE SCHOOL TO EMPLOYMENT TRANSITION

Another sociocultural lens that can be used to filter and thus examine the developmental aspects of transition is Bronfenbrenner's (1979) ecological perspective. As Rogoff (2003) noted, Bronfenbrenner's ecological framework examines the contexts and relationships between settings in which development is occurring. In this view, settings are nested in one another and the barriers or boundaries across settings are permeable. The emphasis on employment for adolescents with disabilities is not only reflective of a dominant developmental view of what it means to be an adult. Additionally, the prioritization of employment is a reflection of macrosystemic ideologies in U.S. governmental policies on education and labor (i.e., exosystemic variables identified by Bronfenbrenner). Throughout special education transition research, scholars invoke federal policy mandates regarding the employment of individuals with disabilities. Legislation such as the Education for All Handicapped Children Act (EAHCA, 1975), related amendments in the 1980s, and the Rehabilitation Act Amendments of 1986 are mentioned throughout the literature, framing the responsibility of employers to create opportunities for adolescents and young adults with disabilities in the workplace (Greenan & Phelps, 1982; Hardman & McDonnell, 1987; Razeghi & Davis, 1979; Szymanski, King, & Parker, 1989; Weicker, 1987).

Federal Policy Links to Employment-Focused Models

One of the first conceptual depictions of transition in special education was Will's (1983) model, which focused on employment as the single most important outcome of education. The dissemination of this model dovetailed with the 1983 Amendments (PL 98-199) to the EAHCA of 1975 (PL 94-142), the legislation currently known as IDEA, which targeted the school-to-work transition, funding related research and demonstration projects on the employment of people with disabilities. Will conceived of services as bridges that make the outcome of postschool employment accessible to all students with disabilities. The first of three bridges (see Figure 2.1) is considered to be generic or typical. This bridge is labeled "No Special Services," and includes resources that all individuals (with and without disabilities) use when they leave high school. This bridge remains an important concept in transition today. For example, adolescents often make connections with their parents' friends and colleagues, securing employment opportunities through these connections. The second bridge is labeled "Time-Limited Services" and captures services that are in place temporarily, providing a push toward immediate employment goals. For example, a training or certification program would be considered a time-limited service under this model. This second bridge is also sustained in contemporary transition models, but its details have been further fleshed out, and currently these supports address needs beyond those in the domain of employment.

Finally, the third bridge, labeled "Ongoing Services," depicts continuing resources in support of working after high school. According to Will (1984), this third bridge represented a "fundamental change" (p. 4) in policy at that time, shifting from postschool programs without an orientation toward the future to programs that would include supports for obtaining and maintaining employment, and thus future independence. Instead of offering assistance with daily living needs without vocational skill development, a staple in transition programs of that time, this shift marked the beginning of transition services for the

Figure 2.1. Will's (1983) Initial Transition Model Entitled "Major Components of the Transition Process"

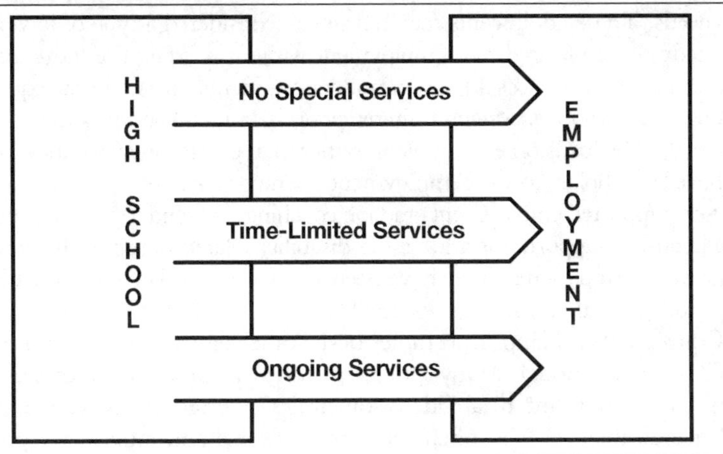

Will, 1983, p. 7

express purpose of supporting employment, including jobs in segregated work settings such as sheltered workshops. Will (1983) identified the third bridge as a noteworthy revision to transition policy because previously, "services are typically designed to be non-vocational, either providing lifelong custodial care or preparing consumers for later vocational services" (p. 7). She critiqued existing approaches for having made little progress toward helping people with disabilities realize the benefits of competitive employment, stating that the programs "actually serve as an alternative to work, functionally excluding participants from both work related services and employment opportunities" (Will, 1983, p. 7).

With this model, Will (1983), and the Office of Special Education and Rehabilitative Services (OSERS) in the U.S. Department of Education, where she then served as assistant secretary, seeded some of the values that continue to be emphasized in special education transition policy today. Transition is conceived of as a process, one requiring coordination between high school and service providers for adults with disabilities (e.g., vocational rehabilitation counselors). A major difference between the early and subsequent models is that the goal of employment no longer serves as the single, exclusive marker of transition success. Another less obvious and perhaps less purposeful shift introduced by this model included a broadening of the population for which transition services were targeted after the release of Will's explanation of transition policy. The OSERS statement clearly focused on individuals with significant disabilities who need extensive transition supports for maintaining employment.

Yet Will acknowledged that individuals with disabilities did not represent a homogenous group and that the type, amount, and duration of support leading to employment should be individualized. The OSERS focus on employment may have pointed administrators, educators, and other service providers toward adolescents with less intensive learning, emotional/behavioral, cognitive disability-related needs. These adolescents may have been considered a type of low-hanging fruit ready to be plucked into employment without needing the more extensive array of transition services and accommodations identified as "special equipment, building modifications, longer training periods, and other investments" (Will, 1983, p. 9). The focus on employment, rather than postsecondary education, may also have led scholars toward employment-oriented research questions about task analyses, supported employment, and job coaching that tend to be associated with more intensive supports for addressing disability-related needs in the context of employment. Employment may have been seen as appropriate for populations for whom college, at that time, seemed unlikely.

Conceptual and empirical studies of the time aligned with or were reflected in Will's (1983) model. Many studies included a sample of adolescents and adults with significant disabilities, sometimes referred to as severe or low-incidence disabilities, who often required extensive and intensive supports to find and maintain employment. Conceptual studies (see, for examples, Holler & Gugerty, 1984; Shroka & Schwartz, 1982; Wehman, Kregel, & Barcus, 1985) focused on delineating the steps necessary to assess, plan, prepare, place, and follow young adults with disabilities in employment settings. Interestingly, some major tenets of vocational preparation and career development are prominent in these conceptual papers, including knowing requisite career-based skills and knowledge, assessing one's strengths and weaknesses in relation to desired careers, and matching skill sets to job settings. As such, these conceptual papers responded to and mirrored Will's primacy of employment as an outcome of high school and focused on the preparation of individuals with disabilities' readiness for employment upon leaving school. Assessing and matching young adults' vocational and other skills to the demands of a particular job were key issues for researchers and practitioners such as vocational rehabilitation counselors and educators (Holler & Gugerty, 1984; Nietupski, Hamre-Nietupski, Welch, & Anderson, 1983; Shroka & Schwartz, 1982). Additionally, the contexts of employment settings and roles of key stakeholders in securing and maintaining employment opportunities were also considered to be important to the process of transitioning to employment during the 1980s. Scholarship engaged discussions of employers' competing needs for an adept workforce and economically viable business plans, as well as their perceptions of people with disabilities. Some conceptual papers acknowledged workplace discrimination (see, for examples, Shroka & Schwartz, 1982; Weicker, 1987). These papers served to expound on Will's model, which had largely described transition as a set of services.

The Roles of Individual Stakeholders and the Importance of Planning

In 1985, Wehman, Kregel, and Barcus reenvisioned a transition model that continued to focus on employment as a sole outcome but added more specificity about services and stakeholder roles (see Figure 2.2). This newer model added several key concepts including input from individuals with disabilities and their families, whom Wehman and colleagues (1985) position as consumers, and related service providers. This model demonstrated another lens that, similar to the ideologies of employment represented in policy, mirrored dominant views about people as consumers, suggesting that individuals' choices and goals should determine which transition services were available to adolescents, young adults, and their families. These connections made visible the relationship between adult services for people with disabilities (i.e., vocational rehabilitation) and services for children and adolescents with disabilities (i.e., special education transition services). In this way, their model populated the initial conceptual model of transition, outlining who was responsible for what and introducing the importance of interagency collaboration. Whereas Will's initial model depicted

Figure 2.2. Wehman and Colleagues' (1985) Transition Model Entitled "Three-Stage Vocational Transition Model for Handicapped Youth"

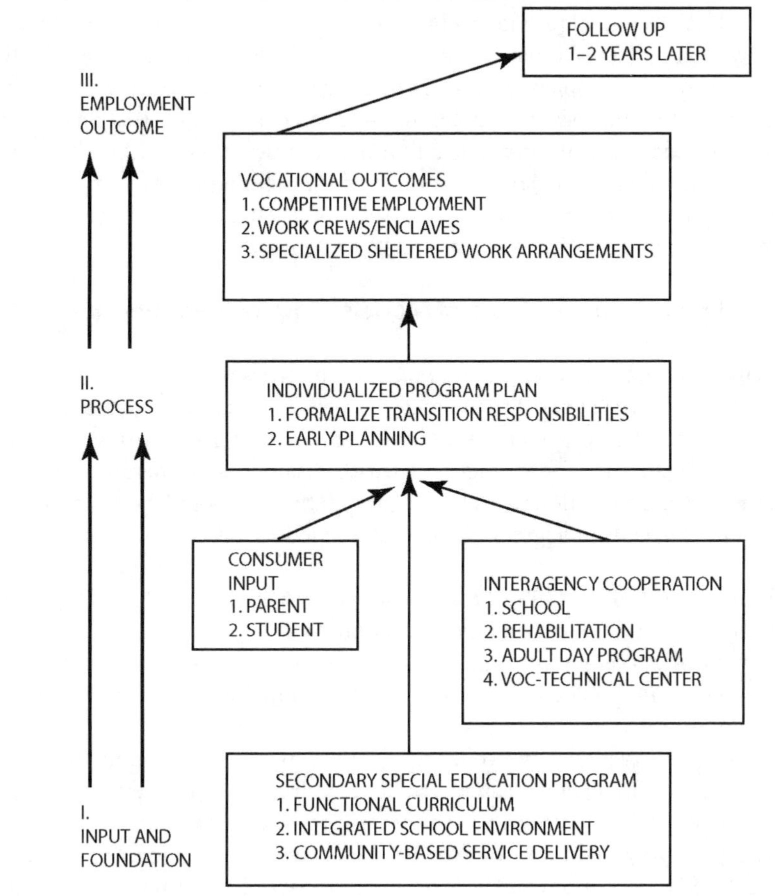

Wehman, Kregel, and Barcus, 1985, p. 28

a system of supports from high school to employment with bridges that did not intersect, Wehman and colleagues detailed the relationships between individuals with disabilities and service providers, both of whom they positioned as key players in planning processes.

Will's (1983) use of the metaphor of bridges depicting services necessary for attaining employment served to organize many of the steps in Wehman and colleagues' model. In Wehman et al. (1985) the representation of "secondary special education program" (the functional curriculum and integrated learning environments) corresponds to Will's second bridge depicting time-limited services to be delivered in high school, while the services such as those provided by "voc-technical centers" and "sheltered workshop arrangements" mapped more closely to the third bridge depicting ongoing services provided by adult-serving agencies after high school. Wehman and colleagues, however, depicted the transition process as one that required interactions of multiple individuals and agencies over time. Further, although employment remained as a culmination of transition efforts in their model, the importance of planning and follow-up were introduced. Will's model provided a bird's eye view of transitioning from school to employment, while Wehman and colleagues established some key steps in the process and focused on planning as a mediating step. These conceptual studies open the door for empirical examination. Wehman et al. emphasized inclusivity and differentiation in transition education for adolescents with LD within the extant general education curricula, stating, "If the school program experiences have been rich in quality and diversity, many mildly handicapped persons will be able to work in a variety of fields" (p. 32).

Empirical Studies as Artifacts of Models' Employment Priority

Research continued to illustrate and reflect the emphasis on employment depicted in both Will's (1983) and Wehman et al.'s (1985) models as a single priority. Many studies used employment as a kind of litmus test for whether school was a successful experience for young adults with disabilities. Generally, research reified the existing transition models by conceptualizing a population that would likely not pursue college degrees. Thus, employment remained the central focus of transition.

Wehman and Hill's (1981), early work in transition illustrates this point. Funded by a state rehabilitation office, vocational services are designed to secure employment of adults with "moderate to severe" intellectual and developmental disabilities. The implementation of the intervention, tested through a single subject design, included multiple components, many of which would later be conceptualized in Wehman and colleagues' (1985) model of transition: assessing clients' work and independent living skills, establishing goals, developing and securing opportunities with employers willing to hire people with disabilities, supervising employment, and evaluating the success of placements. Wehman and Hill (1981) saw employment as an integral part of adult life. Their study provided empirical evidence on which both models would later build, depicting employment as a universal outcome of high school, focusing on a younger population that included adolescents with the most intensive and extensive support needs. Characteristic of this body of research, studies provided descriptions of interventions and employment outcomes. Conceptual research, however, indicated a move beyond employment with position statements and theoretical discussion of postsecondary education.

EXPANDED MODELS OPEN THE FIELD BEYOND EMPLOYMENT

Despite field-initiated research projects' focus on employment, societal attitudes shifted toward postschool education as a necessary step in adult fulfillment. Hence, transition research and practice similarly expanded (Madaus, Dukes, & Carter, 2013). In 1985, Halpern captured the calls of researchers and practitioners who were concerned that employment, as a singular focus, did not adequately depict the richness or the demands of adulthood (see Figure 2.3).

> What the authors (sic) of this [Will, 1983] policy seems to be suggesting is that the nonvocational dimensions of adult adjustment are significant and important only in so far as they contribute to the ultimate goal of employment. . . . Such a position can be challenged both philosophically and empirically. (p. 480)

Halpern (1985) argued that community adjustment functioned as a kind of umbrella over employment, residential environment, and social and interpersonal networks. As Halpern's model illustrates, Will's (1983) bridges of services from high school to employment were retained but their positions were modified. A broader conceptualization of adulthood, one Halpern termed *community adjustment*, was balanced on three pillars that he considered to be of equal importance, arguing that "if any of the three pillars are inadequate and do not carry their own weight, then the entire structure is in danger of collapse and a person's ability to live in the community is threatened" (pp. 480–481). Although community adjustment was not succinctly defined in the discussion of the model, it was clearly linked to the concepts of quality of life and life satisfaction, ideas behind the pillars capturing participation in activities with family and friends, inclusion in community, and social and emotional well-being.

In a detailed discussion of the pillars, Halpern (1985) explained what each entailed. First, the employment pillar adopted, without modification, Will's (1983) components and issues related to career and work. Second, the residential environment pillar emphasized for the first time in the context of transition a set of nested environments (i.e., home, neighborhood, and community) in which individuals with disabilities lived. Third, the social and interpersonal networks pillar introduced the centrality of concepts of self and relationships with others. Halpern made two important arguments while expounding on this

Figure 2.3. Halpern's (1985) Transition Model Entitled "Revised Transition Model"

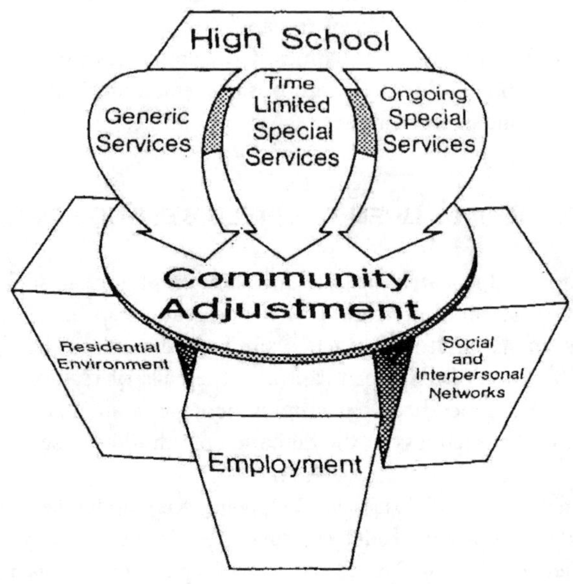

Halpern, 1985, p. 481

model. First, he laid the groundwork for transition research and practice to consider and value interpersonal and social-emotional well-being as a stand-alone and key dimension of adulthood. Second, he strengthened the connections between the general education curriculum, vocational education, and special education. Halpern envisioned these as conduits for transition education, arguing that the general and vocational curricula used to prepare adolescents without disabilities for the typical demands of adulthood (i.e., demands beyond specific job performance tasks) were also appropriate for and should be included in transition education for adolescents with disabilities.

In this way, the Halpern (1985) model, similar to the Wehman et al. (1985) model, fleshed out some of the details of Will's (1983) bridges and began the process of identifying the curricular, service, and instructional characteristics of transition. These models also expanded the image of the population of high school students with disabilities in need of transition services. Prior to this, mostly adolescents with extensive and intensive disability support needs were considered, at that time, to need services for employment and independent living. Those who typically needed less extensive or intensive supports (e.g., LD) were gaining attention in research and practice. Like Wehman et al., Halpern argued that students with disabilities should be included in the array of existing, general education courses that addressed prevocational and vocational education, interpersonal skills, and academics.

Large-Scale and Longitudinal Evidence Bolsters Model Expansion

In the 1980s, larger empirical studies of student outcomes began to emerge in response to questions about the postschool experiences of young adults who received special education services during high school. These studies often used state-level outcome data of adolescents and young adults with a range of disabilities and measured achievement in terms of high school graduation and postschool employment, and they included samples of individuals across the 11 then-recognized disability categories enumerated in the EAHCA. Nationally, high school graduates with disabilities were more likely to be employed (60%) than those who left school without diplomas after age 18 (30%) and those who dropped out prior to age 18 (51%). Across the country, graduation rates for students with disabilities varied, ranging from 44% to 64%, depending on the state.

Analysis of state-level outcomes data illustrated variation, not only in the outcomes themselves, but also in the ways that the data itself was collected, stored, accessed and analyzed. For example, Hasazi, Gordon, and Roe (1985) used a subset of Vermont State Department of Education data to ascertain the graduation status and employment rate of students with disabilities. Approximately 60% graduated, and 65% had paid employment. Similarly, in Colorado, Mithaug, Horiuchi, and Fanning (1985) used state-level data to locate and conduct a follow-up survey of high school graduates with disabilities. Although 82% of the nonrandomized sample self-reported that they were employed at some point since high school, the average number of jobs held was three, most were working below minimum wage and on a part-time basis, and two-thirds reported living with parents. Probing beyond employment, Mithaug and colleagues introduced questions about social relationships and found "a large portion receiv[ing] infrequent or no visits from others" (p. 402). They also included a general question about participants' views of their quality of life and found that 64% indicated satisfaction.

Policy Initiatives Fuel Transition Research and Practice

In 1983, the first amendments to EAHCA were passed and the federal government committed to funding the first of several national longitudinal studies referenced in Chapter 1. The purpose of longitudinal research was to better understand both postschool outcomes of adolescents and young adults with disabilities, as well as their educational progress leading up to graduation or school exit. Although the reports from the first national study of transition-related experiences and outcomes would not emerge until the early 1990s, the field was fueled by the federal initiative and interest in transition. Also included in the 1983 amendments to EAHCA were provisions for developing model service delivery and transition programs [Sec. 626 (a) (2) (b) (2)]. Interestingly, this federal policy was not solely focused on the employment outcomes of adolescents with disabilities. The amendments added several key outcomes of interest including further education opportunities and independent living. Additionally, this policy raised the issue of differing populations of adolescents and corresponding outcomes by calling for demographic studies across disability and age categories. To meet the demands of the federal call for a longitudinal outcome study that also took into consideration the influence of school programs, an expanded conceptual model of transition, one that would more clearly delineate the inputs and the outcomes of transition, was needed.

MODELING TRANSITION AS A SET OF EDUCATIONAL INPUTS AND POSTSCHOOL OUTCOMES

Results from the implementation of the NLTS, conducted in the 1980s, highlighted expanded concerns about the postschool outcomes for adolescents with disabilities. Further, this research greatly influenced the field's conceptual model of transition (see Figure 2.4). Although its publication was limited to research reports (Wagner, Blackorby, & Hebbeler, 1993; Wagner et al., 1991), a number of additional studies employed the NLTS model implicitly, using the dataset. For example, Fairweather, Stearns, and Wagner (1989) conducted an analysis of transition and vocational services offered by schools across the United States, emphasizing inputs rather than outcomes in the transition process. The NLTS (Wagner et al., 1991) model furthered the foundational development of a culture of research and practice upon which the field has continued to build.

As Figure 2.4 illustrates, the NLTS model moved away from Will's (1983/1984) single outcome of employment, also distinguishing itself from both the Wehman et al. (1985) and the Halpern (1985) models by detailing and exemplifying transition variables of interest and furthering the conceptualization of transition as a process. Employing a flow chart motif, the NLTS (1991) model capitalized on an implicit feature of the previous models: transition as a set of instructional experiences and services (inputs) and results (outputs) that required coordination between special, general, and vocational education. Following Wehman et al., the NLTS depicted school programs as one driver of student outcomes, enumerating subcategories such as courses taken, setting of courses, and other services received; it depicted adult programming (e.g., job training, vocational and rehabilitation services) as another driver. Perhaps the most significant conceptual expansion, however, was the enumeration of community adjustment variables. Specifically, the NLTS model went beyond employment to identify other outcomes: postsecondary education, social activities, independence, and community participation.

The NLTS (1991) model introduced several novel transition concepts. For the first time, and in congruence with the 1983 EAHCA requirement to report postschool outcomes by demographic groups, individuals' characteristics were considered as key inputs in this transition model. These included disability characteristics and other sociodemographic characteristics associated with the

Figure 2.4. The 1991 Conceptual Model of the First National Longitudinal Transition Study, Entitled "Conceptual Framework of Transition Experiences and Outcomes of Youth with Disabilities"

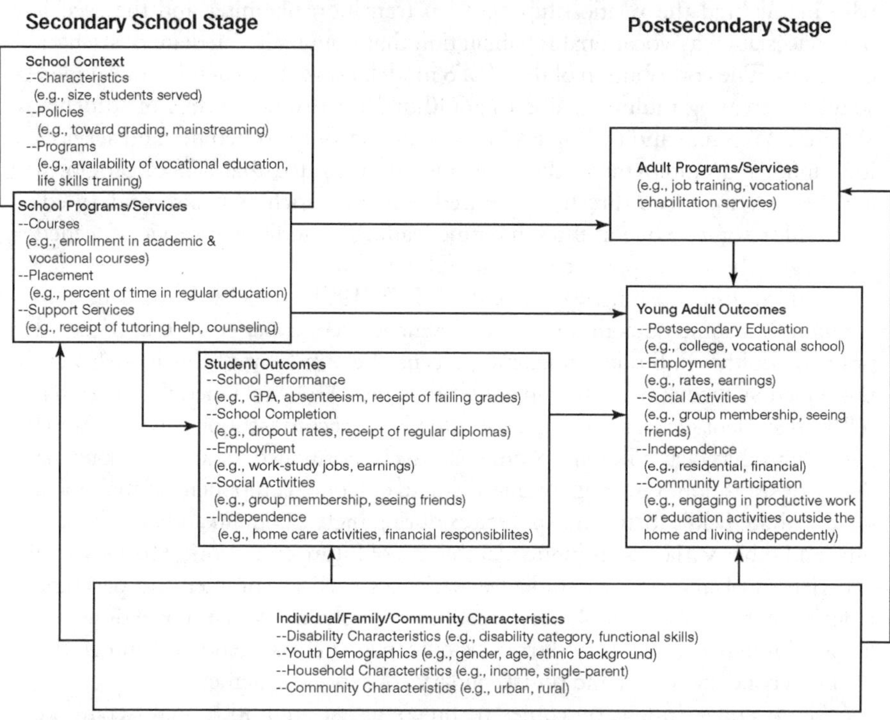

Wagner et al., 1991, pp. 1–7.

individual (e.g., age, sex, and racial/ethnic background), the household (e.g., income, family structure), and the community (e.g., urban, suburban, rural). This revision opened the door to considering intersections between disability and postschool experiences because it identified outcome patterns across groups based on gender, socioeconomic, linguistic, and ethnic backgrounds. It also opened the door to examining intersections between individuals' characteristics and schools' demographic populations, programs, services, and, hence, outcomes. The 1991 NLTS model also illuminated the importance of school contexts that embed instruction and service delivery. The dataset included, for example, school size and amount of time in the full range of educational settings.

Attention in the NLTS (1991) model to school contexts is conceptually related to Halpern's (1985) focus on environment, substituting the NLTS context of school for residence. An important distinction, however, is that the NLTS model positions context as a driver (i.e., transition input) of outcomes, whereas Halpern's model reflected the environment, and the individual's situated success, as an outcome (i.e., output). School context, as conceptualized in the NLTS, also serves as a backdrop for services and programs, which not only potentially drive outcomes, but also potentially predict types of adult services and postschool programs. This is an important feature of the model, and it underscores the point made by early theorizers such as Wehman et al. (1985) who highlighted the relationship between transition planning and the receipt of services such as vocational rehabilitation that potentially mediate postschool outcomes. The contribution of the NLTS model, however, expanded our understanding, creating multiple paths to adulthood for diverse groups of students. Whereas Wehman and colleagues focused on vocational outcomes and services for supporting employment, the latter model illustrated that school programs and services may lead directly to desired outcomes such as postsecondary education for some, while at the same time leading to additional services needed after high school to support employment for others.

A third distinguishing feature of the NLTS (1991) model was the conceptualization that some outcomes (e.g., employment) were experiences that occurred prior to adulthood. Student outcomes, a central component of this model, were positioned as mediating factors in adult outcomes. These included variables that reflected student performance (grades, attendance record, school activities, home and community activities) and were collectively positioned as another potential driver of transition. Creating an intermediate outcome component of the model increased the field's focus on experiences during high school, in addition to planning and other variables, as influential shapers of future endeavors. The in-school experiences of interest (i.e., student experiences such as summer and part-time employment) paralleled adult outcomes. For example, the NLTS model draws relationships between school performance outcomes such as attendance and grades during secondary school and postsecondary education enrollment.

Connecting student outcomes to outcomes in adulthood may seem like common sense; however, it made visible two important expansions in transition models. First, this more detailed version made the field consider a wider range of domains that needed attention during both transition planning and education. Second, it began to disrupt the dichotomization of adult outcomes (i.e., employed/unemployed) that previous models had not begun to address. So, for example, the NLTS (1991) model began to interrogate the importance of a multi-step transition education process that included variables such as earnings and social relationships in relation to postschool employment and community involvement in early adulthood. Taken as a whole, the NLTS model components furthered Halpern's (1985) conceptualization that adulthood amounted to much more than employment, and it began to parse the many moving parts of postschool quality of life.

NLTS Exposes Knowledge Gaps and Issues Requiring Field-Based Research

The NLTS transition model shaped the first national survey of its kind, the purpose of which was to paint a longitudinal picture of how students with disabilities were doing during and after high school. Results from the federally commissioned NLTS were presented in a series of reports from its authors and published by SRI, the institute responsible for implementing the survey. Descriptive results illustrated key findings about the nationally representative sample of adolescents and young adults with disabilities, providing the first snapshot of both their secondary and postschool outcomes for the first time in U.S. education history. The strength of the study was twofold: First, the national sample was randomized and thus the results were generalizable. Second, because transition outcomes are related to maturity and age (e.g., postschool employment often increases over time), the longitudinal nature of the dataset was an illuminating feature. On the other hand, these strengths brought some limitations to the work. Much of the data was self-reported, by individuals with disabilities, their parents, and school/program staff. Response rates over time and participant group varied, affecting the number of complete sets of participant data. Regardless, findings from the SRI reports and the many journal articles that functioned as secondary sources for the NLTS findings mapped new directions in transition research. Hence, the NLTS (1991) model for transition was inculcated in the practice and research of transition even though it was not represented in peer-reviewed special education journals.

Describing who received secondary special education services. Although the annual congressional reports on the implementation of EAHCA provided the incidence rates of disabilities for all youth who received special education, the NLTS data were some of the first to document the national picture of racial/ethnic disproportionality in secondary grades. Wagner and colleagues (1991) found the percentage of Blacks receiving special education was "about twice as high as the percentage in the general population" (p. S-2). They also noted that the population across disability categories (with the exception of deaf/blind) was predominantly male, and more likely than adolescents without disabilities to come from economically disadvantaged backgrounds. Although special education writ large understood disproportionality to be a problem since Dunn's (1968) seminal paper, data for examining the extent of disproportionality in disability identification was just now being spotlighted in the field of transition.

Intersections between bias and/or marginalization and transition are particularly germane because they are closely tied to quality of life. A long history of studying and making policy addressing gender and racial/ethnic equality in the context of labor practices preceded the disability rights movement. The examination of equity, hand in hand with disproportionality, demands the use of the kinds of data the NLTS was generating. Therefore, the NLTS data demonstrating overrepresentation of adolescents of color with specific disabilities, coupled with findings that secondary and postschool outcomes for some groups (e.g., Blacks, girls, young adults from low socioeconomic backgrounds) were subpar as compared to their peers with disabilities who were from the dominant,

White, middle- and high-socioeconomic groups was one indication of an area in need of further study and advocacy.

Describing secondary and postsecondary experiences. Beyond demographic characteristics of students, the NLTS also provided initial national-level data on access to secondary programming and curricula. Adolescents across disability categories were not routinely accessing vocational education, career counseling, job placement, and work experiences; when they did gain access it was often shortly before exiting high school (Wagner et al., 1991). Additional findings raised concerns about access: dropout rates were high among adolescents with disabilities, one-third of whom, as a cross-categorical group, left school without diplomas. Social interaction data was also gathered and these painted a variable picture for adolescents across disability groups. While about 14% were considered socially isolated by their parents (as survey respondents), about 40% were seeing friends and maintaining memberships in social organizations and clubs (Wagner et al., 1991). Residential and financial independence were also measured, resulting in only 12% living away from parents in the first two years following high school.

The NLTS illustrated that for employment, an outcome that had been the subject of previous transition models and numerous follow-up studies, the data were disappointing. Only 46% of adolescents and young adults were employed after high school, as compared to 59% of their peers without disabilities (Wagner et al., 1991). Of those who were employed, 40% were employed only part-time; young women with disabilities were more likely to garner pay at or below the minimum wage. Similarly troubling results surfaced in the examination of postsecondary enrollment. Young adults with disabilities who graduated from high school enrolled in postsecondary education at a rate of 14% during the first two years out of high school. Ultimately, findings from the NLTS signaled to the field that secondary transition experiences and postschool outcomes demanded closer examination and scholarly problem-solving. Additionally, it depicted complex and varied processes by which adolescents with disabilities moved from high school into adulthood. For example, the NLTS showed that some groups of individuals with disabilities (e.g., those with EBD) fared far worse than others (e.g., those with visual impairments [VI]) when accessing secondary programs and services, but that the opposite phenomenon occurred in the world of employment (individuals with VI had lower rates of employment and lower pay than individuals with EBD).

In a subsequent report, Wagner, Blackorby, Cameto, et al. (1993) sharpened the focus of the conceptualization of postschool outcomes, zeroing in on four dimensions: postsecondary education, employment, residence, and community participation. This second report illustrated with greater detail the complexity of the NLTS transition model and its importance for focusing the field's attention on a system of complex inputs and outcomes with multiple paths from high school to adulthood. Also in this second report, the NLTS data were analyzed for the purpose of better understanding the inputs—that is, school characteristics, programs, courses, and services and how these contribute to postschool life. The general finding was that high-poverty schools did not translate into poorer outcomes for all students with disabilities (Wagner, Blackorby, Cameto, et al., 1993). Examining the time that students with disabilities spent in the general education classroom, however, illustrated a different trend in relation to transition outcomes. Controlling for successful school completion, Wagner, Blackorby, Cameto, et al. found that competitive postschool employment was 11% higher for those students with disabilities who spend at least 50% of their time in general education settings. This finding, however, was complicated by the intersection of employment with disability type. Adolescents with either mild or severe cognitive impairments, when compared to their peers with sensory or physical disabilities, did not seem to reap the benefits of inclusive education as a predictor of postschool employment. Perhaps the most perplexing set of findings about school programming was generated by analyzing transition planning data. Results showed that having a formal transition plan did not yield a statistically significant advantage in postschool outcomes. Specific goal-setting, however, did increase the likelihood of goal attainment in significant ways. For example, adolescents with a goal to attend academic or vocational postsecondary education programs were 21% and 11% more likely, respectively, to enroll in such programs than were their peers with disabilities who did not have such a goal statement with respect to competitive employment did not result in statistically significant differences.

Acknowledging issues of inequity. Patterns of outcomes revealed inequality across what the NLTS authors dubbed the "raw ingredients," which represented individual and household characteristics (p. 31). These characteristics included disability, gender, race/ethnicity, individual functional skills and abilities, family composition, education level of head of household, annual income, receipt of governmental financial support such as food stamps, and population and locale of community (Wagner et al., 1991). Neither students' bilingual status nor language spoken at home were examined in detail. Patterns of results are challenging to interpret. The referent group and its comparison groups are not consistently applied throughout related publications.

Some reports use the outcomes of Whites with disabilities as thumbnail sketches of typical postschool outcomes. At other times, the referent group is compared to all other races combined (Wagner, Blackorby, Cameto et al., 1993, pp. 3–17). In multiple analyses seeking to measure observable patterns across the intersection of individual characteristics, the NLTS employed four disability clusters: mild cognitive, sensory, physical, and severe cognitive disability groups. For other analyses, all of the then-recognized 11 disability categories are considered stand-alone categories. Sex is consistently analyzed dichotomously and male–female comparisons are made to either the 11 disability categories or the four disability clusters. Furthermore, intersections of more than two variables (e.g., examining race/ethnicity, disability, and gender simultaneously) are less common. Moreover, results do little to help the field gauge how disproportionate disability identification potentially interacted with transition experiences and postschool outcomes. Although the NLTS drew attention to outcomes differences across groups, it set the stage for basic analyses (i.e., disability and race/ethnicity) without complex and theoretically framed comparisons that detail the convergence of multiple forms and sources of domination and marginalization. Understanding these convergences are essential to understanding experience and outcomes, and to identifying solutions (Crenshaw, 1991). Moreover, such explications help make sense of diversity itself (e.g., inter- and intra-group differences).

The following findings illustrate some of the inequalities that were initially documented through analyses of the NLTS results. Transition presented particular challenges to young women with disabilities in ways that differed from the challenges faced by young men with disabilities. For example, although females with disabilities were considered to have more significant manifestations associated with disability, they performed better academically than their male counterparts (Wagner et al., 1991). Despite this, female secondary students were not more likely to leave high school with a diploma than were their male peers. Further, females had less access to transition programs and services while in school than did males with disabilities. A potential explanation both for leaving high school without a diploma and for limited participation in postschool employment is that females with disabilities were more likely than their male counterparts to be parents before leaving or within the first three years after high school.

Patterns of reduced access to transition education and programming for adolescents from low socioeconomic backgrounds also surfaced in NLTS analyses (Wagner et al., 1991). For example, students with disabilities living in poverty had reduced access to inclusive, general education classes while in school, and they were less likely to receive related services when compared to adolescents from higher socioeconomic backgrounds. Additionally, low socioeconomic background was also associated with diminished rates of postschool employment and postsecondary education enrollment. In Wagner and colleagues' report they elaborated on two intersections (disability x sex and disability x socioeconomic background), noting "The characteristics were not independent of one another, but were often clustered" (S-13). Exploring more complex experiences that required questioning the convergences of structural, political, and representational intersectionalities (Crenshaw, 1991) related to race, disability, gender, and socioeconomic background, occurred to a much lesser extent.

Later, Wagner, Blackorby, Cameto, and colleagues (1993) tried to capture a more nuanced understanding of differential transition outcomes experienced by subpopulations of individuals with disabilities, including young women. Although fewer women with disabilities enrolled in postsecondary education as compared to women without disabilities, the difference was similar when comparing males with disabilities to males without disabilities. Examining wages, however, told a different story. Here, men with mild cognitive or sensory disabilities earned significantly higher wages than women within these same disability categories. Interestingly, young men with disabilities were significantly less likely, despite higher on-average incomes, to live in independent residences. The authors hypothesized that independent living, which included separate households, was higher for women because those who were parents were more likely to live with a spouse or domestic partner (Wagner et al., 1991).

Racial/Ethnic inequalities were also documented in early reports from the NLTS. African Americans with disabilities were 13% less likely to be employed after high school than their peers with disabilities from all other racial/ethnic groups combined (Wagner, Blackorby, Cameto, et al., 1993), they earned lower salaries, and they were less likely to live independently. A pattern of inequality was more difficult to identify when considering the postschool outcomes of Latino students. For example, Latino students were less likely than their Black and White peers to access vocational education in secondary school, but more likely to access postschool vocational training. As a cross-categorical group, independent living arrangements were 19% lower for Latino young adults when compared to their European American peers with disabilities (Wagner, Blackorby, Cameto, et al., 1993).

Reach of the NLTS Findings in Transition Research and Practice

In addition to the widely available NLTS reports, scholars' uses of the findings contributed to a set of papers published in special education journals. Researchers in the field were likely hungry for NLTS results because, as a first-of-its-kind study, major findings identified knowledge gaps and problems, patterned over time, and demonstrated need for additional study. For a handful of studies, the focus was on the inputs and outputs identified in the NLTS model (see Figure 2.4), and research questions were designed to examine predictors of postschool outcomes.

Postschool employment studies. Following the NLTS, studies of postschool employment by other researchers illustrate the survey's influence on research design. Some conducted secondary analyses of NLTS data. For example, Heal and Rusch (1995) examined postschool employment of a subsample of NLTS school-leavers and their outcomes. They identified 22 predictor variables clustered around student, parent, school, and community levels. In addition to finding that postschool employment of individuals with disabilities was significantly lower for those who lived in low-income, high-unemployment communities, they also found that individual characteristics significantly predicted postschool employment. Specifically, males with disabilities were more likely to be employed than females with disabilities after high school, and the same was true of White students, when compared to individuals who were not White.

Other secondary analyses on postschool employment included Rojewski (1999), who focused on a subpopulation of the NLTS who were identified through parent surveys as having LD. A major finding from this study was that young women with LD were six times less likely to have postschool employment up to 2 years following high school when compared to young men with LD. When compared to females without disabilities, the NLTS female subsample was half as likely to enroll in postsecondary education and reported unemployment at four times the rate of those without disabilities. Rylance (1998) also conducted a secondary analysis of the NLTS to study predictors of postschool employment, focusing on adolescents and young adults with EBD. Although results of her study showed that sex and racial/ethnic differences in postschool employment were not significant, she was able to identify school-level predictors of postschool employment such as having a high school diploma and access to vocational education for both male and female young adults with EBD.

Other researchers extrapolated from the national findings in designing smaller studies. Doren and Benz (1998) examined gender inequality in competitive employment and used the NLTS model as a guide for identifying and examining predictive factors in a smaller sample from a follow-up study with participants from Nevada and Oregon. In this study, females with disabilities (47%) were significantly less likely to be competitively employed than their male peers with disabilities (72%), and these differences were not attributable to the range of disability categories. Predictor variables for both males and females included the number of jobs held during high school and thc use of social networks to find employment. For females, additional predictors were identified; these included self-esteem, family income, and the interaction of these two variables (Doren & Benz, 1998). These researchers also focused on programmatic access to vocational education and transition planning as is visually represented in the NLTS model, concluding that access to transition education for females with disabilities warranted further study.

Similarly, Levine and Edgar (1995) compared postschool outcomes in employment and other domains for males and females with disabilities in the state of Washington, as did Sitlington and Frank (1993) in Iowa. Results varied. In Washington, females with LD had significantly lower employment rates than their male counterparts for 1 of 3 years studied, and no significant differences were found between males and females identified with ID and those without disabilities (Levine & Edgar, 1995). In Iowa, differences between males and females were also not found to be significant; however, males earned significantly more than females. Congruent with NLTS findings, both studies raised concerns about the degree to which young women with disabilities were parenting and the possibility that this interfered with their availability for paid employment and/or substantiated females' independent living status correlating with marriage and parenthood (Levine & Edgar, 1995; Sitlington & Frank, 1993).

Rimmerman, Botuck, Levy, and Royce (1996) also examined predictors and used the NLTS concepts of inputs of individual characteristics such as disability, sex, and household income, as well as community characteristics such as population size (e.g., urban, suburban). Their sample included both younger and older adults with ID or LD enrolled in a New York City–based vocational rehabilitation program, and they found that gender did predict employment, with males being twice as likely to be employed. Further, they found that race, in particular being African American, was associated with low job placement, which they hypothesized was connected to "the incalculable consequences of racism" (p. 60) and the limitations in the job market associated with poverty (Rimmerman et al., 1996).

As this handful of post-NLTS studies of predictors of postschool employment illustrates, early transition research followed the NLTS conceptualizations of inputs (i.e., individual, school, and community level characteristics) as variables of influence on the postschool outcomes of young adults with disabilities. Further, these studies show that equal employment outcomes for males and females with disabilities was on the minds of researchers and valued as an important issue in the field. Despite findings that showed significant differences in employment for young women with disabilities, researchers were slow to extend secondary analyses of NLTS postschool employment or other outcomes to race/ethnicity and/or its intersection with sex. In some studies, race/ethnicity was not reported (for example, Doren & Benz, 1998). In others, race/ethnicity was examined separately (Heal & Rusch, 1995; Rylance, 1998) or was not disaggregated in analysis (Levine & Edgar, 1994; Rojewski, 1999). Only Rimmerman and colleagues (1996) disaggregated for race (i.e., Black, Latino, and White) and provided discussion of race/ethnicity as a predictor of postschool employment.

Instead, many researchers used NLTS results and reports as a springboard for launching related, small-scale studies with similar designs. Most focused on disability category or geographic locale. Often these lines of inquiry were used to build conceptual arguments for the development of transition interventions. Race/ethnicity was infrequently or intermittently included or presented as data collection and/or analysis. Discussions of findings most often centered on postschool outcomes research and recommendations for practice based on disability, at times addressing the intersection of gender or socioeconomic background. A strong push toward race-neutral inquiry allowed race/ethnicity to remain unquestioned as an individual characteristic that functioned as a driver of both student and adult outcomes originally presented in the NLTS model.

There were exceptions. In a state-by-state comparison of school-leaving status, Oswald and Coutinho (1996) used national child-count data collected under the directive of IDEA and the U.S. Department of Education to conduct a secondary analysis to better understand the phenomenon of dropping out of high school. They intersected statewide variables of school-leaving with population demographics such as poverty and race/ethnicity. Building on the NLTS transition model, its methods, and its findings, these researchers also examined state-level community characteristics pertaining to the transition variable of high school completion for adolescents with EBD. Findings from this study provided another direction for the study of transition, moving away from individual sociodemographic characteristics toward contextual variables in which schools are embedded. Their contribution to the literature was to demonstrate that the graduation rate and type of completion (i.e., diploma, certificate of completion) varied greatly from state to state, and that patterns of race/ethnicity and socio-economic statuses of statewide populations existed. Questions about equity and models' capacity to support the development of related research studies were just starting to take hold in the field.

Implications for the practice of special education transition education. Following the NLTS reports, secondary analyses, and related original studies, unequal patterns demonstrating diminished postschool employment for women and people of color with disabilities were addressed quite differently. A flurry of follow-up studies examined differential outcomes by disability and gender, amassing implications for practice. The suggestions for changing practices directly addressed reducing gender biases in the materials, programs, and approaches to career development and job placement (Doren & Benz, 1998; Rojewski, 1999; Sitlington & Frank, 1993). Levine and Edgar (1995) recommended pregnancy prevention programs including the assertion "that every female special education student should have a pregnancy-prevention plan specified on her IEP" (p. 298). Studies in this era also addressed specific issues pertaining to disability category studied (e.g., linking to adult counseling for young adults with EBD and career development for high school students with LD), but robust discussions of barriers that might illustrate the convergence of multiple exposures to marginalization were rare. Moreover, ignoring the particular challenges that might correlate with disproportionality, for example, marked a missed opportunity to more closely follow the NLTS conceptual model, which illustrated complex paths to postschool outcomes that included the multiple influences of school- and community-level variables in addition to individual-level variables. Instead, subsequent models of transition dug more deeply into practice, inching the field closer toward the study of intervention.

FROM MODELS TO A TAXONOMY FOR TRANSITION EDUCATION

Federal special education legislation and policy, beginning with EAHCA in 1975 and proceeding through a series of reauthorizations resulting in its current iteration, IDEA (2004), have paid increasing attention to outlining specific transition requirements for adolescents with disabilities. As a result, in addition to funding the NLTS, field-based studies of transition were funded, as were national centers of technical support and transition research. This attention solidified the study of transition into a bona fide subfield of special education. Continuing to the present day, the National Center for Special Education Research (NCSER), a subunit of the U.S. Department of Education's Institute of Education Sciences (IES), commissions national longitudinal studies and funds research and technical assistance focused on special education transition, furthering the development of research and practice.

The Transition Research Institute (TRI), located at the University of Illinois at Urbana-Champaign, was one such federally funded think tank in transition that was funded from 1995–2000 (A. Trammell, personal communication, January 4, 2015), from which emerged another type of model, a taxonomy (see Figure 2.5). The taxonomy served as "a comprehensive, conceptual organization of practices through which transition-focused education and services are developed and delivered" (Kohler & Field, 2003, p. 176). The organizational tool continues to structure a framework for thinking about transition today; an updated version (Kohler, Gothberg, Fowler, & Coyle, 2016) is available from the current federally funded national technical assistance center on transition at the University of North Carolina at Charlotte. Further, the 1996 version has been used as a framework in widely cited reviews of experimental and quasi-experimental transition research to identify evidence-based transition practices (Mazzotti et al., 2015; Test, Fowler, et al., 2009; Test, Mazzotti, et al., 2009). Kohler's (1996) taxonomy, unlike other transition models, does not posit a sequence of steps toward successful transition, nor does it illustrate relationships between inputs and outputs. Rather, the taxonomy turns the field's attention to the practice of transition education and lists the activities in which schools engage in an effort to prepare adolescents who are leaving school and entering young adulthood.

The taxonomy consists of five domains that contribute to transition programming as a cohesive set of practices: *student development*, *family involvement*, *program structure and attributes*, *interagency collaboration*, and *student-focused planning* (Kohler, 1996). As a set, the taxonomy represented a framework of effective practices resulting from multiple reviews of the extant literature, evaluation studies of effective programming from U.S. state departments of education, and federally funded transition research projects (Kohler & Field, 2003). These reviews, however, were made prior to contemporary discussions of standards for efficacy and rigor in research that began to occupy concerns in both education and special education in the early 2000s (cf. Cook et al., 2009). As such, Kohler and colleagues did not limit their review to experimental and quasi-experimental designs as would likely have been done if the review were done today, although the 2016 version does not state this explicitly. The scholarly reviews upon which the original version is based preceded its publication (Kohler, 1993; Kohler, Destefano, Wermuth, Grayson, & McGinty, 1994; Rusch, Kohler, & Hughes, 1992). Similar to the NLTS model, depictions of Kohler's taxonomy (1996; 2016) are primarily disseminated through technical reports.

Kohler and Field (2003) describe each domain's components in some detail, providing the rationale for its inclusion, a sampling of supportive empirical evidence, and alignment with federal transition policies. Within each of the five domains, Kohler (1996) listed characteristics of effective practices. For example, life skills instruction, employment skills instruction, career and vocational curricula, work experiences, assessment, and support services were identified as essential components of the domain of *student development.* Additionally, each component was parsed into groups of effective practices. Thus, life skills, a component of *student development*, included instruction and curricula in the subdomains of

Figure 2.5. Kohler's (1996) Transition Taxonomy Depiction, Entitled "Taxonomy for Transition Planning"

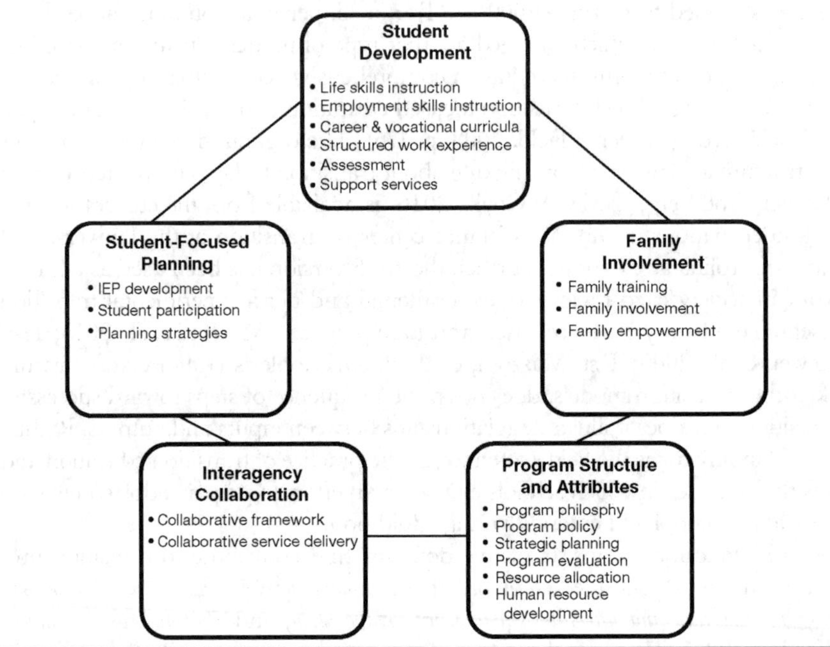

Kohler, 1996, p. 3

recreation, social skills, self-determination, self-advocacy, independent living, and learning. Rationales for the domains and the components, either those included or those omitted, are not fully explicated. For example, about the domain of *student development* the authors broadly stated that the identified practices "emphasize life, employment, and occupational skill development through school-based and work-based learning experiences" (Kohler & Field, 2003, p. 177). Interventions (e.g., Steps to Self-Determination) were also identified and categorized according to the taxonomy's structure in subsequent research (Field & Hoffman, 1996).

The categorical domain focus on practices minimized earlier model conceptualizations of inputs and outputs. Particularly in comparison to its immediate predecessor, the NLTS (Wagner et al., 1991) model, the taxonomy omitted student and family characteristics. As explained above, the previous NLTS (1991) model included racial/ethnic and other sociodemographic individual characteristics, family characteristics such as socioeconomic background, and community characteristics such as community size. Although the previous NLTS model did not explicitly address diversity, culture, and equity, the inclusion of individual and family characteristics in the former model implied that these factors were pertinent to transition education. The inclusion of sociodemographic variables was an acknowledgment that they somehow mattered in unequal postschool outcomes. The taxonomy's (Kohler, 1996, 2016) focus on categorizing practices did and continues to do more to identify and describe extant practices. It is less robust as a tool for asking how and why group differences in postschool outcomes existed. For example, in the taxonomy's *family involvement* domain, subdomains included training, involvement, and empowerment as neutral categories. The extent to which the identification of practices for the taxonomy engaged the extant scholarship on cultural and linguistic diversity and family involvement in special education was not clear. Yet the challenge of family involvement in special education processes was not a new issue at that time (Hanley-Maxwell, Whitney-Thomas, & Pogoloff, 1995; Katsiyannis & Ward, 1992; Mlawer, 1993; Turnbull & Turnbull, 1982), nor were the particular barriers faced by parents who were also members of historically marginalized groups (Boone, 1992; Harry, 1992a, 1992b; Sileo, Sileo, & Prater, 1996; Voltz, 1994).

Moreover, despite concerns about racial/ethnic disproportionality across all ages of students receiving special education documented in early reports to Congress on the implementation of EAHCA, and later IDEA, and continued documentation of disproportionality in the secondary grades noted by Wagner et al. (1991), Kohler's (1996) model did not have an obvious connection to practices that addressed this issue. Disproportionality, on the surface, may seem to have a distal relationship to the research questions and practices typically examined in transition. As the first NLTS demonstrated, however, postschool outcomes varied by race/ethnicity and disability, thereby highlighting the need to examine outcomes with an eye toward diminished opportunity and increased vulnerability for adolescents with disabilities who were also from historically marginalized groups. To illustrate, adolescents with EBD had (and continue to have) some of the poorest postschool outcomes. African Americans were (and are) overrepresented with EBD. Therefore, the poor postschool outcomes of African Americans and the state of their access to education opportunity was and is highly relevant to disability identification and its accuracy.

In the 2000s, annual reports to Congress would also show that disproportionality occurs, not only in the context of disability identification but also in students' access to the general education curriculum, which we also later learned was positively correlated with desirable postschool outcomes (Rojewski, Lee, & Gregg, 2015; Wagner, Newman, Cameto, Levine, & Marder, 2003). These connections, which need to be visible in order to be examined, were potentially obscured with the field's move toward Kohler's (1996) taxonomy as a transition model. It is possible that the domain of *program structure and attributes* provided the conceptual space for the consideration of disproportionality and other equity and diversity related issues, but the subdomains identified by Kohler (1996) and Kohler and Field (2003) were generic: program philosophy, program policy, strategic planning, program evaluation, resource allocation, and human resource development. Moreover, the intended purpose of the structures and attributes was to "provide the framework for implementing transition-focused education" (Kohler & Field, 2003, p. 179). On the other hand, the subdomain of program philosophy was the one place in the taxonomy where diversity was acknowledged with the practice of "cultural and ethnic sensitivity in programming and planning" (Kohler, 1996, model domain/subdomain depiction 12).

A RETURN TO INPUTS AND OUTCOMES MODELS

Although Kohler's (1996) taxonomy has been widely and recently employed as a framework for thinking about transition research and practice, two other important transition models have subsequently emerged.

Broadening the View

The first, a model by Patton and Dunn (1998; see Figure 2.6) blended earlier, pre-taxonomy models' conceptual assertion of directionality and flow. In other words, this model illustrated a process orientation aligned with federal policy and viewed transition education as activities (i.e., processes) resulting in postschool outcomes. The ultimate outcome, similar to Halpern's (1985) community adjustment, was non-specific, labeled *personal fulfillment.* Intermediate outcomes in this model, represented by a block labeled *knowledge, skills, supports,* and *service needs* closely paralleled the NLTS model's depiction of student outcomes, except that achievements (e.g., GPA, graduation) are omitted. Further, similar to Kohler (1996), this model de-emphasized school contexts, perhaps implied as embedded in the categories of leveled *school, family, self,* and *adult-services activities.* The NLTS (Wagner et al., 1991) model identified key inputs forming multiple pathways to life after high school, as well as a range of possible outcomes, but these were lost in this new model. Although the Patton and Dunn (1998) model marked a loss of complexity, it offered two additional insights to the field: emphasis on *activity* as a major input, moving beyond static knowledge and skills including, for the first time, experiences in planning and practicing transition activities (e.g., student-led IEP meetings), and insertion of mediating factors in the transition process, identified by the block *demands of adulthood.*

While the former was not exactly novel (both the Wehman and the NLTS2 models included work experiences), Patton and Dunn's (1998) focus on activity placed emphasis on the actors (individuals, parents, teachers, and service providers). This underscored the role of adolescents with disabilities and their families as more than recipients of services. By adding consideration for the types of knowledge, skills, and experiences required of adulthood (i.e., demands), their model also provided room for expanding conceptualizations of outcomes to those associated with a range of disability characteristics. The historical emphasis of transition education had previously been on adolescents who needed intensive and extensive services such as personal care attendants, job coaches, and independent living facilities for adults. Patton and Dunn were modeling the intermediate consideration of those needs in relation to the goals of personal fulfillment that individuals identified. For example, the demands of adulthood for a

Figure 2.6. Patton and Dunn's (1998) Transition Model, Entitled "Adulthood Implications of the Transition Process"

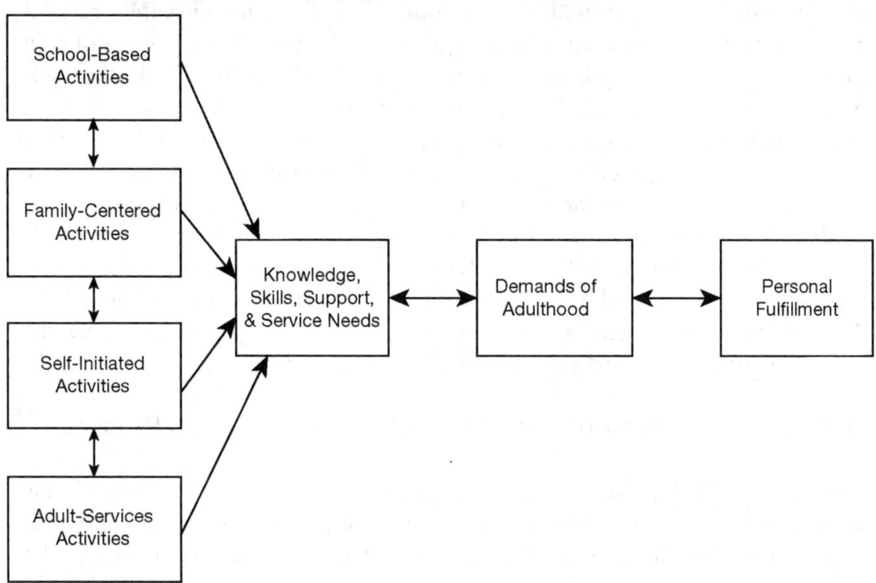

Patton & Dunn (1998), p. 5.

college student are likely different when compared to the demands for someone who is employed and does not intend to pursue further education. Thus, the model showed that transition preparation is mediated by adulthood demands.

The shifts noted in Patton and Dunn's (1998) model recursively reflected shifts in transition research and practice. Focusing on the roles of individuals with disabilities in their own transition processes was fueled by (and fueled) results from numerous federally funded projects that examined self-determination (Field, Martin, Miller, Ward, & Wehmeyer, 1998). The study of the construct of self-determination originated in psychology and remains closely linked to motivation theory (Deci, Vallerand, Pelletier, & Ryan, 1991). Self-determination appealed to both special education scholars and to people with disabilities who were leading the disability rights movement as a way of understanding disability and individuals' rights, roles, and responsibilities. Its invocation in transition scholarship marked the burgeoning of a significant body of research in transition and an important cultural shift.

Patton and Dunn's inclusion of the demands of adulthood in their model matched a then-recent emphasis on the largest emerging subpopulation of U.S. public school students receiving special education services, students with LD. Between the first year after the passage of EAHCA (1975) and 1994, the percentage of students with LD increased from slightly less than one quarter to 51% of all students receiving special education (U.S. Department of Education, 1995). Moreover, the first NLTS raised concerns about the transition and postschool outcomes for all young adults with disabilities and for young adults with LD in particular. Although young adults with LD were gaining employment at rates that exceeded rates of individuals from other disability categories, their rates of postsecondary education enrollment were lower than some, leading to concern about reaching a "ceiling in their progress toward independence" (Blackorby & Wagner, 1996, p. 410). This dovetailed previously voiced calls for expanding the focus of transition research and practices so that planning and education would benefit a larger group of adolescents including those with less intensive and extensive disability-related needs (Knowlton & Clark, 1987). Parallel studies in the LD population growth and their postschool outcomes drove home this message. In fact, Patton and Dunn's (1998) model was originally published as a model specifically geared toward adolescents with LD (Blalock & Patton, 1996). Not only were the content and complexity of transition expanded, so to was its conceptualization as a process with interdependent components.

Reaffirming the Interconnectedness of Components and Process

As conceptualizations became more complex, it was clear that additional information was needed to understand how young adults with disabilities fared after high school. The need for updated outcome data prompted IES to repeat the call for research examining the postschool outcomes of students with disabilities, commissioning the second NLTS (NLTS2). With the NLTS2 came a new depiction of the NLTS model of transition (Wagner, Kutash, Duschnowski, & Epstein, 2005); however, few changes were made to the original NLTS model. The depiction itself became simpler, but the model continued to show multiple paths and connections between inputs (e.g., school programs, individual characteristics) and postschool outcomes, now termed *achievements*. See Figure 2.7.

The relatively unchanged model depicted in the NLTS2 continues to be a driving force in transition, as reflected by the many publication from SRI and secondary analyses in academic journals that employed NLTS2 data. Therefore, its underlying assumptions and model structure are important markers of where we are as a field of practice today. Taken together, both the SRI reports and the journal articles reflect improved postschool outcomes for individuals with disabilities as well as pockets of tenacious challenges that have yet to be fully addressed. The overall rate of employment and postsecondary enrollment of young adults with disabilities has increased over time, and gaps between those with and without disabilities have narrowed. But wages, adjusted for inflation, do not reveal significant gains (Wagner, Newman, et al., 2005). Descriptive reports also show losses and gains for subgroups with a net effect that is challenging to interpret. For example, employment rates of young men and women with disabilities were comparable in the NLTS2, but the data also showed a significant gap in the rates of school-based (e.g., suspensions) and community-based (e.g., police involvement) behavioral consequences (i.e., negative social adjustment). Also, some gender gaps, such as getting married, were sustained as

Figure 2.7. The 2000 Conceptual Model of the Second National Longitudinal Transition Study, Entitled "NLTS2 Conceptual Framework"

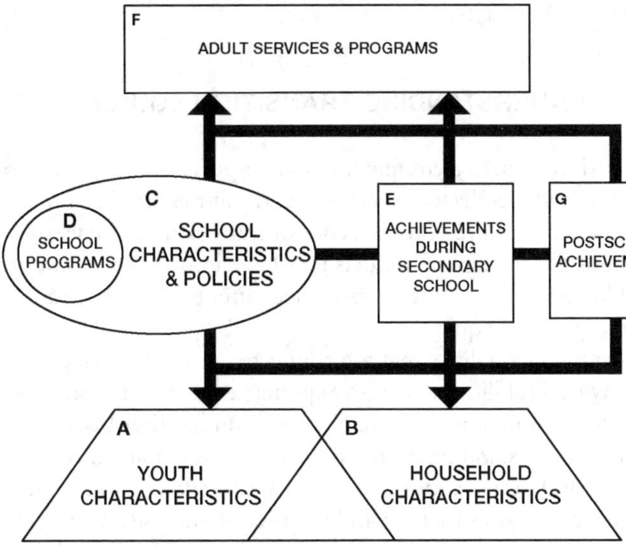

F
ADULT SERVICES & PROGRAMS
C
D
SCHOOL PROGRAMS
SCHOOL CHARACTERISTICS & POLICIES
E
ACHIEVEMENTS DURING SECONDARY SCHOOL
G
POSTSCHOOL ACHIEVEMENTS
A
YOUTH CHARACTERISTICS
B
HOUSEHOLD CHARACTERISTICS

Wagner et al. (2005), p. 32

depicted in the NLTS2, with young women being more likely to be married in the first few years since high school (Wagner, Newman, et al., 2005).

Many secondary analyses focused on predictors of both in-school and post-school outcomes, depicted in both NLTS models (Wagner et al.,1991; Wagner, Kutash, et al., 2005). For example, postsecondary enrollment in vocational and technical education programs was associated with disability type, whereas enrollment in college was associated with both race/ethnicity and socioeconomic background (Fleming & Fairweather, 2012). Additionally, dropping out was associated with significantly lower postsecondary enrollment (Newman, Wagner, Huang, et al., 2011), and it was also associated with individual characteristics such as having EBD, being female, and being African American (Zablocki & Krezmian, 2013). Moreover, some of these complex analyses addressed intersectionality of adolescents' identities based on individual characteristics. For example, Carter, Austin, and Trainor (2012) found that being male was associated with increased likelihood of employment, specifically for young adults with disabilities who were among those with the most extensive and intensive service needs (i.e., severe disabilities). Such analyses, however, were often conducted without an identified conceptual model depicting the position or direction of transition components in relation to outcomes, with explicit consideration for moderating and mediating factors. *Youth and household characteristics* in the NLTS2 (Wagner, Kutash, et al., 2005) model, the *individual/family/community characteristics* in the NLTS (Wagner et al., 1991) model, comprise a collective component functioning as an input, but its significance and path are not visible. Mediators such as teacher knowledge and moderating factors associated with individual, family, and community characteristics are in need of further development in future models.

UNDERSTANDING TRANSITION EQUITY

Postschool transition marks a culmination of compulsory education experiences and is a marker of the collective successes and failures leading up to and into early adulthood. The culture of the practice of transition can be viewed through this discussion of the conceptual models that have informed the work of people in the field. The models reveal that only select attention has been devoted purposefully to questions of equity.

Addressing the inequalities that are connected to the historical marginalization of people with disabilities who also experience poverty, racism, and sex and gender identity discrimination, as well as anti-immigration biases, and so on, requires a better understanding of the theoretical and empirical connections between transition and larger issues and broader contexts of American society. It also requires us to use tools that expand the unit of analysis. The model review demonstrates that much of transition research has focused on the individual without purposeful examination of the historical, social, political, and cultural factors that contribute to postschool outcomes. Augmenting our knowledge and practice also necessitates the use of broader methods of inquiry in addition to those that attempt to demonstrate causality, as well as improved strategies for making sure our research, across methodologies, makes strides toward culturally responsive research (Trainor & Bal, 2014).

Ladson-Billings (2006) challenged scholars and teachers to reconsider the use of the term *achievement gap* and replace it with *education debt.* In this, she asserted the importance of reframing educational inequalities as the result of disparities, not located in the performance of children in schools, but located in the work of policymakers, leaders, researchers, educators, and our society writ large who have been unable, unwilling, or unaware of the kinds of changes that are needed to be equitable and provide all people with opportunity through a strong education. Ladson-Billings' reconceptualization resonates with the purpose of this book. The work of sociocultural theorists such as Rogoff, Bourdieu, Bronfenbrenner, and others will continue to be used in the following chapters to aid our understanding, providing not only new views of the affronts to equality faced by people with disabilities who are also members of other marginalized groups, but also to provide windows through which solutions for improvement can be glimpsed or seen unobstructed.

CHAPTER THREE

Changing the Lenses of Inquiry

Putting the School-to-Prison Pipeline Into Focus

Every day in the United States, adolescents and young adults with disabilities face disciplinary procedures, both in and out of school, that exclude them from instruction. Sometimes disability does influence behavior in ways that limit executive functioning in self-regulation and impulse control. For example, a student with ADHD who deliberately sets off a fire alarm as a joke, either without knowing or without considering the consequences of that action, will likely receive a punitive response from educators and administrators.

But studies of school discipline also demonstrate that educators, school administrators, and law enforcement officials employ biases, introducing vulnerability and exposure to in- and out-of-school disciplinary procedures for youth with disabilities, particularly those from other historically marginalized groups. For example, a teacher might associate classroom disruption with a student who is identified as having EBD without realizing that the disability label itself might be a key factor in who he sends out of class, who he refers to a disciplinary dean, or, in an extreme case, about whom he calls for assistance from a school resource officer (i.e., police).

Disciplinary exclusions, particularly reoccurring incidents, can have a devastating domino effect on an individual's and her family's plans for the future. This chain of negative school-based experiences can set off undesirable community-based experiences such as police interaction and court involvement. From missed instructional time and social isolation to encounters with the juvenile and adult justice systems, each experience chips away at education opportunities while in high school, postsecondary education, employment, and community engagement.

The first domino to fall is missed instruction. Disciplinary procedures interrupt learning to varying degrees. Students sent to an in-school-suspension setting are separated from their peers and their teachers. This likely results in some combination of missed collaborative work with peers, group instruction from general education teachers who are content experts in a given course, and/or assistance from special education teachers who are experts in individualizing instruction to meet disability-related needs. Yet, the payoff for the individual student is low. Exclusionary discipline procedures are not effective in reducing inappropriate behaviors (Noltemeyer, Ward, & McLoughlin, 2015), and repeated exclusions are negatively associated with academic achievement (Morris & Perry, 2016).

A second domino to fall is often an individual's self-concept as a successful student and her presence as an integral member of a classroom community (Gibson & Haight, 2013; Haight, Gibson, Kayama, Marshall, & Wilson, 2014; Kayama, Haight, Gibson, & Wilson, 2015). Deleterious effects on achievement and self-concept likely contribute to long-term effects such as dropping out of school and repeated behaviors that are deemed either delinquent or illegal (Lee, Cornell, Gregory, & Xitao, 2011). Thus, police involvement represents yet another domino in the chain of negative events associated with suspension and expulsion. This trajectory has been named the school-to-prison pipeline (STPP). Both adolescents with disabilities, and those from historically marginalized groups, are vulnerable to involvement in the STPP because, in part, these practices and systems are fraught with biases. Before exploring the STPP and its relationship to transition, it is necessary to step back and examine the importance of field, specifically, general education settings, which often fall outside the notice of special education transition researchers and practitioners.

GENERAL EDUCATION SETTINGS AS FIELDS OF PROMISE

As noted, there are many fields, both metaphorical and actual, that come together in the lives of individuals who are transitioning from adolescence to early adulthood. According to Test, Mazzotti et al. (2009), one setting, that of the general education classroom, is of particular interest because it is a moderate predictor of postschool engagement in postsecondary education (Baer et al., 2003; Halpern, Yovanoff, Doren, & Benz, 1995), employment (Heal & Rusch, 1995), and independent living (Heal & Khoju, 1997). Test, Mazzotti, and colleagues used criteria for moderate evidentiary support authored by IES and included experimental and correlational studies with statistically significant results and measurable effect sizes (Mazzotti et al., 2015; Test, Mazzotti, et al., 2009). For example, there is a positive correlation between general education inclusion and postsecondary education enrollment for students with autism spectrum disorders (ASD; Chiang, Cheung, Hickson, Xiang, & Tsai, 2012). Causal links from inclusion to postsecondary education enrollment using propensity matching methods and a secondary analysis of the NLTS2 students with LD and EBD have also been documented (Rojewski et al., 2015). Further, work experiences in natural settings (where employees with disabilities work alongside employees without disabilities) predict postschool employment both for students with low-incidence disabilities (Carter, Austin, & Trainor, 2012) and those with high-incidence disabilities (Carter, Trainor, Ditchman, Swedeen, & Owens, 2011), who conceivably have differing levels of intensity and extensity of needed supports. Precisely because the evidence supports the benefits of inclusion on transition trajectories, patterns of exclusion in secondary education settings are important to examine.

Patterns of Exclusion

Patterns of excluding adolescents with disabilities from inclusive education settings can be organized into at least two main tracts: disability-related support needs and behavior-related issues. While this division is imperfect, it remains useful in framing why so many students with disabilities are not included in general education settings even though inclusion is a documented predictor of successful transitions. As the previous discussion of field suggests, general and special education settings have different characteristics, are governed by separate and sometimes conflicting rules, and establish distinct roles and responsibilities of the key players.

Inclusive education in the general education setting, particularly for students with the most extensive support needs, has been fraught with implementation questions about physical access to general education classrooms and resources such as texts, technology, and so forth; social access to peers without disabilities and peers with disabilities who have less extensive support needs; and intellectual access to all or a subset of learning standards, activities, and assessments (Ryndak, Moor, Orlando, & Delano, 2009). As a field, the general education setting may be represented both by an actual place (e.g., an algebra classroom taught by a certified mathematics teacher) or metaphorically by "access to" the general education curriculum (e.g., learning algebraic concepts in a self-contained math class taught by a certified special education teacher). In fact, most students from ages 6 to 21, across all disability categories, receive special education services in the general education classroom setting: 62% receive education in the general education classroom for 80% or more of the school day, 19% are in general education classrooms between 40% and 79% of the school day, 14% are in general education classrooms less than 40% of the school day, and only 5% are educated entirely outside of general education classrooms including separate and residential schools, homebound instruction, and detention settings (U.S. Department of Education & U.S. Office of Special Education and Rehabilitation Services, 2015).

Decisions to provide education in restrictive environments can be based on real and/or perceived obstacles to feasibly support students in inclusive settings, and/or to manage significantly disruptive behavior. A closer examination of both disability and race/ethnicity demonstrate that separate settings are disproportionately implemented across subgroups of the school-aged population (ages 6–21) receiving special education (Kurth, Morningstar, & Kozleski, 2014). While 95% of all students across disability categories receive education in the general education setting for some part of every school day, that is true for only 83% of students with EBD and 73% students with ID (U.S. Department of Education & U.S. Office of Special Education and Rehabilitation Services, 2015). Moreover, students with EBD are the third most likely (following students with deaf-blindness and those with multiple disabilities) to be served entirely separately in other settings.

Simultaneously, these categories (EBD and ID) also reflect higher risk-ratios for disability identification for Native American, Hawaiian and Pacific

Islander, and Black students. For example, Black students are 2.14 and 2.26 times more likely to be served as students with EBD and ID, respectively, than are students with other disabilities from all other racial/ethnic groups combined (U.S. Department of Education & U.S. Office of Special Education and Rehabilitation Services, 2015, p. 43). Similarly, Native American students are 1.58 and 1.73 times as likely to be served in these categories, as are native Hawaiian and other Pacific Islanders (1.38 and 1.55 risk ratios, respectively). Therefore, exclusion, or not receiving inclusive education services, is correlated with both disability and race/ethnicity, leading Fierros and Conroy (2002) to dub the phenomenon of general education exclusion of students with disabilities who are also members of historically marginalized groups as "double-jeopardy" (p. 39). More recently, the term double-jeopardy has been used to describe a pattern of risk based on another education contextual variable–urban school settings. Brock and Schaefer (2015) found that schools located in large urban districts were more likely to exclude students with disabilities with extensive support needs (i.e., ASD, ID, and multiple disabilities) from general education settings. Unfortunately, although their study focused on urban schools, Brock and Schaefer limited their analysis to disability without examining race/ethnicity. Yet data from the National Center for Educational Statistics reflect that urban school districts are experiencing a shifting population where children of color represent majority student populations (Maxwell, 2014), making race/ethnicity pertinent to their study.

The annual reports to Congress on IDEA 2004 do not provide distinct, publically available datasets for primary and secondary grade ranges. High school students with disabilities, particularly those from other historically marginalized groups, are potentially more susceptible to being excluded from general education classes and/or access to the general education curricula. For students with disabilities, ages 6–21, African Americans, Asian, and Pacific Islanders are the three least likely racial groups to spend 80% of the school day in the general education classroom. Additionally, these students and their Latino peers are over 1.5 times as likely to spend less than 40% of the school day in general education settings. Important to note, there are implementation challenges to aligning a comprehensive transition plan for a student with a disability who requires an array of services addressing academic, socio-emotional, and independent living goals with learning standards in a general education course. Exclusion may also occur, however, as a result of actual or perceived manifestations of disability (e.g., a teacher's perception that a student with EBD cannot learn to self-regulate in a general education class). As high schools more closely align with college and career readiness standards, and content becomes more intense and challenging for all students, inclusion may seem less feasible. At present, transition education must often be infused into existing general education course content, necessitating input from both researchers and practitioners.

Education environment (i.e., the least restrictive education; LRE) decision-making by IEP teams during high school is not well-studied. Few conclusions can be drawn beyond describing the educational environments where students are served and observing the patterns of exclusion based on the intersection of race/ethnicity and disability. Although an in-depth study of the myriad causes of disproportionality is not the aim of this book, it is important to acknowledge that transition research has not tackled the impact of disproportionate educational environments, at the intersection of disability and race/ethnicity, gender, and socioeconomic status (SES), in the context of moving into adulthood. Further, although inclusive settings have been identified as a predictor of postschool success, the characteristics of learning environments and classroom contexts have not been considered in detail. Considering this, the evidence base provides contradictory guidance: inclusive education predicts postschool success, but evidence-based practices may or may not have been tested in inclusive education classrooms. In fact, teaching life skills, one of the only practices with what Test, Fowler, and colleagues (2009) considered to be strong evidentiary support, is likely not occurring in general education classrooms where common core standards that reflect college preparatory curricula are the focus of instruction.

Using sociocultural tools for examining how and why adolescents with disabilities get excluded from general education during secondary grades and how exclusion disrupts smooth and well-planned transitions to adulthood offers potential in the identification of solutions. Disciplinary exclusions disproportionately affect children of color, and these exclusions carry with them implications for the transition to adulthood that include, but are not limited to, diminished academic achievement associated with missed instruction and criminalization of youth as a result of concurrent or subsequent court and/or police involvement. Further, the involvement of the U.S. Department of Education, Office of Civil Rights has identified exclusionary disciplinary practices as a major concern (U.S. Department of Education & Office for Civil Rights, 2012). This type of exclusion is the focus of the remainder of this chapter.

While not all students with limited access to the general education setting are positioned somewhere along the STPP, decisions, temporary and/or intermittent, to exclude adolescents often appear to be tethered to both behavior and perceptions of behavior (Allen & White-Smith, 2014; Mallett, 2014; Skiba, Arredondo, & Williams, 2014). As children grow into adults, they and the adults in their lives (e.g., parents, teachers) negotiate the degree to which adults both exert control over and foster children's autonomy (Rogoff, 2003). Cultural groups vary in behavioral expectations, rule-setting, and responses to rule-breaking. Without awareness, children learn and internalize the underlying rules of institution-based behavior management, even in cases where there is conflict between dominant ideologies and subgroup beliefs (Rogoff, 2003). Targeting the deconstruction of the STPP provides an opportunity to face concerns about equity and diversity and to improve transition outcomes for adolescents, particularly those from other historically marginalized groups.

OPERATIONALIZING THE STPP

Simply put, the STPP is a series of steps in which both adolescents with disabilities and those from historical minority groups experience disproportionately high disciplinary actions originating in both the institutions of school (suspension) and law enforcement (juvenile detention). These experiences jeopardize students' access to the general education setting when they are of school age, as well as their personal freedom from incarceration, probation, and criminal records as they enter adulthood (Smith, 2009). Some youth continue on this trajectory and enter adult prisons, and some leave with criminal records that may or may not be expunged. Each segment in the pipeline negatively impacts successful transitions to high school completion (Noltemeyer et al., 2015), enrollment and completion of postsecondary education, and employment, career development, and advancement (Waintrup & Unruh, 2008). Court involvement also has the potential to curb an individual's civil rights, such as the right to vote (Kupchik & Catlaw, 2015).

Starting with exclusionary discipline, the STPP has a deleterious effect on the immediate task of learning for adolescents who are, ironically, compulsorily required to be in school. When students are involved in disciplinary procedures along the pipeline, they lose instructional time. They are removed from school entirely, if only temporarily; they receive interrupted and diminished instructional time; and/or they self-select and drop out of school. National survey results show that of the 73% of juvenile detention facilities reporting that all detainees attended school, these facilities represented only 67% of the juvenile offender population (Livsey, Sickmund, & Sladky, 2009). Hence, for adolescents identified as struggling learners, a lack of access to the general education and individualized special education can mean loss of skills or lack of progress toward academic learning standards or IEP goals.

Wilkerson, Gagnon, Mason-Williams, & Lane (2012) surveyed teachers in juvenile detention settings and found that while the teachers were certified and experienced, 40% were new to the detention settings in which they taught. Administrators and teachers in exclusionary settings may be underprepared to teach advanced courses required for graduation, or they may believe that a functional curriculum with a target of a high school diploma is appropriate (Gagnon, Houchins, & Murphy, 2012). Aligned with the latter attitude, teachers in detention settings focus on reading instruction and explicit skills such as phonics, fluency, and vocabulary associated with special education (Wilkerson et al., 2012). Researchers from a critical and culturally responsive perspective have critiqued this approach to reading for its lack of attention to critical literacy skills that support the development of critical thinking skills, creativity, and cultural literacy practices that bolster civic engagement and self-determination for marginalized adolescents (Winn & Behizadeh, 2011).

The STPP, which routinely begins with exclusionary disciplinary procedures, consistently subtracts from the lives of adolescents in additional deep, multilayered, and difficult-to-measure ways. Individual learner identities as competent learners and contributors to school and community, particularly for adolescents with disabilities and those who are also from other historically marginalized groups, can be undermined (Kupchik & Catlaw, 2015; Winn & Behizadeh, 2011). The larger society suffers too. As Winn & Behizadeh point out, the STPP also negatively affects teachers' ability to interact with adolescents who are experiencing trouble at school in creative ways because educators become reliant on more immediate procedures that lead to students' removal from school. Parents whose children are subjected to punitive procedures also experience frustration, and disenfranchisement, and some engage in self-protection by withdrawing from participation in school activities and meetings with teachers (Gibson & Haight, 2013). Entire school climates can be impacted by the frequency of exclusionary disciplinary approaches; multiple studies have demonstrated positive correlations between exclusionary discipline approaches and student disengagement and noncompliance (Christle, Jolivette, & Nelson, 2005; Decoteau, 2014; Lee et al., 2011).

Although definitions of the term vary (Skiba et al., 2014; Smith, 2009), the broad definition of the STPP implicates a set of policies and practices leading to exclusionary discipline practices, both within and outside the walls of school, resulting in missed education opportunities, academic failure, social isolation, and criminalization of adolescents and young adults, particularly those with disabilities and those who identify as students of color (Allen & White-Smith, 2014; Boyd, 2009; Christle et al., 2005; Mallett, 2014). The negative impact of the STPP extends beyond individuals and affects teachers, parents, and entire communities. Eric Holder, U.S. attorney general from 2009 to 2015, reminded Americans that the STPP so significantly threatened the civil rights of students of color that the federal government would intervene and partner with the U.S. Department of Education to create a series of initiatives that addressed school discipline reform (U.S. Department of Education, 2011). As the name suggests, the pipeline is an established pathway out of the field of school and into the field of criminal justice.

UNDERSTANDING THE MECHANISMS OF THE STPP

Students, with and without disabilities, enter the STPP in a number of different ways. The methods of entry, including a criminal offense committed at school or in the community, a status offense following trouble at school or home, or a false accusation of a wrongdoing, necessitate different supports for recovery and exit from the trajectory to incarceration. The STPP may seem intractable, but it is not. Some effort has been made to increase post-detention successful transitions (Cramer, Gonzalez, & Pellegrini-Lafont, 2014; Unruh, Waintrup, & Canter, 2010), but the scholarship in this area is focused on necessary legislation and policy reforms and preventative measures, and it provides few examples of individual-level or group-level data that has demonstrated if and how individuals with disabilities change their paths. Also useful is an examination of the problem using a sociocultural lens, specifically Bourdieu and colleagues' work to identify the importance of cultural and social capital. The following section examines the points of entry into the STPP through Bourdieu and other sociocultural lenses to better understand the implications for leaving it or avoiding it altogether.

School Disciplinary Procedures and Disability

Educators have multiple choices for guiding and responding to student behavior. At the macrosystemic level, education policies have shaped educators' responses to the behavior of students with and without disabilities. Iterations of IDEA have addressed behavior and disability since 1997, stating that positive behavior interventions must be considered by IEP teams and included in IEPs when disability manifests in behavioral challenges for an individual (Wilcox, Turnbull, & Turnbull, 2000). Legislation and policy on student discipline, however, are sometimes seen as contradictory when implemented with students with disabilities because upholding "zero tolerance" policies, which prioritize the removal of students (i.e., suspension and expulsion), potentially violates underlying principles of IDEA such as LRE and "zero reject." Zero reject is a foundational component of federal education policy that prioritizes the inclusion of students with disabilities, including those with serious behavioral challenges, in a general education setting to the greatest extent possible (Skiba & Peterson, 2000; Wilcox et al., 2000).

The IDEA 2004 mandates that an IEP meeting be convened for students with disabilities, or students suspected of having a disability, who are suspended for 10 days or more (Ryan, Katsiyannis, Peterson, & Chmelar, 2007). This special IEP meeting, referred to as a manifestation determination meeting, is a procedure to decide whether a causal relationship between disability and the behavior to which the suspension and/or expulsion is being linked exists (Zirkel, 2010). When the IEP team finds no relationship between disability and the behavior in question, suspension/expulsion and other forms of punishment apply. In cases where the IEP team finds that such a relationship between disability and the behavior in question does exist, provisions need to be made for continuing to address the IEP, and this may or may not include more restrictive educational settings.

Federal, state, and local policymakers have crafted zero tolerance legislation and school policies that pertain to all student behavior regardless of disability, such as the federal law entitled the 1994 Gun Free Schools Act (Kayama et al., 2015). These laws and school policies require immediate removal of students who have been involved in various infractions, but they are often used in response to students' possession or use of weapons or illicit drugs at school (Skiba & Peterson, 2000). Despite the IDEA mandate to individualize behavior interventions, adolescents with disabilities are vulnerable to school removals because the manifestation determination, establishing the causal link between disability and behavior, is difficult to prove and the burden of proof is on the parents of the individual with a disability (Zirkel, 2010). Consider the opening example in this chapter: How does an IEP team decide whether a student with ADHD sounded a fire alarm as an impulsive joke or as an intentionally planned way to disrupt school? Further, a lack of clarity in disciplinary policies has led to confusion and inconsistent implementation of the policies themselves (Taylor & Baker, 2001). For example, teachers perceive that students with disabilities are not held accountable to disciplinary policies in the same way that their peers without disabilities are (Bon, Faircloth, & LeTendre, 2006). Even though students with disabilities are subject to school disciplinary policies, 54% of public school administrators reported that federal, state, and local policies regarding disciplinary procedures for students receiving special education services reduced or limited their ability to prevent crime at school (Neiman & Hill, 2011).

Students with disabilities are vulnerable to the larger cultural context in which they live. Exclusionary disciplinary laws and policies reflect the public's fear of school gun violence as a result of numerous and highly publicized instances of maimed and murdered students and educators (e.g., the 1999 school shooting in Columbine, Colorado, the 2012 school shooting in Newtown, Connecticut) peppering the American education landscape (Heller, 2014). According to the most recent statistics from the U.S. Centers for Disease Control and Prevention, school violence resulting in death by firearms remained constant (less than 2% of all youth homicides) through 2010 (Centers for Disease Control and Prevention, 2012). Importantly, Heller notes that these acts of violence have a tenuous, at best, relationship to students identified as having disabilities and being served under IDEA. Often, adolescents who have committed acts of violence have been subsequently, in some cases even posthumously, identified with mental illness or other disabilities and were not being served by special education at the time of their crimes (Heller, 2014).

Although the most recent iteration of IDEA (2004) has more elaborate provisions for addressing behavior than previous iterations of the federal law did (Ryan et al., 2007), educators' strategies for managing their classrooms and student behavior (e.g., identifying and enforcing rules, implementing direct instruction for behavior change, using behavioral intervention plans and functional behavioral analyses) continue to be challenging to track and measure. Perhaps for this reason, school records of suspension and expulsion rates are often used to provide a thumbnail sketch of disciplinary procedures implemented with students with disabilities. Suspensions and expulsions, though, comprise outcome data and reveal little about how educators work with students with disabilities to transition back into general education settings and, subsequently, into adulthood. Rather, these school-based outcomes are correlated with postschool accounts of dropout and graduation rates (Christle et al., 2005; Lee et al., 2011).

School Suspensions and Expulsions

No single source of in- and out-of-school suspension and expulsion rates for high school students with disabilities across all 50 states exists. In the most recent Annual Report to Congress on the Implementation of IDEA (U.S. Department of Education & U.S. Office of Special Education and Rehabilitation Services, 2014), the rate of in-school suspensions for 10 days or longer (i.e., constituting a change in IEP services) occurred at the rate of 56 youth (ages 3–21) per 10,000 served; for out-of-school suspension, the rate was 98 per 10,000; and, unilateral removals associated with drugs, weapons, or serious bodily injury occurred for 14 of every 10,000 served. These numbers likely represent underestimations of removals because data from the following states were not consistently reported: California, Maine, Nebraska, New York, Utah, Wisconsin, and Wyoming (U.S. Department of Education & U.S. Office of Special Education and Rehabilitation Services, 2014). In a review of case law on the published disposition of manifestation determination decisions that were challenged through due process and not settled out of court, Zirkel (2010) found that in 9 of 14 cases judges upheld the IEP decision that no relationship existed between disability and behavior.

Not only are school disciplinary policies skewed toward the removal of students with disabilities (Krezmien, Leone, & Achilles, 2006), the racially discriminatory application of disciplinary policies and procedures is well documented. The Office for Civil Rights (OCR) in the U.S. Department of Education examined school discipline and the intersection of race/ethnicity, disability, and gender, concluding "with the exception of Latino and Asian-American students" (p.1), one of four males of color with disabilities received out-of-school suspension; the same was true for one in five girls with disabilities with the same racial backgrounds (U.S. Department of Education & Office for Civil Rights, 2014). This evidence is not the first of its kind. In a single-district study of disciplinary referrals and removals, Skiba, Michael, Nardo, & Peterson (2002) found that behavior sanctions of males and African American middle school students were statistically significantly higher than for females and European Americans, and that behavior itself could not account for the differences in referral or punishment. In more recent studies, race/ethnicity and disability status continue to predict higher rates of school removals (Sullivan, Klingbeil, & Van Norman, 2013; Sullivan, Van Norman, & Klingbeil, 2014). Sullivan and colleagues' work demonstrated that students with disabilities, Black students, and those from lower socioeconomic backgrounds were overrepresented in school disciplinary removals, and that this was particularly true of students receiving multiple suspensions (Sullivan et al., 2013). Additionally, nearly 20% of students with disabilities were suspended at least once in a given school year, and African American students were three times as likely to be suspended than European American students (Sullivan et al., 2014).

According to the second National Longitudinal Transition Study (NLTS2), 17% of high school students with disabilities have experienced in-school suspension at least once during a given school year, 11% experienced out-of-school suspension at least once, and 1% were expelled (National Longitudinal Transition Study, 2006). Parent surveys from the NLTS2 illustrated a rate of 73% for students with EBD and 41% for students with other health impairments (OHI; this includes youth with ADHD) to ever have experienced suspension or expulsion during their schooling. In fact, four of the five disabilities with the highest rates of suspension and expulsion are also categories of disabilities that rely, in part, on educator evaluation and judgment for identification (i.e., EBD, OHI, ID, and LD). Students with traumatic brain injury (TBI), the fifth disability category, have the fourth highest suspension and expulsion rates at 30% (National Longitudinal Transition Study, 2006). Similar trends have been documented in smaller longitudinal studies. In Maryland, from 1995 to 2003, students with EBD were the most likely to face suspension. African American and American Indian students with high-incidence disabilities (i.e., ID, OHI, and LD) exceeded the odds ratios for suspensions of Whites, Asians, and Latinos (Krezmien et al., 2006). Further, these judgmental or high-incidence disabilities are the very same categories of disability that are closely associated with racial/ethnic disproportionality (Artiles, Rueda, Salazar, & Higareda, 2005; Losen & Orfield, 2002; Sullivan & Bal, 2013).

Hence, race/ethnicity and disability intersect, not only at the initial identification of disability, but also in the implementation of exclusionary practices of school disciplinary policies. Unfortunately, the field of special education has been slow to respond to research documenting exclusionary disciplinary procedures at macro- and microsystemic levels and how these affect postschool transition and outcomes. While the OCR has issued research briefs and policy recommendations for school districts to use in reforming institutionalized practices that address inequity in discipline, special education intervention research has been nearly silent on the subject. One exception is efforts to improve educators' response to behavior and classroom management through positive behavior interventions and supports (Ryan et al., 2007). Collectively known as PBIS (Positive Behavioral Interventions and Supports; Skiba & Peterson, 2000), this systemic approach has ample empirical evidence supporting its use, including an entire academic journal devoted to the practice. Yet, some research shows that, even in schools where PBIS is implemented, racial/ethnic disproportionality continues to surface and related school disciplinary procedures continue to contribute to diminished access to general education settings (Skiba et al., 2011). In their national study of schools implementing PBIS, Skiba and colleagues (2011) found that African Americans and Latinos were respectively 4 and 2 times as likely to be suspended for minor infractions than students from other racial/ethnic groups at the elementary level, and that these patterns continued, statistically significant but less pronounced, at the middle-school level.

Consequences of School Removals

Chief among the problems associated with exclusionary discipline, whether in or out of school, is academic failure. Although academic failure has multiple causes, grade-level retention is associated with missed opportunities to learn tethered to exclusionary discipline, underscoring the relationship between academic failure, leaving school, and STPP involvement (Townsend Walker, 2012). Using data from a single state, Kentucky, Morris and Perry (2016) demonstrated that African American and Latino middle and high school students were 6 and 2 times more likely, respectively, to be suspended than their European American peers. Asian students were the only racial/ethnic group to be suspended less frequently than their European American counterparts (Morris & Perry, 2016). Special education status was also tested in Morris and Perry's model; however, race/ethnicity remained a salient factor when controlling for this variable.

At the school level, Noltemeyer and McLoughlin (2010) found that urban and low-income schools were more likely to use exclusionary disciplinary practices. When examining the same statewide dataset, Morris and Perry (2016) also found that being suspended was a strong predictor of students' academic performance in both reading and math; further, when comparing students' achievement scores in years where suspension occurred to achievement in years when suspension had not occurred, significantly lower math performance was documented (Morris & Perry, 2016). A similar inverse relationship between every type of exclusionary discipline, including in-school suspension, and academic achievement is documented in a recent meta-analysis of suspension studies (Noltemeyer et al., 2015).

Lost instructional time bridges diminished academic achievement to the loss of specific types of learning opportunities necessary for developing higher-level critical thinking and reasoning skills, too. Winn and Behizehdah's (2011) review of literacy research showed that adolescents who miss instructional time and have a pattern of poor academic performance also lose access to critical literacy instruction and are often relegated to acritical and skills-based reading instruction. Special education researchers and practitioners have focused on the latter skill set, devoting much work to the study and teaching of fluency and word recognition, particularly for students in alternative education settings such as detention. Evidence of this focus can be seen in a recent survey of reading instruction in juvenile correctional facilities conducted by Wilkerson, et al. (2012), wherein skills related to fluency and phonemic awareness, in addition to basic comprehension, predominated both the instructional practices respondents most frequently identified and the recommendations of researchers.

Another consequence of school removals is their potential to shape students' identities and their families' views of schooling in negative ways. Using the National Longitudinal Survey of Adolescent Health, Kupchik and Catlaw found that students who had been suspended were less likely to vote and to be community volunteers in adulthood. They conclude, "The observed negative effect of suspension is because suspension short-circuits dialogue and student involvement; it removes a student from the school rather than responding constructively and therapeutically to problematic behavior" (Kupchik & Catlaw, 2015, p. 116). Although these effects were not more pronounced for the Black and Latino participants in their study, Kupchik and Catlaw point out that these students are more frequently and disproportionately suspended and expelled, and, therefore, they experience the negative impact of school removals more often than do their White peers.

In a study of young women with disabilities who were incarcerated, Annamma (2014) found that the militaristic approach to socialization diminished self-determination by focusing on compliance, and that control measures occurred at the cost of academic instruction. Further, the criminalization of the adolescents' behavior and their life experiences, combined with a silence around cultural responsiveness and critical pedagogies, did not support or sustain their identity development (Annamma, 2014). Similarly, in an interview study of Black males (48% of whom had IEPs) who were suspended, their teachers, and their parents/caregivers, Kayama and colleagues (2015) used discourse analysis and found that participants across groups adopted the language of the criminal justice system to discuss school misconduct, even though students' infractions did not reflect illegal behavior (Kayama et al., 2015). Although the authors do not link their empirical work to Bourdieu's theories of field and *habitus* (Bourdieu's term for rules that govern the field), they identified a parallel concept, that of the hidden curriculum, connecting excluded adolescents to the criminal justice system and potentially disrupting their identities as good students and citizens.

According to Kayama and colleagues (2015), this hidden curriculum is dangerous because it reifies historical and racist conceptualizations of "the criminal self and social identities" (p. 33) of African American males as these adolescents are transitioning to adulthood. While teachers and caregivers also spoke in ways that positioned themselves in loving relationships with these young men, and they acknowledged their responsibility to guide them, the mindset of criminality, punishment, and safety seemed to preclude critical thinking about solutions other than exclusionary discipline. Finally, this research showed that using the language of the criminal justice system also maps to the larger fields of society in which Black adolescents and their caregivers have been subject to biased and racist police and courts. In fact, in more in-depth interviews with caregivers, they articulated that they considered the out-of-school suspensions to largely be overly harsh responses to students' misconduct (Gibson & Haight, 2013). Parents were concerned that educators did not respect the lessons they were teaching their sons and that some of the punishments were racially motivated. Tapping into feelings of mistrust, the effect likely alienated these members of the school community even further. These sentiments are not new, particularly in special education research, where previous research has also found alienation and dissatisfaction among parents of color for similar reasons (Harry, Allen, & McLaughlin, 1995; Harry & Klingner, 2006; Trainor, 2010c; Zionts et al., 2003).

School disciplinary removals and law enforcement proceedings can run together; each of the segments of the STPP dually affects adolescents with disabilities, particularly those from other historically marginalized groups (Kayama et al., 2015; Skiba et al., 2014; Skiba et al., 2011; Skiba et al., 2002; Sullivan et al., 2014). Townsend Walker (2012) notes that the common theme of desensitization among African American adolescents in her study who reported repeated disciplinary and court interactions results from familiarity with punishment efforts that ultimately fail to inspire avoidance. The costs of school removal are high: the loss of opportunities to learn (Morris & Perry, 2016); the loss of opportunities to advance to sophisticated academic skills (Winn & Behizadeh, 2011), perhaps bridging to the loss of identity development as a critically conscious, contributing member of society (Kupchik & Catlaw, 2015); the loss of family and student trust in educational systems (Kayama et al., 2015); and categorically diminished postschool outcomes such as high dropout rates (Lee et al., 2011).

The implementation of many behavior interventions, both those that incentivize and those that punish as a method for shaping the behaviors of students with disabilities, are under the purview of federal, state, and local policies and procedures. Policies and procedures are intertwined with policing, criminal and civil law, and court involvement. Suspension and expulsion are often conceptualized first segments of the STPP, feeding into the next segment where many students shift from receiving punishment meted out by school personnel to interactions with law enforcement.

Court Involvement, Detention, Incarceration, and Disability

In 2013, 1,058,500 juveniles, ages 10 to 18 in most states, were processed in juvenile court (Hockenberry & Puzzanchera, 2015). The exact number of juveniles in detention who are also identified with disabilities upon entry into the system is unknown, and estimates range between 33% and 40% (Gagnon & Barber, 2010). The most recent national data on criminal behavior such as property offences (e.g., car theft, vandalism), person offenses (e.g., assault, rape), and violation of drug laws accounted for approximately 74% of total juveniles detained without being charged as adults (Furdella & Puzzanchera, 2015).

An important reason to consider the paths that contextualize adolescents' criminalization is to understand how to shut down the pipeline itself. Currently, transition research that intersects with the STPP prioritizes changing the behavior of adolescents with disabilities. While this may be one fruitful tack, it is not sufficient for preventing the STPP and related inequities. Educators' discretionary response to behaviors also play a role in the STPP. Physical altercations between students, for example, may be viewed as violations of school rules that are subject to consequences at school, such as in-school suspension for shoving one's classmate. The same physical altercation, however, might also involve police if educators view the shove as physical assault and make a report to law enforcement. Direct paths from suspension and expulsion to court involvement often involve police who are assigned to school campuses, called school resource officers (SROs); 63% and 64%, respectively, of U.S. middle and public high schools have security personnel on duty (Gray & Lewis, 2015). In fact, as American schools have increased their employment of SROs, arrest rates of students have risen (Thurau & Wald, 2009). The paths connecting school punishment to law enforcement are multiple; some are direct and others are more circuitous. Behaviors, both at school and in community, can be subject to court involvement.

Path one: Breaking a law. The most direct path to the STPP is for an adolescent to commit a crime (e.g., shoplifting). The likelihood of engaging in illegal behavior is greater for adolescents who meet peers in segregated settings (e.g., in-school suspension classrooms, detention homes) who also fail to comply with school rules and government laws (Davis, Sheidow, & McCart, 2015). Students with disabilities are more than twice as likely to be suspended as those without disabilities (13% as compared to 6%), and they comprise 58% of all students who are secluded or involuntarily confined even though they represent only 12% of U.S. public school enrollment (U.S. Department of Education & Office for Civil Rights, 2014). Additionally, law enforcement officials infrequently and/or inconsistently receive targeted training to address youths (Shippen, Patterson, Green, & Smitherman, 2012) and individuals with disabilities (Stonebrook, 2016), which may exacerbate or escalate situations leading to the arrest of adolescents with disabilities.

Path two: Committing a status offense. Some of these one-million-plus cases involve minors who commit status offences, treading a well-worn path from school misconduct to court involvement. This second, fairly direct path is for a minor (i.e., age 18 or younger, except in Alabama and Nebraska where the age of majority is 19; http://minors.uslegal.com/age-of-majority/) to commit a status offense. Status offenses, behaviors considered illegal only when committed by a juvenile, fall into five categories: running away, truancy, curfew violations, ungovernability (i.e., noncompliance with an adult such as a parent or teacher), and underage consumption of alcohol, including, in some states, tobacco. Skipping school, for example, is a violation of compulsory attendance policies implemented by schools, but it is also often a violation of local and state laws.

In 2013, the total number of status offenses petitioned in the United States was 105,000, or 3.5 per 1,000 juveniles, ages 10 and older (Hockenberry & Puzzanchera, 2015). Yet, a decades-old, well-established bank of empirical evidence shows that court involvement resulting in detention and other punishment fails to address the underlying issues associated with behaviors such as running away and noncompliance in school contexts. Hence, changes in policy regarding these offences have emerged (Arthur & Waugh, 2009; Coalition for Juvenile Justice, 2011). Since 1974, federal law has incentivized states to deinstitutionalize status offenses using family courts and facilities other than jails to detain status offenders (Arthur & Waugh, 2009); however, at least 30 states continue to have and to use exceptions, incarcerating youth for status offenses in some situations (Coalition for Juvenile Justice, 2011).

Historically, adolescent girls and young women have been more likely than their male counterparts to be detained for status offences (Quinn, Poirier, &

Garfinkel, 2005). Sexual, physical, and emotional abuse reported by girls in detention have been very high (92% in one California state-wide study), and abuse is correlated with status offenses such as running away. Abuse is also correlated with violent criminal offenses such as assault. In fact, the increasing rate of female juvenile in detention is associated with committing violent acts (Sickmund & Puzzanchera, 2014).

Path three: Having a disability that manifests in noncompliance or antisocial behaviors. One of the more challenging paths to both identify and document is the relationship between disability and behavior. The extent to which the manifestation of a disability plays a role in a student's misconduct is difficult to know. As explained earlier in this chapter, IDEA (2004) recognizes that misconduct by individuals with disabilities may not be willful and may be directly linked to a disabling condition. The mandatory IEP meeting–the manifestation determination meeting–is designed to deliberate a causal relationship between the disability and misconduct. The meeting does not, however, prevent vulnerability for adolescents with disabilities introduced through involvement in the criminal justice system. As Zirkel (2010) points out, the manifestation determination process is fraught with inconsistencies, a lack of transparency, and questionable results. Further, the majority of cases that are appealed (and thus have public records for examination) are of students with LD. The direct relationship between LD and behavior is complex as is evidenced by studies that document the courts' reluctance to uphold IEP teams' findings that there is no relationship between the disability and the misconduct. Even when the conduct of students with EBD is in question, IEP teams remain reluctant to associate the disability in any causal way to an infraction (Zirkel, 2010).

In cases where the IEP team decides that disability did not cause the student to break school rules, those with disabilities receive the same punishment as those without disabilities. Further, there are few special provisions excepting people with disabilities from punishment when laws are broken. Nevertheless, disability may manifest in ways (e.g., diminished impulse control) that contribute to or cause behavior in violation of rules and laws. Disability may also cause or contribute to attenuated self-regulation of desirable behaviors; both scenarios may pave the route to court involvement. In fact, students with ADHD have higher suspension and expulsion rates as compared to other adolescents (Centers for Disease Control and Prevention, 2016; U.S. Office of Special Education Programs, 2003) and arrest rates (18%) that are twice that of students without disabilities (9%; NLTS2, 2004).

Students who have been identified as having EBD (6% of the total population of U.S. public school students who receive special education [U.S. Department of Education & U.S. Office of Special Education and Rehabilitation Services, 2015]) may also have disability-related factors that affect their ability to adhere to school rules. For example, pediatric bipolar disorder, estimated to affect nearly 2% of U.S. adolescents and characterized by periods of depression and manic behavior (Youngstrom, Freeman, & McKeown Jenkins, 2009), may result in truancy and/or risk-taking behaviors that result in disciplinary procedures in and out of school. Some estimates of youth with EBD in juvenile detention are as high as 50%, a figure supported by a recent study of adolescents processed in juvenile and adult courts in Chicago, where 68% were found to have psychiatric disabilities (Washburn et al., 2015). Regardless of the safeguard provisions of manifestation determination, adolescents and young adults with disabilities often face the same route to punishment as those without disabilities.

Path four: Responding to victimization or hardship with unsanctioned behaviors. "Research has shown the child's victimization and abuse are linked to problem behaviors that become evident later in life" (Sickmund & Puzzanchera, 2014, p. iii). Thus begins the fourth edition of the Center for Juvenile Justice report aggregating national data for the U.S. Office of Juvenile Justice and Delinquency Prevention. Indeed, not only were children with child welfare involvement 3 times as likely to experience juvenile justice, but 70% of adolescents who had histories of involvement with the child welfare system had additional juvenile justice involvement within 2 years of a previous referral (Sickmund & Puzzanchera, 2014). The recidivism rate for adolescents with no child welfare history was 34%. Based on two databases from the U.S. Department of Health and Human Services, mandatory reports of maltreatment (i.e., abuse of all types and neglect) contained in Child Protective Services (CPS) referrals, the report found that children with disabilities were less likely to be the victims of maltreatment; however, when abused, children with disabilities were more likely than their peers without disabilities to be seriously harmed. Also, for the first time in the 20 years since the first edition of the U.S. Congress–mandated report, researchers found that maltreatment rates of both Black and Latino children were significantly higher than those of White children. Further, poverty continued to be associated with child maltreatment (Sickmund & Puzzanchera, 2014).

Adolescents who suffer maltreatment in the form of neglect and abuse can meet it with resilience, but they can also resist, retaliate (Eisenberg, Gower, McMorris, & Bucchianeri, 2015), and/or withdraw (Dykes & Thomas, 2015; Snapp, Hoenig, Fields, & Russell, 2015). Girls are particularly vulnerable to abuse and response behaviors; parents are frequent reporters of girls' delinquent behavior (72%), and these adults are among those most likely to victimize them (Quinn et al., 2005). There has long been an established connection between female survivors of abuse and behaviors that are considered to be maladaptive or illegal (e.g., underage drinking, running away, participating in sex acts in exchange for money). Vulnerable adolescents may lash out and, in doing so, find themselves facing exclusionary discipline or court involvement (Snapp et al., 2015). In a recent interview study with African American males who had experienced both suspensions and detention, peer pressure, poverty and food insecurity, and estrangement from one's immediate family contributed to these adolescents' decisionmaking and risking school punishment and court involvement (Townsend Walker, 2012).

In a nationally representative survey of abuse of children, Finkelhor and colleagues (2009) found that nearly half of youth self-reported having experienced physical abuse or bullying in the course of the past year. Historically, students with disabilities are considered to be at a higher risk of being both bullied and of victimizing others (Farmer, Lane, Lee, Hamm, & Lambert, 2012; Lochman et al., 2012; Rose & Espelage, 2012). Studies of adolescents with disabilities who experience social isolation and being bullied may react with aggression and anger, which are problematic in the context of school but not pathological (Farmer et al., 2012).

Bullying met with acts of self-protection is also a common theme among lesbian, gay, bisexual, transgender, and questioning (LGBTQ) adolescents (Snapp et al., 2015). While there are no studies documenting the numbers of LGBTQ adolescents who receive special education nationally, students from this historically marginalized group are sometimes vulnerable to developing disabilities (e.g., EBD associated with maltreatment) or challenges to equitable education opportunities (e.g., homelessness resulting from parental rejection). These problems can contribute to status infractions and entry into the school-to-prison pipeline for LGBT youth (Snapp et al., 2015). Further, secondary special educators are unlikely to have received targeted preparation for working with these adolescents–professional development that is warranted because of the likelihood that members of this group experience marginalization during identity development (Arrieta & Palladino, 2015). In special education transition, specific and unique needs of this population have not been fully considered (Dykes & Thomas, 2015).

Path five: Involving police in cases of school conduct violations. A fifth path, one that often surprises students and their families, begins when school administrators, while responding to student behaviors that also violate U.S. law (e.g., possessing an illegal drug at an extracurricular activity), contact law enforcement. Police contact can result in arrest and court involvement. Responses for some rule-breaking behaviors have systematically included school and law enforcement collaboration that reflect increasingly punitive results (Decoteau, 2014). In a longitudinal study across five states (Arizona, Hawaii, Missouri, South Carolina, and West Virginia), police or juvenile justice referrals originating at schools accounted for 10% of all referrals (Krezmien, Leone, Zablocki, & Wells, 2010). These interactions can change the transition landscape.

The presence and invocation of law enforcement in cases of students' misconduct, however, is subject to and representative of inconsistent and biased responses to behavior and social control in the larger society; urban schools frame police–school collaboration as tough discipline, and both students of color and students with disabilities have been disproportionately punished both at school and in courts of law (Cramer et al., 2014; Decoteau, 2014; Rivkin, 2009; Skiba et al., 2014; Thurau & Wald, 2009). The National Association for the Advancement of Colored People, the American Civil Liberties Union, the

National Teachers Association, and the American Bar Association are among the professional organizations that are calling for changes that disrupt this segment in the school-to-police referral phenomenon.

Path six: Associating disabilities with misconduct and crime. A sixth, also less direct and more difficult to document path from school to prison, bears mentioning when considering the population of adolescents with disabilities, particularly those from other historically marginalized groups. This path is one marked by biases that have led educators and, in some cases, law enforcement officers, to wrongly accuse students with disabilities, particularly those from historical minorities, of misconduct and/or illegal behavior. Students with EBD are particularly vulnerable to false accusations for multiple reasons.

Data from the NLTS2 demonstrate that patterns of punishment of secondary students with disabilities for misconduct at school mirror the sociodemographic patterns of adolescents without disabilities. For example, 46% of Black students with disabilities have been suspended or expelled at some point during their school trajectories, while the same was true for 17% and 28%, respectively, of White and Latino students with disabilities (NLTS2, 2006). Further, teacher reports included in the NLTS2 show that educators were more likely to attribute problem behavior in classrooms to Black students with disabilities when compared to their White and Latino peers with disabilities. Teachers said that 26% of Black students with disabilities did not appropriately control their behavior during class, compared to 17% of White students with disabilities and 14% of Latino students with disabilities. Arguing and fighting, 56% and 29% respectively, were behaviors also disproportionately attributed to Black students with disabilities; teachers attributed these same behaviors to fewer White (43% and 19%) and Latino students with disabilities (32% and 13%; NLTS2, 2006).

Whichever the path, the connections between exclusionary discipline and incarceration pose real and perhaps immeasurable threats to successful postschool transitions for individuals with disabilities, creating crises for their families and for the larger society. Surprisingly, the ways and extent to which detention and court involvement affect transition has been studied very little (Kirk & Sampson, 2013), even though 34% of adolescents with disabilities experience disciplinary actions including suspension and expulsion during high school (NLTS2, 2006) and just 79% of juvenile detention facilities offer special education services (Livsey et al., 2009). Of course not all suspended and expelled students enter into detention facilities; some attend alternative schools. But once a student with a disability is on the path to exclusionary discipline procedures and court involvement ending in detention, postschool transition noticeably shifts; the rules for engagement and the types of capital necessary to successfully move from high school to adulthood are expanded and the need for supports becomes more intensive. Without concerted effort to disrupt it, the pipeline is likely to feed into adult incarceration.

Adult Incarceration

Moving through the STPP can have the devastating outcome of becoming an incarcerated adult. For juveniles, particularly those who have committed status offenses, detention may or may not involve locked facilities. And while juveniles who are detained do experience limited personal freedoms and the deleterious effects of police and court involvement, they are also likely to be exposed to some education and health services (Livsey et al., 2009). For 4,000 juveniles in 2015, however, adult criminal charges fast forwarded them to this segment in the pipeline (Furdella & Puzzanchera, 2015). Representing about 1% of all juveniles who were formally processed in the court system, these adolescents were sent by judiciary waiver to criminal court despite being under the age of legal adulthood. Judges make this decision based on likelihood of adolescents' positive response to detention. Repeat offenders, adolescents who commit serious crimes requiring lengthy rehabilitation, and those convicted of person offenses (e.g., homicide, rape, assault) are most likely to face judiciary waivers. Resources are less predictably available in adult facilities and variably accessed by the prison population; those with higher levels of literacy are more likely to access work and educational programming (Greenberg, Dunleavy, & Kutner, 2007).

For juveniles, early, repeated, and violent offending are all associated with offending in adulthood (Loeber, Farrington, & Petechuk, 2013). Estimates of the numbers of adolescents with and without disabilities who continue offending into adulthood and become incarcerated vary widely, between studies that show 16% on the low end and 60% in the high end (Gagnon & Barber, 2010). Federal reports on the U.S. prison census do not include information about disabilities and adolescents' education, obscuring a national picture of this segment of the STPP. Using data from a 2003 survey of literacy rates among incarcerated populations, Greenberg, Dunleavy, & Kutner (2007) found that prose, document, and quantitative literacies were below basic levels for 16%, 15%, and 39% of the prison population, and an additional 3% were considered nonliterate. Seventeen percent of prisoners surveyed reported having been diagnosed with a learning disability (Greenberg et al., 2007). Entering the adult penal system has dense and enduring connections to poor outcomes that include financial problems resulting from lost wages, lost opportunities for career development and networking, and challenges to future employment; diminished physical and mental health and well-being, social stigma and isolation; familial disruption, divorce, absentee parenting, a lack of shared experiences such as funerals, graduations, and weddings; and poor interpersonal relationships and diminished contact with friends. Even if the best-case scenario is accurate with the lower 16% estimate of recidivism and entrance into adult prison rate, the risk of transitioning into adulthood where financial hardship, social turmoil, and diminished self-determination are likely is too great.

EXAMINING THE PIPELINE THROUGH TRANSITION LENSES

Transition, since its inception and first depiction by Will (1983), performs as a bridge from one setting or experience to another. Transitions between exclusionary discipline settings and school constitute changes in educational settings that warrant, at the very least, transition planning. Another compelling reason to consider special education transition for STPP-involved adolescents with disabilities is that these punitive experiences have the potential to change their postsecondary trajectories. Yet little research and few practices have focused on this population or on these transitions. A handful of studies specifically address reentry into school from detention (Feierman, Levick, & Mody, 2009). Beyond this small body of research, postsecondary transition scholarship has focused on adolescents with EBD because this population is associated with maladaptive behavior, and thus, detention. These studies focus on the individual as the unit of analysis. Work that examines punishment itself as a generator of poor postschool outcomes is rare. The sociocultural perspective on the system of treatment of students is missing.

At least three key aspects of broader postsecondary transition research in special education are conceptually linked to research and practices that redirect adolescents' paths along the STPP as they too experience transition. Each of the three are priorities that also reflect the habitus, or macrocontext, of U.S. education: planning, student self-determination and family involvement, and employment. First, transition planning is a prioritized activity in postsecondary transition. A dominant belief associated with U.S. education is that individual and family decisionmaking and preparedness can influence the direction that an adolescent's life takes. Planning connotes an individual's or family's control over the future direction of a life; however, diverse conceptualizations of the future and the extent to which humans exert control on the future exist (Kalyanpur & Harry, 1999).

Second, both the adolescent with a disability and the family are expected to be actively involved in the planning process by, at the very least, stating preferences, needs, and strengths. The importance of choice and self-determination are cultural constructs that are deeply embedded in policy, research, and practice of special education transition. At the same time, the predominance of a self-determining individual who is transitioning into adulthood does not reflect the dynamic and diverse set of values and beliefs of all groups and individuals (Kalyanpur & Harry, 1999). Third, as discussed at length in the previous chapter, employment as a postschool outcome signals the dominant and capitalist-driven value placed on work and ties the value of a person to his identity as an employed person (Manning & Gaudelli, 2006). Even the more recent emphasis on postsecondary education is related to the development of a career; hence, postsecondary education in this context is considered a means to supporting employment that is sufficient for financial independence and a sense of purpose as an employee with opportunities for advancement and benefits. Again, though, not all individuals with disabilities and their families place the same emphasis on work as a key to postschool success (Kalyanpur & Harry, 1999).

The following sections provide examples of special education research and practice that constitute how related problems and solutions have been framed and how these might be relevant and useful to those adolescents with disabilities who experience the STPP. Examining this body of work also reveals methodological and empirical gaps in the special education knowledge base. Therefore, the discussion will also be augmented with research from across disciplines including cultural psychology, social justice education research, and critical theories and pedagogies.

Planning as a Lever for Post-STPP Success

First, transition scholars and educators prioritize planning as a method for preparing adolescents to meet the demands of an unfamiliar field. From policy to practice, planning is valued, even codified, as a way to prepare for the future. For example, a 15-year-old adolescent with EBD-bipolar is transitioning from a detention center where he has been for several months following a recent suspension and court involvement. Now it is time for the adolescent to transition to a high school, one that he has not attended previously. Ideally, the parent, adolescent, and educators at both the exiting detention center and the entering high school plan a schedule of courses, an updated IEP with both a behavioral intervention plan and a postsecondary transition plan, and a medication distribution routine, if necessary. Planning requires anticipating needs and aligning necessary resources. Planning can also demystify the process by disclosing the rules of the new field (e.g., courses to be taken, transportation and logistics, key people). Educators benefit from planning, too; they learn about the new student and IEP members' expectations for moving forward.

In model demonstration research, instate programs in Maryland, Missouri, Arizona, and Oregon, researchers and practitioners have underscored the need to plan transitions between school and detention, and this body of work aligns closely with special education transition planning and education for all students with disabilities. Oregon's Project STAY-OUT, for example, includes the foundational components of postschool transition planning such as assessing adolescents' ongoing career interests, involving a transition specialist, and writing a postschool transition plan (Unruh et al., 2010). These programs emphasize the IDEA-required domains of employment and independent living; yet postsecondary education has typically not been the focus of extant models. Additionally, each of these state programs also includes planning for exiting incarceration or exclusionary discipline settings (Feierman et al., 2009; Nelson, Jolivette, Leone, & Mathur, 2010; Unruh et al., 2010). Planning for this transition is associated with decreased recidivism and increased community engagement (Clark, Mathur, & Helding, 2011; Mathur & Griller Clark, 2014; Unruh, Waintrup, Canter, & Smith, 2009).

Planning for postsecondary education involves ongoing interagency collaboration between educators from high school transition programs, counselors in vocational rehabilitation programs, disability student services providers at postsecondary institutions, adolescents, and parents. In the broader transition literature, much has been made of interagency collaboration due to the transfer from an entitlement to an eligibility-based system (Balcazar et al., 2012; Test, Fowler, et al., 2009). The transition to adulthood signifies the adolescent leaving both a physical setting and a metaphorical field. The adolescent exits high school, both a physical location and a representation of an entitlement system that positions individuals and families as the recipients of services. Subsequently they enter another set of fields (e.g., workplace, college), in which there are new actual places, and there is a new system, one of eligibility where service provision must be actively pursued among collaborators.

Planning is also both short- and long-term, and it is oriented to future goals, some of which will be achieved long after the student leaves high school. In contrast, exclusionary discipline settings for adolescents are often temporary or delimited according to suspension/expulsion policies or court dispositions. In time frames not corresponding to academic calendars, adolescents with disabilities are involved with numerous institutions along the STPP, constituting multiple fields with differing sets of rules and regulations. For this reason, the extant research on the transition both to and from detention settings has emphasized the need to make records transfer more immediate and responsive to adolescents with disabilities' in support of seamless services (Clark & Unruh, 2010; Nelson et al., 2010; Unruh et al., 2009; Waintrup & Unruh, 2008).

Additionally, adolescents with EBD, in particular, are consistently among those with disabilities who do not connect to adult-serving agencies and resources, making a concerted and deliberate effort on the part of educators and transition specialists necessary (Lane & Carter, 2006). Oregon's STAY-OUT model supports the use of a portfolio of documents, called a passport, that houses personal and educational records such as birth certificate, proof of medical insurance, immunization records, work samples, transcripts, IEPs, and vocational assessments (Clark & Mathur, 2009). Other state programs have adopted the passport feature as a key component.

Fostering Self-Determination and Family Involvement

Interventions that promote self-determination and family involvement in transition planning have status in the field of transition as evidence-based practices (Test, Fowler, et al., 2009). Further, both components also have positive correlational relationships with postschool employment and postsecondary education based on smaller-scale studies (Test, Mazzotti, et al., 2009) and secondary analyses of the NLTS2 (Mazzotti et al., 2015). Both components are also reinforced through educational policies such as IDEA (2004). At the policy level, or macrolevel, of the special education transition ecosystem, student and family participation is acknowledged as essential, and teachers are required to seek student and family input during transition planning and education.

Self-determination and family involvement are socially and culturally constructed. They entail some of the most visible examples of cultural and social capital that reflect knowing and accepting self and disability, connecting to supports, and valuing career development (Trainor, 2003, 2005). Additional less-obvious types of cultural and social capital, however, are also at play in this field. Preferring independence and autonomy over interdependence and shared responsibility, and valuing work as an indicator of human value are examples of underlying or foundational dominant cultural beliefs in special education transition (Harry, Kalyanpur, & Day, 1999; Kalyanpur & Harry, 1999; Rueda et al., 2005; Trainor, 2002). Some special education transition research and practices specific to the STPP address both self-determination and family involvement directly. In fact, these programs borrow planning approaches and reflect rhetoric from the field of postsecondary transition, using words such as "person centered" (Karpur, Clark, Caproni, & Sterner, 2005). Strengthening family connections has also been a target of programs such as Project RISE (Mathur & Schoenfeld, 2010). Like much of the work in self-determination research in the broader field of special education scholarship, however, the conceptualization of self-determination is largely focused on choice and goal setting, as well as participation in IEP development.

These studies, similar to self-determination research and practice in the larger field, do not engage the complexities of the construct for adolescents who are often seen, in the eyes of many adults, from a deficit perspective and for whom limited opportunities to practice self-determination are available at school (Trainor, 2005, 2007). Questions about the interaction between adolescent self-determination and family involvement in transition, in which beliefs about disability, work, and autonomy in child development are embedded (Trainor, 2002, 2005, 2007), have yet to be answered by these studies. Without additional focused attention in research and practice, the dominant definition of self-determination is tacitly accepted as a construct that is universally valued. Moreover, in the case of STPP transition, self-determination in the highly regimented and adult-controlled field of detention, a part of which involves locked facilities, is not problematized in this body of work. Further, issues of equity and diversity emerge. Just as adolescents with disabilities are vulnerable to exclusionary discipline, either because of actual offenses connected to some manifestation of disability or because teachers perceive them to be noncompliant, so too are students of color. Racial/ethnic discrimination associated with disciplinary procedures in U.S. schools is amply documented through Civil Rights Data Collection (CRDC) by the Office for Civil Rights in the U.S. Department of Education (U.S. Department of Education & Office for Civil Rights, 2012).

Preparing to Become a Worker

As a linchpin in the postschool transition of adolescents with disabilities, one's identity as worker is connected to a dominant belief held by many Americans across racial/ethnic and socioeconomic backgrounds, closely tied to dominant capitalist and Puritanical planks in our social and historical foundations (Manning & Gaudelli, 2006). As explained in the previous discussion of the evolution of transition models over time, the field of special education has taken up employment as both a desired postschool outcome and as one that normalizes the experiences of young adults with disabilities. There are measurable benefits to employment for individuals with disabilities as well: financial and other material gain, the development of applied knowledge and skills, enhanced autonomy and self-determination, increased density of social networks, and so forth (Jahoda, Kemp, Riddell, & Banks, 2008). Research on adolescents with disabilities who are at various points along the STPP is unanimous in the conclusion that vocational education and career preparation is necessary for successfully exiting detention settings. Employment has also been associated with a reduction in the return to detention (Baltodano et al., 2005; Nelson et al., 2010; Unruh et al., 2009).

The types of employment-related activities and services promoted through research with adolescents with disabilities who are on the STPP largely mirror those used by those not on the STPP. These include recruiting and supporting adolescents' active involvement in transition planning and education, cultivating career awareness and interests, articulating employment-related goals on IEPs; developing soft skills (e.g., professional communication habits), acquiring pre-employment skills, including job search and application strategies (Unruh et al., 2009); and providing job skill development such as computer literacy. Many of these strategies and approaches align with the evidence-based practices identified by Test, Fowler, and colleagues (2009). Other employment-focused transition research and practices focus on disability-specific populations. Some transition research is not transferable to adolescents who experience exclusionary discipline and detention. For example, early work experiences have been identified as a predictor of postschool success (Carter et al., 2012; Test, Fowler, et al., 2009); however, for those who are in detention centers, freedom to work outside the facility may not be granted. For students who are experiencing exclusionary discipline who are suspended or expelled, district policies govern whether work-study placements and other types of school- and IEP-related employment, as well as the services such as transportation and job coaching, can continue during suspension and expulsion. Project STAY-OUT in Oregon focuses on the delineation of in-facility and post-facility transition planning and instruction, promoting job placement and coaching post-release (Unruh et al., 2010).

Related research moves beyond traditional postschool planning, adding components for the transition into school and/or community, including resources that help adolescents and young adults with disabilities meet the requirements of probation, community service, and mental health services. Some of these services go beyond work-related needs but have the potential to influence the sustainability of employment. For example, helping adolescents to stay connected to mental-health service providers is a key recommendation for maintaining emotional and social well-being and treating mental illnesses (Unruh & Bullis, 2005; Waintrup & Unruh, 2008). Mentoring programs have a long-standing positive association with improving the decisionmaking, goal setting, and engagement of adolescents with EBD (Baltodano et al., 2005). Mentors provide guidance and social/emotional support for adolescents who experience challenges with decisionmaking (e.g., staying in school, avoiding negative peer influence). Transition models for STPP-involved adolescents also recommend that transition specialists provide assistance in the adolescents' efforts to meet legal disclosure requirements regarding juvenile detention and court involvement to employers (Waintrup & Unruh, 2008). As Waintrup and Unruh note, disclosure of disability and mental health status is a part of transition education of particular relevance to adolescents who also experience juvenile detention.

Historically, transition specialists (i.e., special educators who work specifically with adolescents on IEP transition plans) have played a central role as job developers. People with disabilities face discrimination and deficit perspectives in the workplace. Many employers lack awareness of disability, have little experience employing people with disabilities, and harbor anxieties about and/or ignorance of compliance with labor and disability policies such as the Americans with Disabilities Act of 1990 (Draper, Hawley, McMahon, & Reid, 2012; McMahon & Shaw, 2005). In particular, adults with mental illness, an imperfect parallel subgroup to adolescents with EBD, face a host of prejudices and discriminatory practices that have the potential to diminish employment success (Russinova, Griffin, Bloch, Wewiorski, & Rosoklija, 2011). Transition specialists meet with employers, assess the requirements for a particular job, and help prepare adolescents with disabilities to experience on-sight employment with a range of supports to meet the student individualized needs. Adolescents involved with the STPP may face additional barriers to employment, so the role of job developer becomes even more critical (Nelson et al., 2010; Waintrup & Unruh, 2008).

In the field of U.S. employment, securing and maintaining employment is also a well-documented challenge for people who experience incarceration, often requiring substantial cultural and social capital resources. According to the handful of studies that address transition and adolescents with disabilities involved in the STPP, implications of detention and disability taken together may have an impact on future career development beyond just getting a job. In Project SUPPORT, an early model transition program for incarcerated youth in Oregon, Waintrup and Unruh (2008) present one of the few references in the transition scholarship to the relationship between having a record and eligibility for financial aid. Their program was unique in considering program provisions for visiting postsecondary educational settings during the post-release phase of adolescents with disabilities who experienced detention.

In grappling with the STPP and transition-related issues and methods of researching and practicing special education, we can draw from a small subset of chapters and articles that specifically examine the transition of adolescents on the STPP. We can also apply and adapt what we understand more generally to be important implications for the transition of adolescents with disabilities as a larger group. Additionally, we also have research and practice scholarship that focuses on the subpopulations where there are likely intersections with the STPP, including transition and adolescents with EBD and transition and racial/ethnic, linguistic, gender/sexual orientation, and cultural diversity as these pertain to equity. Synthesizing and conceptualizing intersections is largely a task that has been left up to consumers of research, so it is important to state future directions for both research and practice so that we can increase the strength of our knowledge base.

MINIMIZING THE STPP THROUGH STRENGTHENED TRANSITION RESEARCH AND PRACTICE

Many individuals with disabilities and their parents, and nearly all educators, researchers, and policymakers, consider enrollment in college and employment central to successfully transitioning into adulthood. These are the exact same outcomes that are so directly and adversely affected by involvement in the STPP. Following the earliest models of transition focused on work for people with disabilities, including vocational education and training, recent transition models and interventions include a more targeted approach to postsecondary education. But, as Halpern (1985; see Figure 2.2) pointed out early on, community adjustment, or as other scholars have discussed a related concept, personal fulfillment (Patton & Dunn, 1998; see Figure 2.6), are broader postschool outcomes that are long-range and inclusive of additional domains of adult living such as interpersonal relationships, community engagement, and self-determination. Employment and postsecondary education function as stepping stones. Neither guarantees success or happiness, but without one or both, some doors to future opportunities swing shut. Both postsecondary education and employment contribute to economic capital and potential for becoming financially secure. Cultural capital is also expanded through participation in work and postsecondary education, and its development is reciprocal to the development of social capital (Bourdieu, 1986). In fact, all three types of capital feed into one another. Memberships in communities on campuses and in work settings potentially create foundations for building connections and dense networks of all types of capital through friendships, coworker interactions, mentorships, and collegial relationships.

Understanding the Limitations of Our Knowledge Base

The examination of the knowledge base in special education transition research around the STPP exposes its limitations and most vividly illustrates the problems of special education research outlined in the introduction of this book: (1) the body of work is largely absent tools to understand power and status and the relationships that intersect with individual and group identities in the larger social, historical, and political contexts of U.S. education; (2) studies of individuals' characteristics and manifestations of disabilities predominate, and too few studies employ sociocultural theories to help explain the interaction of people and the broader society; and, (3) the methodologies and tools for increasing our understanding of both postsecondary transition and the STPP weigh heavy with conceptual and theoretical frames that neglect issues of cultural diversity and equity through the use of objectivist paradigms. Thus, the body of work reflects theory and empirical questions, analyses, and data representative of experimentation and related, mostly research quantifiable methods, as valued by special education writ large. Narrow conceptualizations of the types of transition research with potential for enhancing the complexity of the knowledge base and generating practical solutions creates limitations.

To illustrate these limitations, consider the following: Of the seven special issues published in special education journals relevant to the STPP (e.g., school violence, bullying), the primary focus of the 35 articles is on behavioral manifestations of disability and interventions to remediate or change behavior–both academic and social/emotional–in the context of the classroom. Two articles focus on transition either from various points on the STPP and/or into adulthood (see Baltodano et al., 2005, and Clark & Unruh, 2010). Macrolevel and systemic issues such as policy are given surface-level attention, mostly at the point of introducing the theme of the special issue. The majority of the articles, including those on classroom interventions and/or professional development, do not reference cultural identity theories nor do they delve into culturally responsive pedagogy. These examples do not take up critical epistemologies or challenge deficit orientations of adolescents and young adults who are either labeled as EBD and/or are experiencing exclusionary discipline. Nor do they problematize historical marginalization and its effects.

By way of contrast, special issues on the STPP outside of the field of special education, yielding 16 articles across four special issues, center less on disability characteristics and interventions and focus instead on specific equity issues that disrupt access to the general education system for all adolescents from historically marginalized groups, including those with disabilities. These special issues, published in law reviews, criminal sociology, and general education journals, do not ignore disability. Rather, they expand an examination of the problem to the larger issues such as institutionalized racism and sexism using sociocultural lenses. Racial/Ethnic and gender disproportionality, both in disability identification and in disciplinary referrals and punishment, are central themes in this body of work. Policy and legal analyses are more common in this subset, as are theoretical frameworks that make it possible to interrogate the intersectionality of disability with race, gender, LGBT, and other identities. The methodological tools range and include both quantitative and qualitative research designs. Rather than asserting that special education needs to be more like those other fields, the approach I suggest is two-fold: Engage in scholarship across disciplines and accept a wider range of research methodologies.

Merging Bodies of Literature

The above content analysis depicts a stark contrast between special education research and research in other fields interrogating the STPP. The difference sheds light on limitations in the knowledge base fueling current special education research and practice, particularly in the subfield of transition. Because special education transition is the focus of this book, the implications for this field are highlighted here; however, it is important to acknowledge that work from other fields (e.g., critical race theory in education, general education, education policy, criminal justice) have blind spots where disability is concerned. Nevertheless, these fields shed light on the problem by examining the social construction of disability, policy, and the legal proceedings and decisions that establish patterns in the STPP. The sociocultural nature of these bodies of work help us understand how disability labeling is contributing to the STPP on a larger scale. This body of work and its underlying set of frameworks is similarly helpful in understanding some of the paths to the STPP, especially paths two, four, five and six (above) that are more about marginalization and separation of students of color than they are about disability. Paths one and three are also connected to the conceptual understanding of disabilities as being socially constructed, but a more robust explanation of the adolescents' mental health, behavioral disabilities that manifest in challenging interactions at school, and the availability of resources and other services that would improve adolescents' with disabilities access to general education and inclusive education environments is needed.

The diverse paths to the STPP (i.e., those associated with disability and those associated with marginalization) are not mutually exclusive; adolescents' trajectories may be complex and circuitous. Understanding these paths, both for individuals and for groups of adolescents with disabilities, helps identify steps for moving forward toward the elimination of the STPP. Moving the lens out to see larger and multiple phenomena affords a better view of the playing fields, the rules that govern, and the capital needed to leverage power. In merging the bodies of literature and holding both special education research side-by-side with research across disciplines, we can begin to develop a wider range of solutions and we can benefit from multiple knowledge-generating paradigms. These potential solutions are laid out in the next section.

Targeting Inclusive Education

If general education is the field with the greatest promise for adolescents with disabilities, a first priority for improving transition for all youth, but particularly those with disabilities who are also from other historically marginalized groups and those who experience the STPP, is to strengthen in-school experiences. These adolescent learners must participate in authentic, motivating, and effective education opportunities before and during the transition to adulthood.

Exosystemic changes. Bronfenbrenner (1979) defines the exosystem as the system in which activities connect multiple environments (e.g., Congress' passing education legislation affects special education programs available in U.S. districts and individual schools). Examination of the exosystem shifts focus on context rather than the direct participation of the individual. Disrupting the STPP by increasing access to the general education system in meaningful ways necessitates that schools have an infrastructure to support inclusive education (Wilson, 2014).

One education policy-related change with strong support from scholars and advocates alike is for Congress to fully fund the implementation of IDEA as originally promised (40% of the average per-pupil spending [APPS]) by the federal government when IDEA was first passed as EHCEA in 1975. In 2015, several bills such as the IDEA Full Funding Act, were introduced in both houses of Congress (i.e., House of Representatives bill 551, 2015; Senate bill 130, 2015) that proposed a graduated scaling up of federal funding for the implementation of IDEA to 40% by 2025 (https://www.congress.gov/bill/114th-congress/house-bill/551/text?q=%7B%22search%22%3A%5B%22IDEA%22%5D%7D&resultIndex=8). In 2015, the federal government funded 15.3% of the national APPS, which was the highest amount for any given year since the passage of the original legislation (Council for Exceptional Children, 2015). Continued gaps in federal coverage force state legislatures to address funding shortages. Unfortunately, strategies have been to narrow eligibility criteria and shift costs to families (Council for Exceptional Children, 2015).

Beyond funding, scholarship across disciplines calls for the dismantling of zero tolerance policies in favor of procedures that minimize punishment and promote student learning (Gonsoulin, Zablocki, & Leone, 2012). Disciplinary policies that push students out are deleterious to the education opportunities for adolescents subjected to the STPP, diminishing the likelihood of graduation and the maintenance of a positive self-concept and self-efficacy toward future goals (Kayama et al., 2015; Nelson et al., 2010; Rutherford & Nelson, 2005). Implementing positive behavior supports (Jolivette & Nelson, 2010), restorative justice practices (Wilson, 2014), and mentorship programs (Waller, Houchins, & Nomvete, 2010) are promising alternatives to zero tolerance policies. One important caveat, however, is that research in support of these practices needs augmentation. Many studies have not included people from historically marginalized groups, either as researchers or as participants. Moreover, some employ invisible, dated, or problematic theoretical frameworks for understanding culture, race, diversity, marginalization, and equity; and many over-focus on the individual and/or on disability, espousing a color-blind view of the STPP that does not include a critical analysis of racism.

Microsystemic changes. Assuring there are fully prepared educators to meet the needs of adolescents with disabilities who are among the most likely to face exclusionary discipline also means that teacher preparation and professional development focus on both culturally responsive education practices and the knowledge and skills for effective classroom management and socio-emotional development of students. First and foremost, educators need to understand how racial/ethnic biases contribute to suspension, expulsion, and detention, and they need increased awareness of how to disrupt deficit thinking that feeds into racial/ethnic disproportionate punishment (Osher et al., 2012; Shippen et al., 2012; Townsend Walker, 2012). Developing culturally responsive educators, specifically to address the STPP, is a priority across disciplines, including special education; calls for improved teacher preparation and professional development are pertinent to special and general educators, administrators, and school staff (Shippen et al., 2012).

Related to promoting cultural responsiveness among professionals is the call for addressing social emotional learning (SEL) which includes the development of teachers' skills in building relationships with students and guiding them through learning experiences resulting from maladaptive behavior rather than relying on punishment. In a multi-case study of high schools that effectively supported both SEL and academic learning, Cervone and Cushman (2015) identified key structural and contextual supports of SEL including changing scheduling and class sizes, engaging in community building, and promoting student agency. In fact, supporting both academic and social emotional learning and well-being necessitates reorganizing schools and alotting time for teacher collaboration and the development of interpersonal relationships with students, particularly those who have experienced marginalization (Osher et al., 2012).

In special education scholarship, there is a strong voice calling for the use of evidence-based instructional practices, including those used in detention and other separate settings (Jolivette & Nelson, 2010). Coupled with the presuppositions about the strengths of research methods that include experimentation (i.e. RCT, quasi-experimental, and single subject), the assertion is that these research methods can be implemented with the constantly shifting and relatively smaller populations in detention settings (Nelson et al., 2010). This body of work focuses on reading and other academic instruction (Gagnon et al., 2012; Leone, Krezmien, Mason, & Meisel, 2005; Mathur & Schoenfeld, 2010) without broaching critical literacy or critical thinking skills. Yet, students need these skills to begin to challenge the inherent inequities they face by experiencing exclusionary discipline, or merely by attending underfunded and inadequate schools (Decoteau, 2014; Haight et al., 2014; Winn & Behizadeh, 2011). Three critical questions, at least, should be used to interrogate the value of these assertions: How will these approaches to research begin to employ an understanding of racial/ethnic disproportionality and other discriminatory disciplinary practices? How will these works account for the intersection of disability and other aspects of *both* researcher and participant identities? And, given the resources necessary for experimentation, both material and symbolic, is a one-size-fits all approach in an attempt to establishing causality the best way to solve problems related to the STPP?

School-wide positive behavior and intervention supports (SWPBIS) has been promoted as a sound method of managing students' behavior and shaping classroom environments in both general and special education settings (Gonsoulin et al., 2012). Strategies for PBIS have also been put forth as an effective practice to implement in detention-based education settings (Houchins, Jolivette, Wessendorf, McGlynn, & Nelson, 2005; Jolivette & Nelson, 2010; Leone et al., 2005; McDaniel, Jolivette, & Ennis, 2014). Although PBIS and related strategies address setting standards for students' behavioral expectations and establishing inclusive school climates, their overarching conceptual models for behavioral intervention do not engage cultural diversity or equity and have been, at best, retrofitted with tenets of culturally responsive pedagogy (Vincent, Randall, Cartledge, Tobin, & Swain-Bradway, 2014). Even in cases where PBIS is posited to solve problems of racially/ethnically disproportionate disciplinary practices, its implementation does not consistently ameliorate the problem, particularly for Black children who face disproportionately high exclusionary discipline (Boneshefski & Runge, 2014).

Pinpointing Transition Education

Relatively few scholars have tackled transition education during the STPP, yet transition planning and its domains of assessment and instruction hold promise for changing the trajectory of adolescents with disabilities who experience exclusionary discipline practices. Implications of research addressing the intersection of STPP and transition posit that some type of education portfolio, beyond what is normally documented in students' cumulative school folders, is one way to increase the likelihood that adolescents leaving detention will have the opportunity to demonstrate success and complete school. The contents of the portfolio are broad and are intended to address transition domains such as health, housing, and further education. Documents that track medical diagnoses and medication, eligibility for related services such as counseling and treatment for addiction, and receipt of public housing can prevent loss of services, relapses, and homelessness. Less has been written about documents that are necessary for juvenile records expungement, an important step that typically requires filing of court documents and, often, the assistance of a lawyer.

With its heavy focus on employment, the usual best practices in transition are in play for adolescents with disabilities who experience exclusionary discipline: ongoing career assessments, self-determination education, early work experiences, and job training. These practices increase adolescents' readiness for a transition from high school to work. Transition for adolescents who have been court-involved have additional considerations. One issue is how to garner authentic early work experiences while simultaneously fulfilling the requirements of community service, probation, and/or detention. Coordination of multiple obligations across institutions can be challenging. Further, adolescents need to be coached, in culturally responsive ways, on how to discuss their school and employment records, if and when appropriate, with future employers. Transition specialists, both in detention settings and in neighborhood schools, need to have the time resources to meet with adolescents, parents, and employers. Meetings with the employers must include job development, disability awareness, and information about the STPP so that community members understand the scope of the problem beyond maladaptive behavior, and so that biases and racism associated with the STPP are prevented from reification.

Despite academic struggles associated with both diminished access to the general education curriculum (e.g., teacher shortages in low-income communities) and the manifestation of disability (e.g., difficulty paying attention), IDEA (2004) requires that transition specialists and teachers consider postsecondary training and/or education for all students with disabilities. Exposure to the STPP should not change this aspect of transition planning. Special efforts must be made to access, for example, financial aid. Financial aid and housing may be unavailable to those who have been convicted of specific offenses (i.e., drug-related); however, court records of minors, with effort, can be expunged or sealed. Perhaps a more formidable obstacle is changing the mindset of adults so that they see the potential of adolescents with disabilities, especially those from other historically marginalized groups, to be engaged and to contribute as community members in and out of classrooms.

AN EDUCATION FIELD THAT INCLUDES THE STPP

There are, in the Bourdieuian sense, rules in the field of public school education that includes the STPP. These rules can be examined and used to frame ways to avoid some of the most deleterious effects of detention and court involvement for adolescents with disabilities. Educators, transition specialists, parents and guardians, and individuals with disabilities can and do change their trajectories and move forward as adults who are engaged in their communities, working, learning, and living alongside their peers without disabilities into adulthood. Doing so necessitates the cultural capital required for identifying both the rules and the strategies for working around them or with them to improve outcomes and deconstruct the STPP itself. Leveraging such power requires other types of capital too. Teachers and other educators need capital, both cultural and social, to challenge how biases and discrimination work to create dominance, whether it be situated in ableist, racist, sexist, anti-gay, English-only, or other similar ideologies. This includes knowledge and skills necessary for self-reflection and relationship building across groups. Connecting with others and forming the trust and rapport necessary for social capital requires strengths-based disability and asset-based inclusion conceptual frameworks, the historical, cultural, and political knowledge of the United States, and social-emotional skills to sustain shared learning and responsibility for change.

Interrupting specific instances of STPP involvement requires supporting adolescents' and their families' images of the future, to set goals, to plan for how those goals will be supported, and to assess progress on an ongoing basis. These activities are the cornerstones of transition planning in general; however, the STPP can seem insidious and intractable, making future planning and advocacy all the more crucial. The following are priorities for transition education: (1) raise educator awareness of the STPP and foster critical problem-solving to address disability, racial/ethnic, gender and sexual identity, and other biases in disciplinary decisionmaking; (2) increase educators' strategies for advocacy on behalf of adolescents who are in danger of being sent to segregated or restrictive educational environments; (3) implement culturally responsive pedagogy in transition education that addresses both the academic and socio-emotional growth of adolescents; (4) develop educators' knowledge and skills in the area of behavior and classroom management so that exclusionary discipline such as suspension and expulsion is avoided to the greatest extent possible; (5) focus adolescents' school trajectories on access to the general education curriculum that supports academic preparedness for postsecondary education; and (6) use teaching and learning tools that prompt development of students' critical and self-determined thinking to augment the development of competent and contributing young adults who have a sense of belonging to communities in which they identify belonging.

The responsibility for system change does not rest solely on the shoulders of school officials and educators. All stakeholders must be involved and invested in problem solving. Political engagement on the part of adolescents and adults is needed. At a systems level, dismantling the STPP began and continues with the involvement in 2014 of the U.S. Department of Education Office of Civil Rights, and efforts to collect data on the racially/ethnically disproportionate use of exclusionary discipline. Detaining adolescents and young adults can increase the likelihood of physical and psychological harm associated with incarceration settings, and it can diminish access to academic instruction and social networks of peers and adults who do not exhibit behavioral problems. In 2015, two bills were introduced for approval in both the U.S. Senate (the Juvenile Justice and Delinquency Prevention Reauthorization Act [JJPD] of 2015) and the U.S. House of Representatives (the Youth Justice Act [YJA] of 2015) to reform the ways that states handle detention-based discipline and punishment of young people. Both the JJPD and the YJA, under continued consideration in the U.S. Congress, strengthen previous legislation requiring alternatives to housing minors in locked facilities for status offenses. Both proposals would remove court authority to detain youth for status offenses within 3 years after their enactments (Congressional Research Service, Library of Congress, & U.S. Congress, n.d.-a, n.d.-b). Both acts also require states to actively seek solutions to racial/ethnic disproportionality in the punishment of juveniles and to develop community-based alternatives to detaining juveniles.

The policies, coupled with education policies, are the backdrop in the field of education opportunities throughout the schooling lifespan of students. During periods of transition, particularly the transition out of high school and into adulthood, the field needs to have a broad grasp of both society-level and individual-level mechanisms that support agentive change.

Chapter Four

Adjusting the Scope

Gaining Perspective on Self-Determination and Health Care

Maintaining health and well-being is at the heart of living a good life. Poor physical and mental health can lead to illness and pain, medical expenses and reduced earnings, diminished activity and social isolation, and depression. Adolescents with special health care needs, many of whom are served in special education, experience health disparities (Lotstein, Kuo, Strickland, & Tait, 2010). The U.S. Department of Health and Human Services defines health disparities, which can be tracked in both access to health care and health status of individuals or groups of people, as

> a particular type of health difference that is closely linked with social or economic disadvantage. Health disparities adversely affect groups of people who have systematically experienced greater social or economic obstacles to health based on their racial or ethnic group, religion, socioeconomic status, gender, mental health, cognitive, sensory, or physical disability, sexual orientation, geographic location, or other characteristics historically linked to discrimination or exclusion. (U.S. Department of Health and Human Services & Office of Disease Prevention and Health Promotion, 2008, p. 28)

Health and well-being are components of transition that intersect with disability, equity, and diversity. Diminished access contributes to health status disparities and postschool outcome inequality. In the field of health care, disparities are associated with income and level of education (National Academy of Sciences, Engineering, and Medicine, 2015), two major targets of transition education. Another commonality between the two fields is the prioritization of individual engagement in complex processes such as IEP design and medical treatment plans. In special education, self-determination has been bolstered by empirical, theoretical, and ideological scholarship (Algozzine, Browder, Karvonen, Test, & Wood, 2001). Likewise, the U.S. health care system and its members have had threads of patient decisionmaking and engagement woven throughout their culture of practice, referred to as patient-centered care, since the 1970s (Robinson, Callister, Berry, & Dearing, 2008). Discourse and practice endorsing patient-centered care is similar to the transition culture of practice known as person-centered planning, which is centrally linked to self-determination (Wehmeyer, 2002); the dominant, macrocultural value of individualism is foundational to both.

Active collaboration between those responsible for serving (e.g., teachers, administrators, nurses, and doctors) and those receiving services (e.g., students, patients, people with disabilities) requires capital resources across the two groups. In addition to the economic capital required for health care, cultural and social capital are necessary for understanding how the systems work, how to leverage power (i.e., self-determination), and how to get one's needs met. In medicine, patient-centered care specifically addresses the role of the patient and doctor in shared decisionmaking (Epstein & Street, 2011; Stewart et al., 2000). In education, IDEA 2004 and its earlier iterations also address the roles of the individual with a disability and parents as decisionmakers (Algozzine et al., 2001). These cultures of practice explicitly embrace agency.

Under the surface of the practices of education and medicine, however, lie strong undertones of the medical model of disability, which positions disability as an anomaly, a condition that needs intervention for the purpose of either improving or eradicating it (Kalyanpur & Harry, 1999). Since the proliferation of RCT as a gold standard (and quasi-experimental and single subject designs) in education research, special education has arguably become more closely aligned with the medical model, using jargon such as "dose" and "intervention" to describe educational practices. For examples, see Fraker et al. (2016), Fuchs et al. (2015), Parker McGowan et al. (2014), and Solari and Gerber (2008). Simultaneously, the fields of medicine and rehabilitation have moved toward a more comprehensive model of disability endorsed by the World Health Organization (WHO). This model is known as the International Classification of Functioning, Disability, and Health (ICF) and it integrates medical, functional, and social models of disability (Chan, Gelman, Ditchman, Kim, & Chiu, 2009).

ANSWERING AND QUESTIONING THE CONCEPT OF OPTIMAL ADOLESCENCE

Health and disability, and thus transition education, are connected in multiple ways. If the most optimal outcomes for postschool life are built upon healthy foundations, increasing opportunities for adolescents with disabilities who have specific vulnerabilities and needs for health-related services and supports has the potential to improve postschool outcomes. Understanding the need for health-related transition education and its potential for promoting equitable postschool outcomes, particularly for students who are also from historically marginalized groups, requires an understanding of the bidirectional relationship between disability and health/disability and health/well-being. Examining the scope of the interaction between transition and health highlights opportunities for improving transition education outcomes.

The aforementioned vision of self-determination and independence as universal states of being, coming to fruition during adolescence, may be more representative of a cultural practice than a natural or uniform developmental stage (Rogoff, 2003). Similarly, efforts to promote the development of self-determination in schools are part of an educatation-related cultural practice in the United States. In considering diverse populations and inequitable access to postschool opportunities, as well as the range of values, definitions, and approaches that are included under this umbrella, the conceptualization of self-determined adolescent deserves attention. All adolescents experience changes associated with growth and maturation, and these changes have implications for both healthy physical and mental development. Yet research on the universality of adolescence, including its construct and its biological, psychological, social, and sociological implications, has also been critiqued as ethnocentric (Rogoff, 2003). Hence, developmentally and irrespective of disability, adolescence is seen by many dominant-group scholars as a normative period of life in which increased self-determination and risk-taking meet and impact health status and other life experiences (Ryan & Deci, 2000; Steinberg, 2008; Wehmeyer, Abery, Mithaug, & Stanciffe, 2003).

The view that adolescence is predominantly, if not solely, defined by increased self-determination is critiqued for being too narrow, informed primarily by individualistic and Western paradigms (Kagitcibasi, 2013). Balancing the notion of adolescence as a universal developmental stage with an understanding that contexts influence normed expectations, responses to those expectations, and development itself, is critical to being culturally responsive yet it is not without tension. In Kagitcibasi's review of scholarship on autonomy and adolescence, the role of such balance is underscored:

> While emphasizing different developmental pathways that are adapted to different contexts, this study [the aforementioned review] has also stressed universal basic needs and optimal models deriving from them. It could be claimed that there is a tension between these two perspectives. Although there may be some truth in this claim, the more constructive approach would be to search for a balance between these two perspectives. I referred to this goal at the beginning as "achieving cultural contextualism without complete relativism." From a theoretical perspective the key is to both recognize what is basic and also to be cognizant of contextual–environmental demands on the growing person that would impact how the basics are realized or manifested in different ways. (p. 231)

This balance is an important aspect in achieving equitable outcomes with adolescents with disabilities from other historically marginalized groups. One tension is a lack of dialog between bodies of knowledge. Whereas developmental psychology and related fields have been contextualizing adolescent development and employing sociocultural lenses, particularly in education research and racial/ethnic identity, disability has been largely absent from consideration.

Similarly, special education research has used a dominant-group view of adolescence as a yardstick by which to measure the experiences with those identified with disabilities, failing to examine interactions and contexts associated, not only with racial/ethnic identity development, but also other environmental factors associated less with the individual and more with their embedded communities and the larger macroculture (Rivas-Drake et al., 2014; Umaña-Taylor et al., 2014; Williams, Tolan, Durkee, Francois, & Anderson, 2012). Becoming an adolescent and being treated as an adolescent, including tensions and variations associated with population diversity, are cultural practices across multiple fields. Examining them exposes both a chink in the foundations of equitable education opportunity and an opportunity and strategies for closing the fissures.

DISABILITY, HEALTH, AND TRANSITION INTERSECTIONS

The most obvious disability and health intersection in U.S. public schools is for adolescents with specific health conditions that make them eligible for special education, provided they demonstrate education-related needs. At the same time, adolescents are growing and their bodies and minds are maturing, opening opportunities for addressing changes in disability specific needs, their general health, and the preferences and strengths associated with such changes.

Disability-Related Needs

As with the general population, people with disabilities are living longer than in previous generations. In previous generations, adolescents with disabilities manifesting in chronic or acute health problems often did not survive into adulthood and transition was not a priority; currently, an estimated 90% now transition into adulthood (American Academy of Pediatrics, American Academy of Family Physicians, American College of Physicians, & American Society of Internal Medicine, 2002). This has prompted the medical field to address Health Care Transition (HCT) services (American Academy of Pediatrics et al., 2002). Paralleled with education transition plans, HCT services are person-centered plans that address medically and developmentally appropriate health care for adolescents with special health care needs, bridging pediatrics to adult service providers and physicians.

Needs associated with other health impairments. Some adolescents with disabilities have identified health-related acute or chronic health conditions such as cancer, HIV, spina bifida, kidney disease, sickle cell anemia, and asthma, to name only a few. Students with disabilities served in the public school system who have a primary handicapping condition related to health are classified as having other health impairment (OHI). Fourteen percent of all students ages 6–21 served under IDEA were considered to have a specific health impairment as the primary reason for IDEA eligibility (U.S. Department of Education & U.S. Office of Special Education and Rehabilitation Services, 2015). The establishment of OHI as a category of eligibility in IDEA occurred in the 1990 reauthorization; one year later ADHD was officially recognized as a disability that could be served under OHI if considered to be the primary handicapping condition (U.S. Department of Education, 1999). As a result, the OHI category has steadily increased (Centers for Disease Control and Prevention, 2016; Wagner, Cameto, & Newman, 2003). Like other health conditions, the issue of ADHD diagnosis, which requires access to a physician and, at times, medication, is salient to equitable transition opportunities.

ADHD as a prevalent health disability. In the discussion that follows, ADHD as a primary handicapping condition is understood to be served in the OHI disability categorization structure laid out in IDEA 2004. For some students, ADHD is a secondary handicapping condition that accompanies other disabilities, making the exact number of students receiving services related to this specific health condition difficult, if not impossible, to estimate (National Longitudinal Transition Study, 2004). Most recently, the U.S. Centers for Disease Control (2016) estimates that 11% of American children ages 4–17 have been diagnosed with this condition.

As a medical condition, ADHD is considered to have an impact on stamina, sleep, memory, attention, cognition, and social-emotional functioning (National Longitudinal Transition Study, 2004; Wei, Yu, & Shaver, 2014). In a nationally representative sample, parents reported that 69% of their school-aged youth with ADHD were taking stimulants and other types of medication (Schnoes, Reid, Wagner, & Marder, 2006). Both diagnosis and medication require access to health care and prescriptions; yet Shnoes and colleagues found that 43% of school-aged youth with ADHD received free and reduced-price lunch and potentially public health care coverage. Interestingly, children living in poverty, those where the head of household had a high school diploma but no postsecondary degree, and those who were Medicaid-insured were more likely to be identified as having ADHD than their peers from higher socioeconomic backgrounds (Visser et al., 2014). Nationally, White and Black students were more likely to be identified than were Latinos or students of other, non-specified racial/ethnic groups; additionally, children from households where English was the dominant language were four times as likely to be diagnosed with ADHD (Visser et al., 2014). Raising further questions about diversity and equity, the most common primary handicapping conditions with which ADHD is associated are LD, EBD, and ID, all of which have high degrees of racial/ethnic disproportionality (Schnoes et al., 2006).

Mental health as a part of total health. Mental health is an important component of overall health and well-being during transition, a period often marked by change and increased freedom and responsibility. Mental health conditions vary in the extent to which they impact individuals' lives, and thus transition-related education. Some mental health issues are tethered to other disabilities. For example, a student with LD or ADHD might experience anxiety associated with school performance and assessment. He may receive therapy or accommodations to relieve the stress. Relatively mild anxiety may not contribute to additional education needs and may not warrant a second disability diagnosis. On the other hand, anxiety can be debilitating and result in numerous school absences or maladaptive behaviors such as walking out of class or leaving campus during school. In fact, the anxiety might require an intensity of services for this student that exceeds those related to his LD; thus, a secondary handicapping condition such as EBD is considered.

Some mental health issues are addressed as types of EBD, the 6th most prevalent category served as a primary handicapping condition under IDEA 2004, representing 6% of all students served in special education (U.S. Department of Education & U.S. Office of Special Education and Rehabilitation Services, 2015). The transition-related mental-health needs of students with EBD are challenging to address given what some might describe as a sparse landscape of effective, accessible, and seamless mental health services for children, adolescents, and adults. Postschool outcomes for adolescents with EBD are among the worst. Only 55% of adolescents with EBD, and 58% of those with OHI, many of whom have OHI/ADHD, complete high school (Wagner, Newman, Cameto, Garza, et al., 2005). Thus, these two groups of students with a range of mental and/or physical health conditions are the most likely to drop out of high school. By other postschool measures of success in the first eight years following high school, slightly over half of adolescents and young adults with EBD, 53%, enroll in any postsecondary education, but they are among those who complete the fewest college credits, and they are more likely to experience police interactions and court involvement (Newman, Wagner, Knokey, et al., 2011). For adolescents and young adults with OHI, the outcomes were slightly better; 66% enroll in postsecondary education programs, but by measures of postsecondary credits earned, this group performed similarly to students with EBD (Newman, Wagner, Knokey, et al., 2011). Police interaction and court involvement for this group was among the top four disability categories.

The types of transition services that adolescents with EBD who have been diagnosed with serious mental health conditions need are frequently located in the fields of mental health and medical care (Davis, Koroloff, & Johnsen, 2012). The range of therapeutic programs (e.g., behavioral, psychological), pharmaceutical interventions, and other health and social services that are often necessary to address depression and other internalizing behaviors, aggression and other externalizing behaviors, self-injury, addiction, and other issues that link well-being to treatments are often beyond the purview of schools. These needs underscore the importance of addressing health-related needs during transition.

The barriers to mental health services within the current U.S. health care structures also reinforce the priority of transition in this domain, particularly for this group of adolescents. Challenges include difficulty establishing eligibility, underdeveloped adolescent-specific services, and a lack of bridging between adolescent-serving and adult-serving programs (U.S. Government Accountability Office, 2008). Additionally, as discussed in the previous chapter, adolescents with EBD are more likely to be eligible for child welfare services for neglected and abused children, compounding the transition education and services needed. They are also more likely to reside in institutional settings away from their immediate families (e.g., juvenile detention, foster care) and to experience homelessness. These life circumstances require navigation of systems with different cultural orientations toward care, childhood, family involvement, and disability (Davis, Green, & Hoffman, 2009). The use of multiple systems can also evidence gaps between systems of care, making interagency bridging necessary, which is particularly important during transition.

Other disabilities with health care needs. In addition to adolescents with OHI, ADHD as a secondary disability, and EBD, adolescents with ASD (Cheak-Zamora et al., 2014), orthopedic impairments (OI), multiple disabilities (Targett, Wehman, West, Dillard, & Cifu, 2013), and TBI (Wehman, Chen, West, & Cifu, 2014) are also likely to have health-related needs that should be addressed during the transition to adulthood. Additionally, some adolescents with ID have health conditions (e.g., diabetes, heart conditions) that sometimes co-occur with congenital disabilities such as Down syndrome and fragile X syndrome.

Using the NLTS2 results on prevalence (Wagner, Cameto, et al., 2003), these combined disability categories would account for about 17% of adolescents who receive special education, but the reality is that health is an appropriate domain to address in transition education both because of the breadth and scope of specific disability-related needs, and because of the common biopsychosocial changes that are universally experienced during periods of growth and maturation. Additionally, access to health care addresses the human conditions of illness and aging. Considering the multiple intersections of disability and health helps establish the scope of the need for addressing this transition domain. Therefore, the remainder of this discussion will assume a cross-categorical stance unless otherwise noted.

The Relationship Between Health Disparity and Disability

Health and well-being entail both exposure to everyday risk and protective factors associated with, among others, diet, exercise, education, work, community, and financial security. These all interface with the broad domains of transition, too. Access to both preventative and responsive care is an important factor for all people, but for people with disabilities who have related and/or atypical health needs, the frequency and intensity of health care interactions may be greater. Further, some people with disabilities have an increased need for appropriate care because they are more likely to have been exposed to multiple risks (e.g., poverty, unemployment, social isolation) than their peers without disabilities. For adolescents who are in the midst of transitioning to adulthood, additional considerations include not only changes in health status associated with growing up, but also changes in the culture of practice between adolescent- and adult-serving institutions and systems (Lollar, 2010). Health disparities stem from both biological differences and social inequities; however, those rooted in inequality are "avoidable and inherently unjust" (Adler & Rehkopf, 2008, p. 237).

Poverty as an Interaction with Disability and Health

The deleterious effects of poverty can be documented both as a contributor to disability incidence (e.g., malnutrition during gestation resulting in very low birth weight, a factor associated with some disabilities) and diminished postschool outcomes (e.g., limited opportunities for employment in economically depressed communities). Health, a domain of transition education, is similarly negatively influenced by poverty. Health status and health care are tethered to one another; status drives need for care and access to care affects status. During transition, both status and quality of care can be negatively impacted by diminished access to a medical home (i.e., an accessible and collaborative physician or nurse who knows the patient's needs through regular contact and refers to additional medical services as needed) and by fewer opportunities to develop a health care transition plan (Lotstein, McPherson, Strickland, & Newacheck, 2005). In short, poverty can expose children to environmental, health, and safety risks that negatively affect wellness.

Poverty is associated with limited outcomes. In the U.S. capitalist economy, human capital and individualism are predominant concepts and ideologies that coalesce, promoting employment as a means by which to be financially secure (Manning & Gaudelli, 2006). More than twice as many adults with disabilities (28%) live in poverty as compared to their peers (12%) who experience the same (DeNavas-Walt & Proctor, 2015). For adults, disability may impact employability, type of employment, salary, and benefits. Although the employment rate for people with disabilities (35%) appears to be about half of that for people without disabilities (72%), it is lower because this estimate does not take into account the number of people with disabilities who are not in the workforce (Brault, 2010). The confidence in work as a method for avoiding poverty, however, is shattered for some Americans; 7% of adult workers live in poverty (DeNavas-Walt & Proctor, 2015). One third of all young adults with disabilities who obtain postschool employment work part-time, and about half of those want to work full-time (Newman, Wagner, Knokey, et al., 2011). Employed people with disabilities, up to 8 years out of high school, have average hourly wages that are significantly lower ($10.40 per hour vs. $11.40 per hour) than their peers without disabilities (Newman, Wagner, Knokey, et al., 2011). Further, for young adults with disabilities, the average wage for part-time workers with disabilities ($9.00 per hour) was significantly less than the average wage for full-time workers ($11.10 per hour).

Returning to the NLTS2, a secondary analysis of predictive factors related to postschool outcomes demonstrated that for students with disabilities from the lowest socioeconomic bracket (i.e., head of household had a high school diploma or less and the family income was less than $25,000), poor health status and disability severity were both associated with lower odds of obtaining a high school diploma and securing competitive postschool employment (Wagner, Newman, & Javitz, 2014). This finding revealed poor health as a factor in postschool outcomes for students with disabilities whose low socioeconomic background was already predictive of poorer postschool outcomes (i.e., graduation, college, and postsecondary education enrollment). Nevertheless, the results from analyses of mediating factors and intersections of sociodemographic variables revealed complexities in need of further study.

For example, in this same study young men from the lowest socioeconomic group were more likely than young women to graduate from high school, gain employment, and enroll in college. An analysis of race/ethnicity showed inconsistent relationships to outcomes, with Blacks positively and significantly associated with education outcomes (i.e., high school graduation and college enrollment) but negatively associated with having a job after high school. Latinos were significantly less likely to graduate and find a job after high school. The authors conclude that poverty does not predict postschool outcomes consistently. Yet in a separate survey study of 500 adolescents with autism, health status and severity of disability were also negatively related to postschool outcomes, as was being poor and Black or Hispanic (Shattuck et al., 2012). This array of findings demonstrates the importance of considering intersectionality, which has been neglected in special education research and practice (García & Ortiz, 2013).

The transition to work becomes inextricably related to health though insurance. Historically, full-time employed Americans have had increased access to health care primarily through private insurance paid in part by their employers; 60% of Americans have health insurance through their jobs (Milliman, n.d.). The passage of the Patient Protection and Affordable Care Act of 2010 (ACA) recently expanded access to medical insurance. Under the ACA, adolescents transitioning into young adulthood through age 26 and people with preexisting conditions (e.g., childhood illnesses and disabilities with health implications) have options for, and are required by law to, purchase private health insurance (Lotstein et al., 2010). The costs associated with purchasing insurance, however, disproportionately affect people with disabilities who are also from historically marginalized groups and are experiencing poverty. The PPACA also eliminates some of the previous barriers to eligibility for young adults with disabilities who are living close but not under the poverty line by increasing access for people living within 133% of the federal poverty guideline (Lotstein et al., 2010).

Further, it is well understood that postsecondary education is associated with opportunity for increased and improved employment opportunities. Poverty, then, sets up another barrier: Adolescents and young adults with disabilities are less likely to enroll in and complete postsecondary education (Karpur, Nazarov, Brewer, & Bruyère, 2014; Wagner, Newman, & Javitz, 2014). Obvious benefits include the opportunity to further develop knowledge and skills and to translate this advancement into a better job with additional benefits. The employment rate for people ages 25–64 with college degrees is 82%, as compared to 72% for people without college degrees and 55% for those without high school diplomas (Kena et al., 2015).

Whereas 70% of adolescents with disabilities attended any type of postsecondary education, that was only true for 50% of those from the poorest backgrounds and 58% of those from household incomes in the $25,000–$50,000 range (Newman, Wagner, Knokey, et al., 2011). According to this same NLTS2 report, differences in postsecondary enrollment were nearly imperceptible across racial/ethnic groups (i.e., 61% of Whites, 60% of Blacks, and 62% Latinos), as well as across sexes (i.e., 60% of both males and females with disabilities enrolled in postsecondary education programs). Data from the National Center for Educational Statistics illustrate that, at the intersection of sex and race/ethnicity, White, Black, Latino, and Native American females are more likely that their male peers to enroll in 2- or 4-year postsecondary education; only Asian and multiracial males were more likely than females in those respective groups to enroll in postsecondary (Kena et al., 2015). Across all racial/ethnic groups, 43% of females enrolled in postsecondary education as compared to 37% of males. Access to health care, similar to housing, food, and other needs, is influenced by household earnings. Earning potential is linked to the advancement of postschool employment and postsecondary education; in turn, these are associated with in-school experiences, which also vary across subgroups of the U.S. population.

Poverty is associated with diminished early education experiences. For many people with disabilities who also experience poverty, the negative effects of being poor do not begin in the transition to adulthood. The experiences of living with limited resources, institutionalized barriers, and discrimination associated with marginalized populations can mean that membership status (i.e., at multiple intersections of disability, poverty, sex, race/ethnicity, immigration, language background, sexual identity, and so on) signifies childhood poverty (Hughes, 2013). More U.S. children (21%) experience poverty than do working-age adults (14%) between the ages of 18 and 64; and children are twice as likely than are retirement-age adults (10%), ages 65 and up, to live below the poverty line (DeNavas-Walt & Proctor, 2015). According to the NLTS2, 35% of adolescents with disabilities live in families with annual incomes in the lowest bracket (< $25,000), and an additional 30% lived in families where the annual income was between $25,000 and $50,000. Between 11% and 16% received

Temporary Assistance for Needy Families (TANF), food stamps, social security income (SSI), and other government assistance (Wagner, Cameto, et al., 2003). Circling back to health status and access to health care, life expectancy studies demonstrate the potential devastating effects of poverty with the gap between those in the lowest and highest income and education brackets widening (National Academy of Sciences, 2015).

Poverty affects people of all races/ethnicities; however, the disproportionately higher rates of poverty for many groups of people of color are striking. As a group, Latinos across age groups are more likely to experience poverty than are European Americans in all 50 states; and, in 49 states (Hawaii being the exception), the same is also true for African Americans (Grusky, Mattingly, & Varner, 2015). Not surprisingly, African American, Latino, and Native American children are more likely to experience under-resourced schools and they are more likely to be identified as disabled. A connection between both achievement disparities and the identification of some disabilities (i.e., LD and EBD) and inadequate instruction at school is a known problem yet one that is understudied (National Research Council, 2002a). Poorly performing and underfunded schools are representative of macrolevel issues folded into tax laws, employment patterns, labor policies, and the availability of resources such as transportation, to name only a few (Anyon, 2005).

Simply put, the economic health of a community is one factor in residents' access to quality schooling and opportunity for postschool success. Access to the best education opportunities and services that are associated with successful postsecondary transition shrink in under-resourced communities, and this lack of opportunity has a negative impact on transitions to adulthood (Hughes, 2013). Yet evidence of the consideration of these factors in transition research is sparse, thus creating gaps in the knowledge base. The 2014 special issue of *Career Development and Transition for Exceptional Individuals* (CDTEI), the official journal of the CEC Division on Career Development and Transition (DCDT), opened the door to expanding and contextualizing transition research and practice.

Historical Marginalization, Education, and Outcomes

Poverty should not be defined as a single or simple causal factor in diminished postschool outcomes for adolescents with disabilities, including those from other historically marginalized groups. Poverty is often intertwined with discrimination based on race/ethnicity, gender, language, disability, and other factors. This is true for people from other historically marginalized groups including people of color, girls and women across racial/ethnic groups, immigrants and people who speak languages other than English, LGBT individuals, and so on. In the fields of health and medicine, life course models are being used to explain the ways in which racism and discrimination have the potential to contribute to negative health status and, ultimately, to reduced life spans of people from historically marginalized groups (Gee, Walsemann, & Brondolo, 2012). Health status and access to health care and education opportunity are not as separate as their disciplined fields of research might suggest. According to life course models, segregation is a source of inequality that contributes to the collective effects of racism (Gee et al., 2012). Patterns of post–*Brown vs. Board of Education* segregation in U.S. schools have long been documented and critiqued by many (Alexander, 2011; Anyon, 2005; Blanchett, Mumford, & Beachum, 2005; Ladson-Billings, 2006; Madrigal-Garcia & Acevedo-Gil, 2016; Smith & Kozleski, 2005).

Yet neither the consideration of marginalization, in its sociocultural and historical contexts, nor its connections to individuals' identities at the intersection of disability, socioeconomic background, race/ethnicity (and other pertinent markers of identity such as sex or gender identity), are consistent or sophisticated in transition research and practice. Unfortunately, this pervasive limitation in the field has allowed for conclusions about postschool outcomes to overlook opportunity inequity. (See, for example, the citation from Newman and colleagues' [2009] NLTS report, a claim that potentially has the effect of downplaying differences in postschool outcomes across racial/ethnic groups). Our understanding of employment, postsecondary degree attainment, and other postschool outcomes of adolescents with disabilities is built upon an uneven foundation: Theory and empirical evidence located at the level of the individual stands tall and sturdy while theory and empirical evidence about sociocultural and historical phenomena that contribute to transition experiences is underdeveloped.

The uneven foundation of transition research is also tied to our methods of knowledge generation (i.e., research). The analysis of the effects of poverty has been consistently based on the individual as a unit of analysis, absent theorizing, questioning, or measuring the effects of the phenomenon of marginalization. While the secondary analyses of national or state databases published in the aforementioned special issue of CDTEI (see Karpur et al., 2014; Rabren, Carpenter, Dunn & Carney, 2014; and Wagner et al., 2014) do not focus solely on student- and family-level SES variables (e.g., disability, income, parent high school education, parent receipt of welfare) as predictors of postschool outcomes, they use these factors as principal drivers of research questions.

In their examination of individual characteristics associated with disability and mothers' welfare recipient status as predictors of postsecondary education, Karpur and colleagues (2014) found that welfare receipt predicted one-third of the disparity in postsecondary education attendance. These researchers concluded that government assistance of parents "could likely create an environment of low expectations for pursuing postsecondary education" (p. 26), and "reduce belief in stigma about welfare" (p. 26). Although the authors do not state who might have low expectations, their stated research implications, engaging families in financial literacy training and increasing adolescents' independence and motivation, suggest that this problem is rooted in the home (Karpur et al., 2014). While Wagner and colleagues (2014) found that poverty had a significant but small effect on graduation, postschool employment, and postsecondary education, they, too, identified parental expectations as a mediating factor. In their conclusions, these authors call for additional examinations of the intersection of race/ethnicity, SES, and disability, and they warn that focusing on individual and family SES may result in placing too much of the responsibility for poverty associated with poor postschool outcomes on the people who are most affected by the problem (Wagner et al., 2014). This is a step in expanding our understanding of the central problem: Equity in postschool outcomes has not been achieved across groups and this negatively impacts transition education and outcomes.

Nevertheless, the lopsidedness of transition research foundations amounts to tacit agreement that racism, sexism, and ableism are either invisible and removed from transition or their effects too difficult to measure and that connections to problems such as disproportionality and poverty can be bracketed as we look for potential solutions. Further, the implication is that these stressors on education opportunities are neither significant nor malleable contributors to continued poor postschool outcomes.

To illustrate this point, consider that the EBD category has both some of the poorest outcomes and pronounced markings of racial/ethnic disproportionality, making this group of adolescents with disabilities among those in greatest need for improved transition education. A full discussion of racial/ethnic disproportionality in identification, service delivery, and exclusionary discipline is beyond the scope of this chapter; however, disproportionality is a tenacious interrupter of equity and a complex cross-disciplinary problem in which both under- and overrepresentation impact education experiences and outcomes. As for health care, it is widely acknowledged that mental health care services are challenging to access and inadequate for addressing the needs of many adolescents with EBD (Davis, Koroloff, & Ellison, 2012; Davis et al., 2015; Forness, 1988; Klodnick et al., 2015; Maynard et al., 2015). Despite repeated calls for policy changes that support interagency collaboration (e.g., mental health care and school), empirical questions about access and collaboration, or a lack thereof, are often acknowledged but not carefully studied in transition research.

Further, non-consideration of sociocultural and historical factors in transition may also reinforce a subconscious belief that postschool outcomes of some groups of adolescents with disabilities (e.g., those with EBD, Black males with EBD and ID, Native Americans with EBD and LD, adolescent girls with EBD, etc.) are intractable. The conceptual disassociation from processes external to the individual and family can be traced to incomplete or inaccurate conceptualizations and conclusions about postschool transitions, diversity, and equity. When the intersection of race/ethnicity, sex, disability, SES, language, and so on, are taken into consideration, the object of study is flipped or turned, at least in part, to the examination of common factors across marginalized groups. Doing so is an initial step in strengthening what we know about transition and in making room for identifying the tools of marginalization, their functions, and strategies for dismantling them.

HEALTH AS A DOMAIN IN TRANSITION EDUCATION

Health-related transition needs have not been a major focus of special education transition research and practice, even though at least half of all disability categories in IDEA 2004 have specific, intersecting health-related issues and needs particularly during adolescence and the transition to adulthood. For adolescents with disabilities who are also from other historically marginalized groups, health status and health care during transition can warrant additional planning and education measures to ensure access to services that support the move to adulthood.

Interventions for Addressing Health Needs

A relatively small number of studies address health during transition and those that exist have been largely focused on transition planning in the domain of health. In-school interactions for students with disabilities that manifest in health-related needs require information sharing between students, their families, and teachers. In survey research, stakeholders (students, families, and their teachers) have repeatedly responded that sharing information about health conditions is key to effectively providing appropriate services, including transition planning, during school (Repetto, Jaress, Lindsey, & Bae, 2016). In a review of transition-related IEP goals, Repetto and colleagues found that while health concerns were noted on IEPs in some detail, there was little indication that these needs were connected to the transition goals in substantive ways. For example, the impact on daily activities of specific health conditions, such as how stamina and attention, pain, depression, and changes in ability might affect attendance, performance, assessment, and progress, was generally missing from goals for employment, postsecondary education, and independent living.

Health and transition connections have emerged as a part of broader research studies aiming to address transition more generally. In a comprehensive review of transition research, Test, Mazzotti, and colleagues (2009) identified three health-related predictors of positive postschool outcomes. These authors considered evidentiary support to be at the "potential" level for all related predictors, meaning that the practices were "promising" but lacked the empirical support necessary for drawing conclusions about causality (Test, Mazzotti, and colleagues, 2009, p. 164). The first predictor is self-care and independent living. Studies of this construct demonstrated that teacher- and self-ratings of strong self-care skills predicted, albeit with small effect sizes, a greater likelihood of acquiring and/or maintaining an independent household, employment, and postsecondary education. This emergent evidence that self-care, one aspect of the transition domain of health, has potential for improving transition outcomes for all adolescents with disabilities is most salient for those who have been marginalized by limited access to health care.

Self-determination, the second predictor, includes component skills such as autonomy and self-advocacy that have consistently been identified as predictors of employment. Employment and postsecondary education were also predicted by one experimental study on self-determination (again with a small effect size) as assessed before high school exit and correlated with postschool employment for students with LD and ID (Test, Mazzotti, et al., 2009). Extending the findings of the 2009 systematic review, Mazzotti and colleagues (2015) found additional evidence, based on secondary analyses of the NLTS2 dataset, that autonomy predicted employment and postsecondary education for adolescents with a range of disabilities. Self-determination and its components are inextricably interwoven into patients' rights approaches to increasing health care and health status for young people transitioning to adult service providers (American Academy of Pediatrics et al., 2002). Nevertheless, little analysis across diverse populations (i.e., disability intersecting with race/ethnicity, sex and gender identity, language) within the special education studies' samples or across learning environments (i.e., urban, suburban, rural; high poverty, low poverty) has been done. Such work has the potential to illuminate sociocultural factors that contribute constructs such as autonomy and its function as a predictor of postschool success.

Interestingly, Mazzotti et al. (2015) and Test, Mazzotti et al. (2009) found mixed results for the predictive accuracy of the third predictor, interagency collaboration, conceivably including collaboration between medical, mental health, and other health-related services, and the prediction of postschool education and employment. The later review of correlational research, Mazzotti and colleagues (2015), found that interagency collaboration in high school was negatively correlated with postsecondary education, contradicting findings of the first review that showed interagency collaboration as being positively associated with successful postschool transitions. Most recently, a meta-analysis of transition predictors by Haber and colleagues (2016) reinforced the need for interagency collaboration as it is centrally important to postsecondary education trajectories for adolescents with disabilities. To be clear, both reviews addressed the broad domains of transition, neither focusing on the domain of health. This work, however, begins to identify possible paths between transition outcomes and students' health-related knowledge and skills, the importance of transition education practices that can affect health, and gaps in our knowledge base that are worthy of further exploration.

In addition to examining what predicts transition outcomes, Test, Fowler, and colleagues (2009), conducted a similarly systematic and comprehensive review of experimental and single-subject transition research to identify evidence-based practices. This study employed criteria for stratified levels of evidence (potential, moderate, or strong), based on quantity of experimental and single-subject results with effect size reports and an absence of counter-evidence.

No studies of instructional practices or interventions directly addressing health needs in the category of student development (i.e., student-centered knowledge and skills included in transition curricula) were included. Neither were health status and health care visible in the remaining areas of Kohler's (1996) transition taxonomy (i.e., student-focused planning, interagency collaboration, family involvement, and program structures). This absence was acknowledged by Test and colleagues (2009), who called for research establishing an evidence base in several transition domains including the general category of interagency collaboration, healthy living, and physical fitness–all of which could be linked to health status and health care access. The authors also prioritized a call for additional research to bolster the extant literature base in health-related transition domains such as self-determination and self-advocacy, family involvement, and community-based instruction (Test, Fowler, et al., 2009). Additionally, Mazzotti and colleagues (2015) recommended that research continue to address the identification of predictors to clear up the contradictory findings across the two studies. They also recommended the study of evidence-based practices with population subgroups, but they did not proffer suggestions about the groups to which they were referring.

These systematic reviews, authored by scholars from the federally funded National Technical Assistance Center on Transition (NTACT), reflect the field's predominant criteria for evidence-based practices associated with experimental, correlational, and single-subject design. One purpose of the NTACT reviews is to infuse local education agencies with evidence-based transition interventions through publications and through dissemination at conferences and working meetings such as their annual institute for state teams to engage in transition professional development. Both reviews deserve and are held in high regard for their rigor and transparency in determining both the studies and the criteria used to qualify the strength of evidence. Nevertheless, two limitations of this work are important to note because they were not mentioned in either study, despite the authors' careful discussion of constraints. Both studies are based on the presupposition that non-experimental research has no relationship to causality. This assumption decontextualizes research. Nonexperimental studies get compartmentalized or excluded from parallel review, resulting in the loss of contextual information that can be paired with or compliment the experimental, quasi-experimental, and single-subject studies' results, essentially becoming lost knowledge. This contextual knowledge is difficult, but not impossible, to measure or include in experimental, quasi-experimental, and single-subject research because of the nature of sample and variable control and perceived objectivity (Bal & Trainor, 2016), allowing for the omission of sociocultural and historical factors, often linked to sociodemographic variables. Thus, the reviews can only paint a partial picture of what is happening in the field.

A second limitation stems from a different yet related problem. The narrow application of culture as a set of variables that can be controlled or held constant obscures our understanding of historical and social contexts that influence education opportunities and experiences (Artiles, 2003). Sociodemographic characteristics associated with individuals are important considerations within any design that attempts to demonstrate causality. As Meehl (1971) states,

> The reason we worry about the "influence" of nuisance variables like social class is that we want our investigation to shed light on what influences what, and the presence of nuisance variables in the system is believed to complicate matters interpretively. (p. 144)

In instances where Test, Mazzotti, and colleagues pay attention either to program characteristics (Test, Mazzotti, et al., 2009, Mazzotti et al., 2015) or to the sample's individual characteristics (Test, Fowler, et al., 2009), interpretation of the evidence is not exhaustive regarding what works for whom and under what programmatic conditions. The significance of each of these limitations in regard to diversity and equity in transition is discussed below.

Limitations of the Intervention Evidence Base

First, descriptive studies in particular, and qualitative designs in general, augment a field's understanding of the context in which experiments are conducted. Without considering the breadth of studies simultaneously, intervention identification of what works is promoted without interpretation of how and why something works. In this scenario, the practice of adhering to the standards of the federally-defined subset of methods belonging to a family of approaches that demonstrates causality and correlation overshadows the situated and non-experimental practices that occur in the field (Schwandt, 2005). Trainor and Bal (2014) examined the six studies identified by Test, Fowler, and colleagues (2009) to have the strongest evidence-based transition interventions, and they found that without context, at least one had diminished applicability in the lives of most students. Specifically, the study (see Nelson, Smith, and Dodd, 1994) examined an instructional intervention for completing job applications more neatly, a task that, given the omnipresence of online applications, word processing tools, and editing software, is arguably a less-pressing instructional need now than in 1994, when the results of the study were first disseminated.

Second, individual characteristics such as disability, gender, and race/ethnicity were not the subject of scrutiny for these systematic reviews, none of which were meta-analyses, or in the original, primary studies. In fact, some studies did not follow minimum APA guidelines for sample description that includes the gender or race/ethnicity of participants (American Psychological Association, 2010). Moreover, most of the original studies did not have sufficient sample sizes for disaggregating effect sizes for subsamples. Therefore, in secondary analyses these factors were considered as nuisances that, if controlled, intervention efficacy could be held constant across subpopulations. In other words, the very idea that what works for some will work for all is promoted by this assumption.

In a subsequent meta-analysis using the same transition taxonomy as a framework (Haber et al., 2016), the question of which intervention works with what population begun to get addressed. Similar paradigmatic assumptions, however, continue to constrain results and their implications. Although what role a person's race/ethnicity plays in educational attainment continues to be questioned, conclusions and evidence about the deleterious role of biases and discrimination in the formation of education opportunities are advancing outside of education intervention research. For example, Kirkland (2013), Stanton-Salazar (2001), and Valenzuela (1999), to name only a select few, have provided detailed ethnographic accounts of the ways in which sociocultural factors such as historical racism and discriminatory policies, irrespective of disability identification, are connected to limited education opportunities for adolescents transitioning into early adulthood.

These limitations encapsulate a significant struggle within the fields of education and special education research to define what is known (in this case about how best to educate students with disabilities during the transition to adulthood). Know-how that drives action in any field, according to Bourdieu (1974), is instantiated with both obvious and hidden value judgments that reproduce power differentials within a given society. At the heart of this struggle are questions about the practices of education research that include how to prioritize research questions, how to define acceptable standards for research methods, how to understand results in a field with diverse groups of constituencies, and how to disseminate and translate these findings into practices that are effective for diverse groups of students. The dominant view in special education research is represented by those who favor causal questions and define rigor as objectivist. Additionally, the dominant view embraces disability identification as an indicator of diversity deserving of attention in study design, while simultaneously de-emphasizing diversity in race/ethnicity, socioeconomic experience, sex and gender identity, and so on. Some scholars, both within and outside of special education, have questioned to varying degrees the proliferation of objectivist research such as experimentation as a gold standard and the simultaneous eschewing of descriptive and qualitative methods as limited (Arzubiaga, Artiles, King, & Harris-Murri, 2008; Connor, Gallagher, & Ferri, 2011; Eisenhart & Towne, 2003; Lather, 2006; Trainor & Leko, 2014). Schwandt (2012) eloquently makes the point that *diversity in practice* is what is needed:

> It is a rare day indeed in which we do not find ourselves having to experiment with something, analyze something, or count, measure, enumerate, or calculate. It is an equally unusual day where we would find ourselves not having to "read" a situation, make sense of or interpret what we are seeing or hearing, or "grasp" the circumstances in which we find ourselves. . . . We need multiple ways of knowing and multiple methodological capacities, so to speak, to successfully navigate everyday life. (p. 127)

Addressing these limitations and making both research and practice in transition more responsive to health status and health care needs across disabilities has the potential to positively affect postschool outcomes, particularly for adolescents with disabilities from other historically marginalized groups. Doing so would address some of the high economic and social costs associated with poor health status. Moreover, the process of involving adolescents in decisionmaking, supported in both education and medical scholarship, would provide opportunity to practice self-determination. Self-determination, however important, needs to be understood not only as a universal component of human nature and development, but also as a response to the social conditions that shape a person's life experiences. The tension inherent in enacting self-determination in contexts of marginalization has not been fully explored in special education research and practice, even though people with disabilities face discrimination on a daily basis. Self-determination has been mostly conceptualized and studied from within an ontology of individualism; however, the concept can be mapped to the conceptualization of agency in sociocultural theory, which employs an ontology of interactionism. In the following section, Bourdieu's understanding of internalized dispositions (i.e., habitus) is presented as a tool for expanding our understanding of self-determination (i.e., agency in Bourdieu's way of thinking) and how best to support its further development.

SELF-DETERMINATION AS DISPOSITION

Self-determination has been operationalized in the field of psychology as intrinsic motivation and self-regulation (Ryan & Deci, 2000). In the adaptation of self-determination theory in special education, led by Wehmeyer and colleagues, the focus is on autonomy in exercising choices and making decisions, setting goals, assessing progress, and realigning goals with one's strengths and weaknesses (Wehmeyer et al., 2003). As previously discussed, self-determination theory, and subsequent empirical support, has played a significant role in transition research and education. The thrust behind this work prioritized self-determination associated with individual development, component knowledge and skills, and/or disability-related implications. Less emphasis has been placed on understanding the attitudes, or dispositions, that support self-determination development, either for individuals or for people in society. A missing piece of the puzzle is the role of membership and identity in sociocultural contexts that promote or thwart self-determination opportunity and development.

The habitus of self-determination is consistently valued across research and practice in both the fields of health care and education, as a promising way to promote equitable postschool outcomes for adolescents with disabilities. Self-determination, as conceptualized in special education research, requires self-reflection and acceptance of disability. How one sees oneself, as an adult with a disability, in relation to adulthood requires a thought exercise that projects into the future. Therefore, dispositions of self-determination include both the ways one thinks about the future (e.g., belief that enrolling in college is an attainable goal, that college is affordable) and the way one communicates this to others (e.g., sharing this goal with teachers at an IEP conference). Dispositions also include nonverbal communication; self-determination curricula often address the body's role in communication, promoting dominant-group views, for example, of the importance of eye contact and posture in communicating assertiveness (see *Whose Future Is It Anyway,* Session 26, on "Communicating: Body Language and Assertiveness," Wehmeyer, Lawrence, Garner, Soukup, and Palmer, 2004, p. 237). Further, self-determination is more than reflection; one must set goals and take action toward their attainment. Thus, one of the many layers of self-determination in special education research is that of construct, a strategy or tool for transition instruction and a set of skills that can be directly taught in addition to dispositions, or habitus, that exist as a type of backdrop to skill development. Most often this scholarship addresses employment, but employment is not far afield from health status and health care.

Layers of Self-Determination

In transition research and education, efforts to intentionally shape habitus by directly instructing students on both the cultural capital and the embedded values that define one's identity as a worker are plentiful and a part of the staid connections between transition and employment. For instance, the National Collaborative on Workforce and Disability, funded by the U.S. Department of Labor's Office of Disability Employment Policy, provides curricular materials for teachers, transition specialists, and vocational rehabilitation counselors. Much of the curricula centers on work readiness, preparing youth with disabilities to find and maintain employment. One such publication entitled *Skills to Pay the Bills* (U.S. Department of Labor & Office of Disability Employment Policy, n.d.) is a material source of cultural capital that provides a direct enumeration of some of the dispositions that are most effective for getting and maintaining a job. In a section entitled "Enthusiasm and Attitude," the following passage underscores what it means to be a good employee:

> There are many ways in which an individual might demonstrate enthusiasm in the workplace. For example, in a job interview, he or she might smile, sit up straight, make eye contact, and discuss training and work experiences in an upbeat manner. Once hired into a position, an enthusiastic employee will typically show up on time, show interest in his or her job, and demonstrate willingness to listen, learn, and try new things. In customer service settings, an enthusiastic employee will approach customers proactively and offer assistance or seek out tasks and projects when there is downtime. This positive attitude helps employees go above and beyond to get along with coworkers and managers—even difficult ones—and respond to constructive criticism with maturity and willingness to improve. Overall, an employee with

> enthusiasm comes across as someone who wants to be at work who is willing to do what it takes to get the job done. (p. 35)

Maintaining a "positive attitude" and demonstrating this through posture and other nonverbal cues are elements of habitus and parallel the skills that the work itself (e.g., serving customers) requires. As adolescents with disabilities receive transition education and services, they are exposed to multiple types of cultural capital that may reinforce habitus as a worker. This particular example can be considered representative of a dominant perspective because it is seen from the perspective of the employer, who arguably has more power than the employee in determining who will be hired and who will be rewarded with continued employment.

On one hand, using dominant-group curricular materials to build cultural capital makes sense because it provides a clear delineation of what is needed to succeed in a world that is shaped by hierarchies of power and privilege. The argument could be made that this supports self-determination because it gives students with disabilities tools for reaching their goals. On the other hand, an uncritical focus on the demands of the workplace, and other environments, without consideration for human diversity (e.g., in culture, in ability) does not serve to develop a habitus of self-determination and autonomy in the pursuit of goals that are outside the dominant–and often deficit–view of what is appropriate for people who are not members of the dominant group.

For example, transition specialists often focus on competitive employment for students with disabilities as a postschool goal. Adolescents with disabilities, however, may not value and maintain jobs when those opportunities, often arranged by transition specialists, do not match their self-determined view of themselves as workers or as adults (Trainor, Carter, Swedeen, Cole, & Smith, 2011). Some adolescents exercise self-determination to *not* work in instances where the employment setting did not meet their expectations, and some maintain goals in postsecondary education despite failure and discouragement experienced in high school (Trainor, 2005, 2007). Even in cases where early work experiences are considered positive, follow-up studies indicate that entry-level competitive employment positions do not consistently afford opportunities for advancement in career development or financial security (Lindstrom, Hirano, McCarthy, & Alverson, 2014).

Importantly, building adolescents' knowledge of the dominant group's cultural capital may be necessary but not sufficient in the practice of conveying a habitus of competitive employment. Moreover, what is understood to be cultural capital and who are in the dominant group should be seen as constantly in flux based on the diversity of community members and other sociopolitical and historical factors at both micro- and macro-levels. Material sources of cultural capital such as *Skills to Pay the Bills* prioritize a specific set of communicative skills that are associated with the dominant group, yet decades of cross-cultural communication research have established the importance of accepting diversity in communication with an awareness that difference is not deficit (Gudykunst & Kim, 1997). Additionally, from a disability studies perspective, these communicative skills also embody dominance (Edwards & Imrie, 2003); the embedded message in these curricula is that diversity in ability is negligible and people with disabilities must learn to make their bodies adhere to the dominant-group communicative styles in order to convey a valued disposition. First-person accounts of disability have critiqued this embodiment of dominance and explained to people without disabilities that a difference in communication (e.g., reluctance to make eye contact) may signify preference or ability, but not *in*ability (Grandin & Panek, 2013). From both research and practice perspectives, inability has signified the need for instruction, remediation, or intervention.

Some research has documented students with disabilities' decisions to question their identity as a person with a disability and to resist participation in IEPs and transition planning (Connor, 2009; Trainor, 2005, 2007). Although the high dropout rate, particularly of students with high-incidence disabilities and those who are also from other historically marginalized groups, has not been examined as a phenomenon of resistance, dropping out of school requires self-determination. Resisting a system in which one feels undervalued and ineffective may very well lead to nonparticipation.

Nonparticipation is also visible in young adults' decisions to forego disability services in postsecondary education. Nearly two thirds (63%) of college students who received special education in high school did not "consider themselves to have a disability" (Newman et al., 2011, p. 31). Autonomy and psychological empowerment self-determination scores, subscales of the Arc's Self-Determination Scale (SDS), did not correlate with the receipt of accommodations in college for young adults included in the NLTS2 (Newman & Madaus, 2015). Further, self-realization, also assessed for this population using the SDS, *negatively* correlated with the receipt of accommodations by students from 2-year colleges. While this finding could plausibly be interpreted as a lack of understanding about disability and eligibility for postsecondary resources (Newman & Madaus, 2015), more research is necessary to explain the extent to which nonparticipation might indicate self-determination and a habitus of resisting disability labeling. Such resistance, however self-determined, can backfire and be deleterious to postschool outcomes. Additional self-determination scholarship is necessary to develop practices that support adolescents with disabilities' acquisition of cultural capital for the purpose of resistance in ways that promote attainment of their postschool goals.

If self-determination is to be considered more than a series of steps for setting and reaching goals as part of intervention or instruction, motivation and self-regulation in the context of diversity and equity need to be better understood. We need to merge our understanding of the individual with a disability as a worker with our understanding of the conditions of U.S. workers in general. In alignment with federal policy and macrolevel values that support the ideals of human capital, many stakeholders agree that work is an important indicator of postschool success. The United States has a legislative history that has protected the right of people with disabilities to work (e.g., the Americans with Disabilities Act of 1990, the Carl D. Perkins Career and Technical Education Improvement Act of 2006, the Rehabilitation Act of 1973). Limited employment often means limited access to resources that are necessary for meeting one's basic needs, including food, shelter, transportation, education, and mental and physical health care; however, understanding that there is in fact a range of perspectives about disability, adulthood, employment, and other postschool pursuits affords an understanding of which transition practices are most helpful and why some do not seem to be effective.

From Self-Determination as Construct to Self-Determination as Habitus

Understanding cultural diversity is key to supporting self-determination in equitable ways because motivation and self-regulation, from a socialcultural perspective, are a part of something larger than setting goals and working to attain them. Self-determination is habitus, a set of ways of knowing and doing. By definition, habitus is an accumulation of the internalized knowledge and beliefs (i.e., cultural capital) about the rules that govern specific fields. Whereas the individual, psychological models of self-determination incorporate the ecology of its practice (i.e., the conditions) as essential to its development (Ryan & Deci, 2000), this emphasis has largely not transferred to special education self-determination models. Not only are special education models tied to individualistic and rational theories of human behavior, they have de-emphasized the component of context or condition. Viewed through Bourdieu's and others' sociocultural lenses, the universality of self-determination as habitus is not in question. Rather, the question is how do individuals with disabilities who are also from other historically marginalized groups and consistently pushed to the margins of education opportunities develop a habitus of self-determination?

To examine self-determination through sociocultural lenses, a series of additional questions emerge. First, without serious consideration of context, can we be sure that self-determination is valued in the larger habitus (i.e., culture) of U.S. schooling? The disenfranchisement of both students with disabilities and students who are also from other historically marginalized groups is well documented, either as evidenced by the poor postschool outcomes such as the high numbers of students with disabilities and students of color who drop out of school, or as evidenced by the rhetoric of schooling as a method of social control such as the STPP (Decoteau, 2014; Ferri & Connor, 2005; Reid & Knight, 2006; Valenzuela, 1999). Deficit perspectives of students' abilities and their behaviors are ribbon-like themes interwoven across research and practices in education. How does self-determination flourish and gain support under these conditions?

Second, what are the effects of special education processes and labels on self-determination for this specific group of adolescents who are struggling in school? Given the tenacious obstacles of racism, ableism, and other biased thinking linked to the marginalization of all adolescents with disabilities, but especially those from other historically marginalized groups, how is the development of adolescent learner identities contributing to the habitus of self-determination? There is evidence across education and psychology demonstrating that identity development is harmed by labeling processes, whether that be through the instantiation of low expectations of self or from others, learned helplessness, social isolation, and/or stereotype threat (Flore & Wicherts, 2015; Higgins, Raskind, Goldberg, & Herman, 2002; McDermott & Varenne, 1999; Wasserberg, 2014).

Third, how are the complexities of the different ecologies of adolescents' lives intertwined and influential as individuals generalize self-determination across contexts such as school and work? Bronfenbrenner's model (1994) emphasizes interaction, not only among people, but also across systems, however remote from an adolescent's daily experiences. At the federal level, self-determination research and practice is supported in research funding and policy, yet both funding agencies such as IES and federal legislation such as IDEA 2004 employ narrow and low-context conceptualizations of self-determination often prioritizing individualized choice and IEP participation. Empirical evidence shows, however, that parents and their children with disabilities have micro- and exo-level experiences that either do not align with federal policies and do not mirror research-promoting dominant views of self-determination, or occur in contexts other than schools (Cavendish, 2016; Kayama et al., 2015; Martin et al., 2006; Repetto et al., 2016; Shogren et al., 2007; Trainor, 2005, 2007). If the ideal is far from the reality of practice, what must be done to ameliorate the culture of the practice in addition to and alongside expanding the knowledge and skills of the individual with a disability?

Fourth, what is the role of variation in human development and disability in self-determination maturation? Early on in the adaptation of self-determination theory, Wehmeyer asserted that the universality of self-determination as a component of human development also applied to people with disabilities, including people with intellectual disabilities who were most often disregarded as causal agents in their own lives. These early studies showed that people with disabilities could learn to make choices and decisions, and that they could understand their preferences, strengths, and needs (Palmer, Wehmeyer, Shogren, Williams-Diehm, & Soukup, 2012; Wehmeyer, 1992; Wehmeyer, Palmer, Shogren, Williams-Diehm, & Soukup, 2013). Once learned, what are the opportunities for self-determination practice and how are these honored or accepted when self-determination interferes with adult decisionmaking, for example, a student's resistance to attending an IEP meeting or a student's decision to become a parent during high school?

Despite lingering questions, self-determination as habitus, inclusive of the special education-adapted construct, retains value in addressing postschool inequity. Self-determination habitus is theoretically connected to agency and the disruption of social reproduction. An ecological view of self-determination is not conceptually distant from a sociocultural theory of agency. The social, cultural, and historical patterns of marginalization of people with disabilities present some of the most deeply rooted barriers to postschool success. Poor health status and limited access to health care are far-reaching obstacles in the pursuit of transition goals in postsecondary education, employment, and independent living. These barriers are sufficiently grand in scale that the limitations manifesting as a result of a condition, illness, or disability can seem less significant in comparison. Understanding and facilitating adolescents with disabilities' resistance to marginalization in ways that are self-determining and agentive have the potential to be transformative. Simultaneously, unearthing and targeting context-based factors that need to be addressed to augment the cultures of research and practice have the potential to strengthen our development of equitable education opportunities and postschool outcomes.

Known School-Based Obstacles

Special education research and practice has produced a substantial knowledge base in support of self-determination development and practice (Anctil, Ishikawa, & Tao Scott, 2008; Lee, Wehmeyer, Palmer, Soukup, & Little, 2008; Morningstar et al., 2010; Powers et al., 2012; Russo Jameson, 2007). But research has also shown that opportunities to practice self-determination at school are thwarted by a number of factors including limited time for practice, lack of curricular infusion, omission of culturally responsive home–school interactions, and limited educator understanding of supportive self-determination development (Carter, Owens, Trainor, Sun, & Swedeen, 2009; Shogren et al., 2007; Trainor, 2005, 2007). Therefore, at the microlevel, cultivating teachers' understanding of self-determination and the integration of curricular materials that support its development into the general education curricula are essential. Teachers' efficacy in supporting students' self-determination knowledge and skills can be considered a type of professional cultural capital that potentially leads to the increase of students' cultural capital. Moreover, as Field and Hoffman (2002) pointed out over a decade ago, teachers' self-determination practices must also be cultivated and supported if they are to implement this approach with their students.

Supporting adolescents with disabilities during transition and cultivating a habitus of self-determination also requires a broad view of ability and the rejection of deficit thinking. Disability studies scholars have long been concerned about the effects of pathologizing disability, especially in the context of school, and they have suggested that teachers can foster students' self-concept (part of the self-determination model in special education) by supporting adolescents' understanding of the range of human ability and by debunking stereotypes of disability, race, class, and gender (Connor, 2009). For example, students with disabilities may identify high-profile career goals such as professional athlete or performing artist. Supporting a habitus of self-determination means avoiding labeling goals as unrealistic, instead taking the time to understand the importance of the goal to the student. Increasing self-determination means bridging related career options to the original goal and expanding adolescents' views of the future and how he/she can make it in the world. Instead of squashing self-determined expressions of who students want to be, affirming those goals and providing related cultural and social capital increases opportunity and thus agency. Understanding the cultural values and beliefs that are embedded in self-determination and welcoming a broader swath of those values and beliefs also builds both educators' cultural capital and support of students' self-determined development. Thus far, self-determination and agency have been discussed in the special-education context of transition, but parallel to this knowledge base has been their development in health care, largely separate from the fields of education research.

DEVELOPING SELF-DETERMINATION AND AGENCY FOR HEALTHY AND EQUITABLE OUTCOMES

At the beginning of this chapter the argument was made that improved health status and access to health care potentially can improve postsecondary transitions in all domains. In the field of health care, recent changes in access to health insurance through the ACA (2010) signified changes that affect health transitions. The ACA is complex legislation that has been challenged in the U.S. judicial system; a thorough and technical discussion of the act is beyond the scope of the chapter, but several key affordances are important to acknowledge because the act has changed the field of transition to adulthood and access to health care for many people, including those with disabilities. Although the act has met with resistance from various political groups, as well as criticism from Americans who are now legally required to have insurance but for whom the cost continues to present economic hardship, its passage has meant increased eligibility for adolescents and young adults with ongoing health issues related to disability (Altman, O'Connor, Anapolsky, & Sexton, 2014). Additionally, some states declined federal funding, and access to health insurance in those states continues to be limited. These macro-level struggles, the political struggles, and policy initiatives that accompany them clutter the contexts in which adolescents with disabilities, their families, and the professionals that serve them, as well as all citizens, must negotiate and navigate as they transition into adulthood.

In states that have fully implemented the ACA (2010), increased coverage, and thus access to health care, has been most impactful in the lives of adolescents with disabilities, particularly those from low socioeconomic backgrounds. Health care coverage has been extended beyond age 19; parents across socioeconomic groups who provide their children with health insurance can continue to do so through age 26 irrespective of continuing education, to which previous health insurance coverage had been linked. This is important because only 60% of adolescents with disabilities enroll in postsecondary education up to eight years after high school (Newman, Wagner, Knokey, et al., 2011). Also, Medicaid, public health insurance, was expanded through ACA (2010) and no longer requires both low-income status and disability. Having low-income status is sufficient for coverage. Additionally, preexisting disabilities are no longer cause for denying coverage (Altman et al., 2014).

These new paths created by the ACA (2010) have also included additional requirements for supporting self-determination in health care. At the macrolevel of policy, the act itself required transition planning for the move from pediatric to adult care through a primary care physician (McManus et al., 2013). In addition to involving the adolescent with a disability in self-determined decisionmaking about health care, this type of transition planning is considered essential for establishing a medical home (i.e., consistent, lead service provision by a medical professional who has a relationship with the patient with a disability and/or chronic health care needs). Even before the ratification of ACA (2010), such planning was considered to be within the responsibility and purview of doctors and other providers, as was evidenced in position statements of multiple professional organizations' position statements on transition planning (American Academy of Pediatrics et al., 2002).

Ideally, health care transition planning (the development of formal health care transition [HCT] plans) occurs during the course of medical treatment that includes this transition service. National surveys revealed, however, that initial efforts in health care transition planning for adolescents with disabilities were not commonplace (Lotstein et al., 2005). More recently, gains in HCT are most pronounced for White young women who come from high socioeconomic backgrounds (McManus et al., 2013). The limited application of HCT for adolescents with disabilities who are also from other historically marginalized groups has led to calls for pediatric professionals to take a more proactive role. Recommendations are to actively engage these adolescents in their health care through the development of written plans and systematically sharing these with adult providers whose practice can serve as a medical home. This model has also been posited as a way to address socio-emotional health-related needs associated with psychiatric conditions and illnesses (Sacco & Twemlow, 2014). A well-articulated need for interagency collaboration to meet the needs of young people with serious mental health conditions has long been identified as a way to improve mental health, transitions between settings (e.g., hospital and school), and postschool outcomes (Forness, 1988). Unfortunately, access to mental health providers continues to be inconsistent, limited, or both.

Health care providers do not have the luxury of a daily classroom setting in which to prepare adolescents for this transition. In an absence of structure, they may assume responsibility and consider the context of their practice as a limitation in support of fostering patients' self-determination. At the same time, teachers are not always privy to the health status of their students nor all of their health care–related needs. Medical and social services require coordination with multiple institutions such as schools, juvenile detention facilities, hospitals, homeless shelters, and therapeutic providers (Davis et al., 2012). Nevertheless, the discussion of these linkages and opportunities for bridging are less common than expected, given the extent of the needs of this population and the lack of dedicated preparation of educators to meet these specific, disability-related needs (Davis et al., 2012; Forness, 1988).

Therefore, coordinated efforts between schools and other institutions in promoting a habitus of self-determination is important. This includes more than the sharing of information through interagency collaboration, as Lollar (2010) has suggested. Supporting adolescents with disabilities in gathering information about their health status, and knowing when and with whom sharing that information is in their best interests is also a part of developing the necessary cultural capital to increase healthy transitions. Further, family practices need to be well understood and considered so that variation in beliefs about adulthood and disability are a part of increasing self-determination.

One way to address this, albeit through low-context communication, is to ensure that transition plans on IEPs are comprehensive. Congruent with findings from other reviews, Repetto et al. (2016) found that IEPs rarely directly addressed health concerns and that the accommodations were neither individualized nor clearly aligned with health-related needs. Yet, accommodations and modifications, particularly those related to both health status and health care during transition, can be essential for documenting what will likely be needed in employment and postsecondary contexts (Lollar, 2010). Additionally, support for meeting these needs may rely on invoking knowledge of civil rights and antidiscrimination laws (Lollar, 2010). For example, accessibility to transportation and housing is often a critical component to transitioning to employment and postsecondary education. This suggestion also aligns with improving transitions for other populations of adolescents with disabilities including those who have also experienced juvenile justice, poverty, homelessness, and foster care. Addressing health care coverage into adulthood, and other resources such as housing and transportation are necessary to ensure equitable opportunity for positive postschool outcomes.

Chapter Five

Inclusive Postschool Success and Equal Opportunity for Fulfilling Adulthoods

Transition from high school to adulthood is a time of great flux; new possibilities seem to be around every corner. Strident, weather-worn obstacles, however, continue to impede access to equal opportunities for students with disabilities, particularly those who are also from other historically marginalized groups. Examining the culture of the practice of researching and teaching transition is instrumental in identifying what needs to change to make opportunity to succeed available to *all students.* The phrase *all students* underscores the need to acknowledge, investigate, and address marginalization anchored in, not only ableism, but also in racism, sexism, homophobia, and other biases. When adolescents start to move into adulthood, marginalization steps up its game, magnifying its deleterious effects on individuals with disabilities as they move into adulthood. For adolescents with disabilities who have also been denied equal access to education opportunities and other necessities that make up the bricks and mortar of a safe and secure foundation, marginalization ratchets up its potential to impede success. Carter and colleagues (2013) posed an "enduring question" following a recent review of 35 years of transition scholarship: "What must be done to make a meaningful and sustained difference in the in-school and possible outcomes of young people with disabilities?" (p. 16). This question should be paired with another enduring question: What must be done to eliminate marginalization, thus contributing to meaningful and sustained differences in in-school and postschool outcomes of young people with disabilities who experience additional marginalization and associated obstacles?

BETTER EQUIPPING TRANSITION RESEARCH AND PRACTICE TO PROMOTE EQUITY

Marginalization is not an individual characteristic; rather, it is a social phenomenon with roots in the shared and separate histories, politics, and cultures of dominant and nondominant groups that are situated variously in geographic, institutional, social, and other contexts. Identifying the culture of transition practice with a focus on marginalization has required some tools infrequently called upon in the field itself. Deliberate consideration through sociocultural frameworks herein has entailed the operationalization of culture as defined by Rogoff and Cole, the contextualization of embedded and chronological interactions as conceptualized by Bronfenbrenner, and, foremost, the functionalization of capital by Bourdieu and descendant scholars.

Transition is a multidomain, interdisciplinary, broad field of practice and scholarship. I have purposefully used a two-pronged focus to narrow this synthesis, making space for exploring the culture of practice. One prong captures the contemporary state of the field and the historical use of models that drive scholarship and practice (Chapter 2). This prong represents an attempt at epistemic reflexivity, not of a single study, but of the culture of practice, reflexivity necessary to understand the role of transition research and its relationship, or lack of a consistent one, to tackle marginalization. The other prong, the investigation of two barriers exclusionary discipline (Chapter 3) and health and self-determination (Chapter 4) illustrates how the culture of practice simultaneously addresses and ignores marginalization, preventing effective deconstruction of barriers to equity in postsecondary transition. This prong also spotlights the crevasses in the knowledge base that need to be traversed in order to improve transition education for many adolescents with disabilities who are also members of other historically marginalized groups, illuminating paths most likely to lead to equity in opportunities for postschool success.

The synthesis of scholarship herein has illuminated a culture of practice largely absent a framework for considering how diversity and equity intersect and should be addressed in transition. The question posed by Carter and colleagues (2013) underscores the neutrality of the field. Deep-seated beliefs among a majority White population of scholars demonstrates a legacy of the conflation of scientific objectivity and non-consideration of the role that racism, not race, and other biases and inequalities play in the transition education of adolescents with disabilities. Scholars outside the field of transition, many of whom have experienced both marginalization as people of color and power as leader-scholars in their respective fields, have identified this problem and potential solutions (Artiles, Kozleski, Trent, Osher, & Ortiz, 2010; Arzubiaga et al., 2008; Bonilla-Silva, 2014; DeCuir & Dixson, 2004; Gutiérrez & Penuel, 2014; Gutiérrez & Rogoff, 2003; Ladson-Billings, 2006; Sullivan & Artiles, 2011). In the sections that follow, I discuss the implications for transition research and practice generated from this synthesis of transition research and sociocultural theories addressing the major question posed by Carter and colleagues in 2013, but with the explicit objective of also addressing equity and diversity.

ADDRESSING MARGINALIZATION WITH INTENTIONALITY

Transition education is not a panacea for inequality, yet bolstering our collective understanding of the obstacles and strategies to address them has the potential to improve postschool outcomes across the racial/ethnic, gender, linguistic, and socioeconomic backgrounds of adolescents identified with disabilities. Ensuring that all adolescents with disabilities have equal opportunity to education, both an academic and functional core set of knowledge and skills and those related to career, college, and independent living preparation, maximizes opportunities for smooth passage into adulthood where dreams are within reach and adolescents face open doors through which to walk, en route to fulfilling their life goals. As a field, we can improve our knowledge base in several key ways so that we fully understand how transition education should work, does work, and does not work for adolescents with disabilities who are also from historically marginalized groups.

Expanding Research Paradigms

Augmenting the research base is essential in transition research because so little work has directly addressed questions of marginalization: how it is introduced and sustained, as well as how it can be stopped and how equity can be achieved. Multiple calls for increasing experimental and other quantitative research designs across special education and transition research (Carter et al., 2013; Cook et al., 2009; Council for Exceptional Children, 2014; Mazzotti et al., 2015; Test, Fowler, et al., 2009; Test, Mazzotti, et al., 2009) overshadow the need to ask questions and study problems that are not comprehensively addressed by these designs. Questions about equity and diversity may be getting quietly shelved, perhaps owing to both the tenets of objectivity demanded by RCT and a rudimentary understanding of how to examine a fluid, multiple, and dialogic construct such as culture. Parallel with research, teaching practices are also heavily steeped in the discourse of experimental research. Teachers are called upon in federal policies such as IDEA to adopt evidence-based practices that have demonstrated causality wherever possible. Teaching has become the delivery of interventions in increments referred to as doses (see, for example, Parker-McGowan et al.'s [2014] discussion of milieu language teaching).

Focused on establishing a knowledge base of evidence, and thus evidence-based practices, resulting from a specific objectivist research paradigm, RCT is at the top of a hierarchy of practice (Borman et al., 2005; National Research Council, 2002b, 2005; Slavin, 2002, 2003) and this ideal is visible in special education research. Currently, one of the embedded values in the culture of practice, or rules guiding the field, seems to be that tightly controlled intervention studies will evidence a set of practices that are causally linked to successful postschool outcomes. While some scholars in transition have been careful to acknowledge the importance of a well-rounded set of methodologies (Carter et al., 2013; Lindstrom et al., 2014; Trainor, Lindstrom, Simon-Burroughs, Martin, & Sorrells, 2008), a close association between causality demonstrated through experimentation and the solution to transition problems–largely associated with the individual with a disability–remains dominant. Carter and colleagues (2013) conclude the following about the state of transition research:

> Although descriptive studies make an important contribution by enhancing our understanding of issues and phenomena in the field of transition, descriptions alone do not provide adequate scientific evidence to judge the efficacy of policies or interventions. (p. 21)

On the surface this is a reasonable claim; however, given the primacy of experimentation and the limited resources in support of education research more generally, the prioritization of one methodology or set of methodologies can effectively eliminate the feasibility of conducting other types of research. Moreover, research itself constitutes a set of cultural practices instantiated with values and beliefs, a type of cultural capital that can be used to leverage power. Beliefs about being (i.e., ontologies), and thus human conditions such as disability; ways of knowing what is true (i.e., epistemologies); and ways of knowing what is morally and ethically acceptable (i.e., axiologies) all fuel any given methodology. While some scholars point out that, despite the calls for experimentation, this type of research continues to be underrepresented in transition research publications, the underlying assumptions of this paradigm can be seen across other methodologies.

For example, a plethora of transition research intervenes at the level of the individual with disabilities, promoting preemployment skill acquisition, student and family involvement in transition planning, self-determination, and vocational education, to name a few. Far less common are studies that address contextual and societal-level barriers to the employment of individuals with disabilities. An argument could be made that the underlying ontology of this body of work elevates normalcy over difference, directing intervention for change to the individual with a disability rather than to the society with biased views of who counts. Finally, the overarching predominance of experimentation and desire for causal knowledge illustrates a deep desire for certainty. But, as Erickson and Gutiérrez (2002) point out, "the accumulation of science is not at all continuous" (p. 22) and the "causal analysis must identify the specific mechanisms that generate specific outcomes within particular structural circumstances" (p. 23).

Paradigm expansion has the potential to shift the culture of transition research and practice toward a more inclusive view of what it means to improve transition for all students, making room for research designs that address the mechanisms and circumstances to which Erickson and Gutiérrez (2002) referred. First, multiple paradigms afford the opportunity to ask different types of questions and to employ a wide range of tools necessary for addressing those questions. Examining complex problems (e.g., lack of equal access to high-quality education for students across racial/ethnic, socioeconomic, linguistic, and ability groups; barriers resulting from inequities embedded in larger social phenomena such as institutionalized racism) requires what Lather (2006) calls "paradigm proliferation." Schwandt (2012) calls this flexibility "methodological diversity." Furthermore, using education research to inform policy requires researchers to take action, to accept experimentation as one tool, and to recognize when other tools are more feasible, practical, and paradigmatically aligned with research questions in need of answering (Schwandt, 2005). Thus, a recommendation for moving the field forward is to prioritize research designs, of all paradigms, that directly address questions of equity and diversity in the scope of the project. This would include, for example, building in the capacity for the disaggregation of efficacy data in intervention studies for multiple subgroups of the study's sample, breaking out sex and/or race/ethnicity as these intersect with disability. Where the sample size precludes doing so, the limitation should at least be explicitly acknowledged.

Second, expanding paradigms has potential to include a wider range of research participants. Sampling methods that meet special education criteria for rigor in experimentation and other quantitative studies can limit inclusion criteria to those associated with disability, rendering participants' identities as members of other historically marginalized groups (e.g., race/ethnicity, sexual orientation) invisible. Moreover, voluntary participation ethics would indicate that volunteers accept the disability category as a part of their identities, but some disability categorizations and labels are disputed or rejected in some subpopulations. It seems unlikely that a mother who does not accept the EBD label for her son would participate in a transition study about adolescents with EBD.

Relatedly, as previously discussed, an inherent bias or limitation of experimentation and other objectivist or positivist methods is a demand for control of variables associated with a sample's sociodemographic characteristics. Artiles (2003) identified limitations in special education research resulting from the narrow applications of culture as a set of variables that can be controlled or held constant rather than broader conceptualizations addressing historical and social contexts. These demands create limitations that are particularly salient to minority populations who are included in research. Adolescents with disabilities experiencing transition represent a minority population. For those who are also members of historically marginalized groups, additional minority statuses may apply. In terms of transition intervention research, or even quantitative descriptive studies such as the large number of secondary analyses of the NLTS2 data, the focus on sample identity and homogeneity has largely been at the level of disability. At present, researchers have been more responsive to criteria for rigor of experimental and other quantitative designs when it comes to disability, and less so when other considerations for sample variation exist (e.g., race/ethnicity, home language, sex, socioeconomic background).

Two recommendations for further research are linked to this second issue. The limitation is a reminder that when engaging in research that is representative of the predominant paradigms, criteria for rigor in sampling should be applied to a prioritized set of characteristics, rather than disability being employed as a single identifying characteristic of participants. This same limitation is also reminder that sampling based on a set of characteristics may not be feasible, partly because disability affects a small part of the total population and partly because additional characteristics associated with marginalized experiences are also tethered to minority group status. Research biases are not only anticipated, they are tolerable, insomuch as the method in play is one of many approaches to answering a research problem (Lather, 2006; Schwandt, 2005, 2012). Therefore, it is important for us to make room for other research methodologies, and thus the paradigms, from which they originate.

Third, paradigm expansion should include designs that entail close and non-objectivist relationships between those doing the research and those being researched. Related methodologies allow for including individuals with disabilities and their families, either as participants, consultants, or as members of a research team. Positivistic approaches to knowledge generation such as experimentation require a clear division between researchers and participants (i.e., subjects), but other paradigms allow, or even require, the inclusion of participants as conceptualizers, decisionmakers, investigators, analysts, and disseminators of research. Designs in these paradigms prioritize trust and rapport, essential for circumventing the mistrust and reluctance that communities of color, and others from historically marginalized groups, sometimes feel toward research and researchers, stemming from their historical and contemporary experiences of objectification and marginalization across fields of academic and scholarly study (see, for example, Skloot, 2010). The inclusion of individuals with disabilities and their families, as well as people who have experienced marginalization as racial/ethnic, linguistic, and other minorities, as researchers, informants, or brokers connecting communities to research, and as critical consumers of research products, increases participation in research (Ashing-Giwa, 2005). This is a longstanding recommendation for addressing issues of equity and diversity through scientific research across disciplines. In fact, connecting to other fields of study provides a fresh angle from which to tackle improving our culture of transition practice.

Pushing Forward with Interdisciplinary Capital

Beyond the critical examination of the ways that current and dominant paradigms have both afforded and limited our understanding of disability, education, and adulthood, the field needs to draw on scholarship outside of special education. Bringing sociology, cultural psychology, critical theory, anthropology, law, and other fields into consultation with the special education transition knowledge base can afford new solutions. Addressing problems of equity and diversity in special education transition requires a synthesis of research from other fields of practice, as well as collaborative efforts to generate new solutions. Fortunately, such interdisciplinary collaboration is not new to the field; scholars in transition have established relationships with fields such as vocational rehabilitation, career, vocational, and technical education and development, labor and education policy studies, and various disciplines in the field of medicine, to name only a few. Working across scholarly fields is indicative of strengths in flexible thinking, creativity, and the ability to solve problems through divergent thinking. Both strengthening ties across disciplines and forging relationships with new fields that are specifically poised to contribute expertise in culture in its many entities and manifestations has the potential to improve our ability to address inequality. For example, transition scholars should explore cultural studies of identity, institutions, language and communication to identify explicit theoretical frameworks for culture. In addition, both comparative education studies and critical studies in disability, race, and gender can afford new perspectives on the examination of culture from other fields.

Cultural diversity and educational equity are constructs with synergistic relationships to the histories, geographies, economies, politics, and sociologies associated with groups of individuals (Bourdieu, 1974, 1990; Bronfenbrenner, 1979, 2005; Cole, 1996, 2010; Rogoff, 2003). These complexities are too infrequently invoked in transition research, as is evidenced by conceptualizations of culture that are conflated with race/ethnicity. Current conceptualizations are also often missing the multidirectionality of perceptions instantiated with insider/outsider and majority/minority statuses, and equally absent a broader contextualization that includes power, dominance, and agency. Special education transition scholars do not necessarily need to theorize and operationalize culture and diversity in original ways. Rather, a more deliberate use of established theoretical frameworks for culture, diversity, and equity from other social sciences has the potential to offer our field flexibility in addressing tenacious problems in research and practice. Hence, the recommendation here is not to advocate for a single, correct theory or definition of culture or diversity, but to advocate for the study and transparent application of existing frameworks for which extensive support has been disseminated across other fields. Doing so exposes foundational assumptions, making them obvious and available for interpretation of theoretical tenets and empirical results in transition research. Currently, theoretical frameworks for culture, diversity, and equity employed in transition research remain largely unacknowledged and unnamed and often are without clearly developed connections to research questions.

For example, in Griffin's (2011) study of "CLD (culturally and linguistically diverse) students" and self-determination and participation in transition planning, diversity is seen as a quality associated with racial/ethnic groups of color, excluding "Anglo-Europeans" (p. 154). Further, culture is conceptualized as an approach to communication and interpersonal interactions, a unidimensional binary: either individualistic or collectivistic. The study is a synthesis of 17 published intervention studies–a justification for excluding all descriptive studies from review (Griffin, 2011). Cultural match-mismatch theory, a prominent theoretical framework in Griffin's (2011) paper, is a hidden driver of several assumptions operating without attention from the researcher. The author uses the word "mainstream" to represent White or European American culture, engaging in a kind of othering and dominance without examining the role of power in the phenomenon under examination. Further, the author does not explore the contexts of the studies in which participants' IEP and transition planning were being measured. In so doing, Griffin draws problematic conclusions, one of which locates the onus of transition success on the shoulders of historically marginalized groups by hinting that the "level of acculturation" can explain varied results (p. 161). While Griffin makes some important points about teachers and families sharing of cultural preferences and styles (i.e., a type of cultural capital), the frameworks she employs do not require her to go beyond assimilation and cultural congruency theories, thus limiting the implications of her work.

Relatedly, the field would benefit from a stronger, more transparent effort to connect transition research about culture, diversity, and equity to larger theories of power and broader sociocultural lenses. This is critically important for practice as well. In fields of cultural studies, such as cross-cultural communication, immigrant populations and assimilation is strongly critiqued. For example, Kim (2003) notes that assimilationist views are preferred and reinforced by members of the dominant group rather those subgroups who have been marginalized. In other words, Griffin's (2011) analysis lacks empirical studies and the theories from other fields whose focus is culture. Although these studies may be outside the field of special education, they demonstrate that the identities and languages of immigrants and their communities, particularly those who also have minority status, can be lost through the process of assimilation. Further, this type of stance does not take into consideration students' resistance to assimilation and loss of cultural identities (Kirkland, 2013; Pyscher & Lozenski, 2014). Other fields of education have moved forward, understanding that identifying the problem potentially foists deficit notions upon individuals of color and their families (Gutiérrez & Rogoff, 2003; Valencia, 1997).

Interdisciplinary connections potentially provide a broader palette of tools to use, moving beyond mismatch to research issues of equity and diversity. With the exception of bilingual special education research, special education research has not been widely or intentionally tethered to extant knowledge bases in studies of diversity from other disciplines such as sociology, anthropology, cultural studies, disability studies, economics, communication, criminal justice, legal and policy studies, and so forth. Yet the transition to adulthood is both theoretically and practically tied to each of these fields, and many others, as we consider what it means to be an adult with a disability trying to make it in the world, especially for those who face additional challenges associated with marginalization, historical and contemporary.

In the previous chapters on exclusionary discipline and health in transition, through-threads from other disciplines of research are interwoven to augment this synthesis of the transition knowledge base. These through-threads include the sociocultural theories commonly used in the larger field of education research, increasing the complexity of the questions we ask and identifying solutions that more accurately fit the problem under investigation. Sociocultural lenses are themselves interdisciplinary and can include literature from psychology, education, disability studies, and other fields. Sociocultural theories have been useful in exposing educational inequity for several decades. For examples, see Angela Valenzuela's (1999) *Subtractive Schooling*, an examination of

Mexican-origin urban youths' limited access to effective education in the United States; David Kirkland's (2013) *A Search Past Silence,* an exploration of Black males' identities while being schooled in places and by people who perceive these students as disengaged, lacking knowledge and skills, and threatening; or Jean Anyon's (2005) *Radical Possibilities,* an analysis of the economics of education as depicted or represented in policy and practice. One recommendation that can be gleaned from a close read of these studies is that culture, a broad concept with popular and scholarly meanings, can be defined in a range of ways and that the definition can drive an examination of culture in the context of research. Moreover, incorporating this knowledge base with transition research affords the tools necessary to consistently examine inequality rather than to bracket or set it aside.

Employing the wealth of scholarship on culture to transition education research also allows for comparative studies in transition research that are foundational to studies of inequity. Given the field's preference for experimentation and positivism, culture is too often reduced to a single sociodemographic variable associated with individuals so that it can be discretely measured, as previously discussed. This gives rise to two additional recommendations. First, in special education research, particularly in experimentation, accuracy in labeling (e.g., how an adolescent was identified as ID) should include other identities or sociodemographic information associated with the same participants. The American Psychological Association (APA; 2010), the organization to whose publication criteria the majority of special education journals adhere, requires specificity in participant description as well as avoidance of biased language. Similarly, the American Educational Research Association (AERA; 2006) demands accuracy and specificity in providing descriptions of participants and sites of research. Unfortunately, much of the literature still fails to consistently meet the basic requirement of reporting descriptive characteristics of participants.

A second, more substantial challenge for researchers is to go beyond culture's conceptualization as a tag or a label for an individual or group of individuals, expanding its operationalization to align with the purpose of the transition study and its research question. Doing so would allow us to move beyond the important but simplistic first step of correlating transition outcomes with racial/ethnic, sex, and socioeconomic classifications associated with people with disabilities. Doing so has created a call to action for researchers who believe that all students are equal, to ponder how race/ethnicity is associated with a postschool outcome such as dropping out. Without further questioning, resident theories about race and intelligence, race and student identity, and race and motivation are problematic, incomplete at best or, at worst, laden with the trappings of racist ideologies. More complex theories and definitions of culture can create more space to study phenomena such as racism because these have traction around issues of intersectionality, inter- and intra-group variation, habitus and agency. Continuing along these lines of argumentation, operationalizing culture and employing theories from other fields also illuminates the need to consider extraindividual conceptualizations of culture–culture in other forms such as the culture of practice, cultural capital associated with resisting oppression, or the institutional cultures of schools and communities.

In special education research, *diversity* is similarly problematically defined. Diversity is frequently tethered to culture, as in *cultural diversity*. Most often the phrase is used to mean people of color, but at other times the term includes members of the dominant group in the United States: White adolescents, their families, and the majority of educators who are from middle and upper socioeconomic backgrounds. When cultural diversity is objectified as some characteristic that one group (e.g., Black and Brown adolescents) has and one group (e.g., White adolescents) may or may not have, confusion about the meaning of diversity and the conflation of the term with race results. Moreover, the current use of *diversity* obfuscates intragroup differences while overemphasizing intergroup differences. The student and community population is diverse, and the culture of practice must be cultivated to respond to that diversity. In research, single and surface-level classifications serve to mask or minimize our understanding of both diversity and related marginalization. A necessary step in expanding our understanding of cultural diversity is to incorporate the knowledge base from other fields on intersectionality.

Intersectionality is commonly the subject of both theoretical and empirical work in other fields; incorporating this work into transition research can afford ways to frame and examine problems of marginalization that are rarely straightforward or simplistic in nature. For example, examining the dropout phenomenon and high school students with EBD requires disentangling the experiences of different subgroups of this population, adding depth to our understanding of diverse experiences and outcomes. Males and females, for instance, may develop the capital necessary for sustained achievement toward a high school diploma differently, and this might also vary across racial/ethnic groups.

Moreover, the contextual demands of subgroups of students may require differing responses to their transition environment. For example, Black adolescents with EBD who are from high socioeconomic backgrounds may experience the high parent and teacher expectations associated with college preparatory secondary programs, whereas their same race/disability peers at impoverished schools may not. A careful read of intersectionality studies and the incorporation of related findings would also create opportunities to expand our thinking beyond binaries that serve as a backbone of classification systems. The needs of LGBT adolescents, who are vulnerable to be classified as EBD and who experience high rates of dropping out of high school, have been all but ignored in our field. In the above example of a study on EBD and dropping out, for example, sex and gender identity need to be studied. This is not to advocate that all studies need to ask every question. The assertion is, however, that all studies should acknowledge the related questions that cannot be answered and more carefully enumerate implications for future research about subgroups that the study cannot address, particularly when issues of equity are conspicuous.

Finally, interdisciplinary research can bring transition research closer to understanding identity theories from fields such as cultural studies, linguistics, ethnic studies, anthropology, and others. The current use of sociodemographic terms to identify participants demonstrates a habitus among special education researchers of accepting disability classifications largely without questioning or problematizing the deleterious effects of labeling. In an area such as transition, where many student-focused interventions promote independence, goal setting, and self-reflection, a more critical approach to the classification of adolescents with disabilities is warranted. It is important to consider the implications of labeling on participants' identity formation and its relationship to transition, its orientation toward the future, and its perception of adulthood. Once labeled as an adolescent with an intellectual disability, how does a person conceptualize his future as a life-long learner? What agency does he have in transition planning? How do teachers reflect upon the use of a label and its symbolic and material capital? The recommendation to delve into identity scholarship is for the purpose of opening and bridging transition research to include theory and empirical evidence about resilience and critical approaches to education, such as critical literacy and community-based organizing, that dovetail with transition researchers' existing investments in the study of constructs such as self-determination.

Balancing Foci: Individual and Context

As discussed, the connections between a philosophy of individualism in U.S. education, including special education, is part of our larger habitus. Accordingly, it is not surprising that both research and practice in special education have deep historical, legal, and professional roots grounded in methods where the individual is both the focus of intervention and improvement, and the unit of analysis for knowledge generation across many methodologies. For instance, single-subject methods and individualizing instruction are both legacy practices from conceptual and theoretical frameworks that prioritize the individual with disabilities and her family as recipients of intervention and as key decisionmakers (Horner et al., 2005). These ideas have long been codified in special education policies such as IDEA in all of its iterations, stressing that educational programming should be tailored to the individual's preferences, strengths, and needs.

Education policy such as IDEA 2004 has been a driver of practice and research, but it is also responsive to the research base. Returning to the example of self-determination research and practice, the theoretical framework for which originated in cognitive psychology (Ryan & Deci, 2000), provides an illustration of this point. Following a 1995 call for special education research proposals from U.S. federal funding sources in the Office of Special Education

Programs, research developing self-determination conceptual frameworks, assessments, curricula, and descriptive studies has comprised a vibrant strand in transition research. The majority of this body of work has examined and tested individuals' self-determination characteristics and/or their capacity, after having been given an intervention for developing students' self-determination knowledge and skills, as referenced in Chapter 4. Few examples of self-determination research examine teacher perceptions of the construct and associated practices of students' self-determination (for an exception, see Field & Hoffman [2002]), or the larger sociocultural contexts in which adolescents with disabilities are encouraged to practice self-determination with the guidance of key adults in their lives.

In some ways, the push to understand how the individual can be taught or how disability-related needs can be addressed may overshadow the interactional contexts in which individuals with disabilities live, learn, and work. The use of sociocultural lenses is one strategy for better understanding context, without losing sight of the individual. Doing so can address concern about the field's hyper-focus on the individual as a unit of analysis and the ways in which this focus has served to obscure systemic and institutional challenges to equity that may influence self-determination (Arzubiaga et al., 2008; Bal & Trainor, 2016; Reid & Valle, 2004). How, for example, is disproportionality considered in transition research? In what ways are the economic and labor profiles of communities used to contextualize postschool outcomes and thus the interventions that are designed to improve transition? If the evidence-base in transition research is constructed with the characteristics of a specific disability in focus (e.g., an intervention designed to promote access to postsecondary education for adolescents with autism), to what extent are community and context considered? How do researchers design studies that avoid generalizations that prioritize one aspect of a person's identity and/or group membership and instead focus on intersections of identities and membership?

A national-scale issue such as disproportionality potentially affects transition education in multiple ways, yet it is infrequently problematized, either centrally or tangentially, in transition research. For example, high school students of color, in particular Black males, are overidentified with ID. In instances where this is true at a local level, a possible implication is that some Black males classified as having ID do not, in fact, have ID. Interventions designed to address specific transition needs, for example receiving life skills instruction, may be inappropriate for a number of students in this group. Yet there is little evidence in the extant body of intervention research that researchers have considered this issue, even though accurately identifying disability classification of the research sample is a criterion for rigor (Odom et al., 2005). Moreover, the extant body of work on transition to postschool employment tells us that approaches for planning and skill development for students with ID is distinct from career development for students without disabilities, or even for students with other disabilities. Therefore, using the tools of sociocultural research approaches and paradigms to study phenomena such as disproportionality in the context of transition interventions and other types of research holds promise in the effort to improve transition education.

Additionally, many students of color experience poverty and underfunded, urban schooling in communities where prospects for postschool employment for adults, much less for adolescents and young adults with disabilities and few work experiences, are severely limited and require solutions such as transportation to employment in other locales. Examining contexts such as high community-level unemployment as a variable or as a factor is essential to addressing the types of questions raised in transition research. Expanding the unit of analysis and/or contextualizing individuals' experiences does not preclude the design and implementation of RCTs or any other approach to research. Rather, it necessitates a careful consideration of these factors, and in most cases, a broad examination of a set of studies and associated results to fully understand any problem or viable solutions. Perhaps this assertion seems obvious; however, the current state of transition and special education research is so strongly focused on establishing causal evidence through very specific methods that calls for disregarding the review of descriptive and qualitative research are routine.

By focusing on discrete variables and correlational and causal relationships, study results may get decontextualized. Without descriptive research, either as stand-alone methodologies such as ethnography, or discourse analysis, or as methods for data collection (e.g., interviews and observations), we lose sight of how processes are implemented, under what local conditions, and how key stakeholders make meaning of research results, what it took to get them, and what implications can be derived from them. We must challenge the narrow primacy of research associated with causality, as promoted here by the Council for Exceptional Children (2014):

> Although CEC recognizes the important role that correlational, qualitative, and other descriptive research designs play in informing the field of special education, the standards do not consider research using these designs because identifying evidence-based practices involves making causal determinations, and causality cannot be reasonably inferred from these designs. (p. 505)

Balancing individual and context in transition education is also necessary for addressing the interaction between labeling and identity. We have many interventions that aim to cultivate students' plans for the future, particularly in the area of employment. At the same time, these interventions rarely include components that address the deleterious effects of labeling and classification. The label as an identity for adolescents with disabilities is taken as a given, a type of baseline fact. But descriptive research paints a different reality where adolescents who receive special education question their identities as people with disabilities (Connor, 2009; Trainor, 2005, 2007) and where young adults with disabilities do not identify and seek services from collegiate offices that serve students with disabilities (Newman & Madaus, 2015). Classifications and labels interact with identity, and outside of special education they have long been recognized as concepts instantiated with meaning and assumptions that have historically served to further marginalize people of color, people living in poverty, and people who speak languages other than English (Dunn, 1968; McDermott, Goldman, & Varenne, 2006; McDermott & Varenne, 1999; Reid & Valle, 2004).

Resistance and agency, in the face of labeling, has also been studied, often in other disciplines of research, many of which apply sociocultural lenses. Employing critical paradigms, such as critical race theory, will augment our field's understanding of the opportunities for equity that exist during transition and how these need to be expanded, supported, and improved. This is particularly important for addressing the strengths and needs of adolescents with disabilities who are also from other historically marginalized groups. For example, how do we target interventions to harness and support the employment– and postsecondary education–related strengths of Black males identified with ID, who, as a group, also experience disproportionately high rates of exclusionary discipline and police involvement? How can we support goal setting for future employment and education by fostering their critical thinking skills and agency?

Balancing the context and the individual as foci of research and practice is also essential for documenting disruptions of equity, deconstructing them, and producing solutions. At present, inequity is not consistently visible, beyond statements that simply acknowledge unequal outcomes, most often in the form of achievement gaps. Presenting information and discussion that illuminates the larger social biases and systemic problems that potentially affect the sample and the results of the research is critical (Arzubiaga et al., 2008). For instance, if the study includes a nationally representative sample of adolescents with disabilities, racial disproportionality and its impact on sampling is part of the backdrop of the study and is pertinent to the interpretation of results. Descriptions of researchers and contexts pose a jumping-off point for discussion rather than a separate descriptive task to be completed irrespective of question formulation, study, and analysis. In this way, research (design, implementation, and results) should be examined as situated in sociocultural contexts and with respect to history and timing so that we can better understand phenomena of interest, and in particular how equity is disrupted in educational contexts (Bal & Trainor, 2016). Achieving context/individual equilibrium in our examination of transition questions, and our interpretation of results, paves the way for our ability to promote equity by examining power differentials, acknowledging existing agentive capital and associated practices, and promoting further agency for adolescents with disabilities who are also from other historically marginalized groups.

Examining Power and Agency

Thorough examination of ability, culture, and equity begs examination of historical, social, political, and other connections and layers (e.g., temporal, geographical) that convey privilege and power (Artiles, 2003). As adolescents move into adulthood they experience degrees of newfound freedoms and obligations. The literature in special education transition has not extensively tackled issues of power and agency in transition. With the exception of the ostensible connections to self-determination scholarship, the topic rarely surfaces. Adults, and specifically teachers, may be unprepared to share power and decisionmaking at IEP meetings with students, despite students' preparation to be actively engaged in meeting procedures (Martin et al., 2006). Further, this work provides only a glimpse at a bigger issue; agency and power are necessary for attaining fulfillment in adulthood, far beyond the context of school-based processes in special education.

Also important, current scholarship isolates the discussion to individual expressions of agency, failing to consider a range of cultural and societal responses to adulthood: familial obligations and roles as well as able-ized, raced, and sexed perceptions of power and agency. All of these are linked to the fields of practice, its governing rules enacted in the habitus of the stakeholders, and the cultural and other capital constituting the experiences of adolescents with disabilities. In particular, deficit and biased perceptions of adolescents with disabilities may subtract from their motivation to set goals (e.g., learned helplessness, defeatist orientation) or their efforts to reach goals (e.g., stereotype threat). What does it mean for adolescents with disabilities to set goals and candidly discuss strengths and weaknesses when they are consistently reminded of deficits associated with disability and poor academic and social performances at school? What are the effects on adolescents with disabilities who are also from other historically marginalized groups that witness parent–school conflict of the kind amply documented in research on schools and the participation of families of color (Harry & Klingner, 2006; Horvat et al., 2003; Trainor, 2010c; Zionts et al., 2003)?

Power and agency have iterative and generative relationships within any field of practice. The field and its capital can fuel interactions that lead to change and support equity. On the other hand, conditions such as the access to capital or the habitus for action can be insufficient for change in the form of the destabilization of structural obstacles to equity. Acknowledging and supporting power and agency among adolescents with disabilities and their families uncovers only a part of the view of the transition landscape. In fact, researchers and educators are also stakeholders, themselves representing variable access to power and agency in transition education.

Research itself is a way to leverage influence, pushing beyond evidentiary results–or knowledge products–functioning as reproducers of inequity or producers of equity. As purveyors of the cultural practice of research, researchers should acknowledge and reflect on their personal and professional values and beliefs about research and the subject under examination, including ways in which their own identities and experiences shape their work (Bal & Trainor, 2016; Trainor & Bal, 2014). Transparency in research is critically important because researcher and educator identities and lenses help shape the field's understanding of research results (Arzubiaga et al., 2008; Bal & Trainor, 2016; Trainor & Bal, 2014). In the field of transition, leaning toward objectivist research paradigms does not currently demand this type of disclosure. This stance is reinforced by other standards in the larger field, with neither the APA nor the AERA guidelines requiring or even suggesting that the most basic description of researchers' sociodemographic background be included in research reports. The rules and habitus of the culture of practice reinforce what Arzubiaga and colleagues (2008) identify as "a view from nowhere" (p. 319).

The current climate demanding causal evidence through experimentation and other sophisticated quantitative designs such as hierarchical linear modeling and propensity matching has infused objectivity with power. The elevation of select research paradigms over others influences what gets funded, what gets taken up as rigorous, what gets published, and what gets translated into practice. Narrowly defining efficacy in research methodology is shortsighted; the instantiation of power has translated to a type of dominance in special education research. The onus is on transition scholars of all paradigmatic positionalities to do the work it takes to examine the limitation of the extant transition scholarship and practices, and to develop a deep understanding of other approaches, resisting the move to curb the implementation and dissemination of other research designs–designs that provide rich contextual evidence and answer questions beyond causality, such as *why* and *how*.

Grasping the power, and thus agency, to address the work of expanding the field's understanding of transition requires reflection on and critique of both one's own contributions and the contributions of others that collectively comprise the base of knowledge and practice. It requires consumption of a wide range of scholarly work from multiple disciplines, and it requires an unbashful and unapologetic commitment to equity. Invisibility and narrowness in our theoretical positions, ignorance or disregard for research from related fields, an over-focus on the individual at the expense of context, and the absence of an analysis of power presuppose that teaching and learning in special education transition are a-cultural or neutral (Arzubiaga et al., 2008). Culture-free approaches to research disrupt the production of transformative knowledge (Artiles, 2011); understanding culture and its relationships with diversity and equity has the potential to make our research more impactful, and, hence, more powerful.

EMBRACING AND LEARNING FROM DIVERSITY INTENTIONALLY

Achieving equity in opportunity for adolescents who are transitioning to adulthood, particularly for those who are from other historically marginalized groups, requires action and targeted efforts to solve complex problems, some of which have been around for a long time. Dismantling obstacles and promoting equal education opportunities for adolescents of color, those who experience poverty, those who speak languages other than English at home, and those who face discrimination of any kind are important steps in moving forward. Perhaps it is this work that weighs heavily on the minds and words of people who discuss diversity as something to be handled or "dealt with." That phrase, however, belies the deficit orientation that many of us, particularly those of us who are White and holders of assorted privileges associated with U.S. citizenship, relatively stable and comparatively high socioeconomic background and/or status, level of education beyond high school, English language literacy and communication fluency, heteronormative sexual orientation and gender identity, and other group memberships and experiences find so difficult to discard.

A final, yet pivotal, recommendation here is that we, transition researchers, educators, and other stakeholders, embrace diversity for the strength that it is. Doing so requires rewiring ourselves to think differently about diversity itself, applying what we know about deficit thinking and learning from the very people and groups we disregard as being "disabled," "disadvantaged," "culturally impoverished," in the "gap," and "at risk." What is known about deficit thinking is that it is pervasive in education, rooted in theories of poverty and pathology that ultimately lay blame for the problems created by larger societal inequities at the feet of those who are most negatively affected by exclusion and exclusivity (Valencia, 1997).

Embracing diversity means letting go of meritocracy and taking a place at the table with all others, without demanding to sit at its head. For example, Think College (thinkcollege.org) is a strong force in postsecondary education for young adults with disabilities. More importantly, the movement and the scholarship behind it are challenging what it means to go to college and, in some cases, to get a degree or another type of credential. In what instances do we support open enrollment in universities? How do we advocate for the Deferred Action for Childhood Arrivals (DACA), formerly introduced as the Dream Act, for individuals who entered the country as undocumented children? What efforts do we support in reduction of costs associated with university and vocational programs without the burden of loans? We have to engage in the challenging work of defining how we will contribute to sharing resources more broadly.

Embracing diversity also means learning from communities who have experienced marginalization. Churches in African American communities have long been a source of cultural and social capital in promoting postsecondary education to their adolescent members, and these resources should be linked to transition planning when that is the choice of the individual with a disability and his family. Religious and cultural institutions that serve similar purposes in other minority communities should also be seen as potential partners when identified as such by community insiders. How do we increase responsiveness in instances that suggest blurring the line between religion and public education? Responses to these questions do not come without careful deliberation across groups, where capital is generated by knowing one another and sharing perspectives of the field is the hallmark of collaboration.

More specifically, in transition research we can begin by problematizing group differences in postschool outcomes in more complex ways. First, we can dig down to the sources of the education problems we are studying, locating the root of the problem more precisely. Rather than identifying race, or even diversity, as the source of a problem or the object of study, we must be more pointed and acknowledge racism, or the failure to be inclusive in response to diversity, as the target for examination. For example, multiple transition studies have interrogated the relationship between individuals' racial group membership and self-determination. Examining the role of racism and discrimination in self-determination practices, however, may provide more useful information for targeting solutions, and doing so aids in the rejection of deficit notions that one group is inherently more self-determined than another.

Second, we can address the underlying mechanisms that correlate with the beliefs and practices (i.e., habitus) of people. Rather than drawing connections to reductive cultural identities as the source of beliefs and culture, we must understand identity as intersectional and context-dependent. For example, studies of poverty and parental expectations of college enrollment for students with disabilities have examined relationships between low socioeconomic background, low expectations for postsecondary education, and low enrollment rates. Augmenting this line of work entails acknowledging and probing the roles that income disparity across generations, inexperience with higher education, and attitudes about disability play in the formation of parental expectations.

Third, we can envision education for what it is, a part of a solution to greater societal inequity. Rather than engage in the mythology that education fixes all inequity, we should recognize education as necessary but not sufficient for redressing the discrimination that individuals with disabilities face daily. For example, the large majority of studies in the domain of employment are classified as "student development" in transition taxonomies of research, focusing on adolescents' skill development. In addition to designing and testing interventions that support the career readiness and work-preparedness of individuals, we must do the same in the areas of job development and boosting the cultural and social capital of employers so that hiring people with disabilities becomes more common and sustained.

Fourth, we can recognize agency and more actively examine how it is fostered in the context of discrimination. Rather than exclusively focusing on instances of risk, gap, and failure, we should borrow from resilience studies, maximizing our methodological capacity to investigate how and with what supports, both institutional and personal, emerging adults harness strength and demonstrate goal attainment. For example, research amply documents the relationship between exclusionary discipline settings, academic failure, and poor postschool outcomes. We must also turn our inquiry to success, and to the ways in which resources and individuals coalesce to attain positive postschool outcomes following separation punishment.

Finally, we can be purposeful, transparent, and reflective about our application of theory. Some scholars have been troubled by the application of Bourdieu's capital theory that seemingly contributes to deficit orientations, highlighting what types of capital people from historically marginalized groups lack or need to develop while struggling to attain, for example, positive postschool outcomes. Indeed, upon retrospective self-reflection, I can see how my own work has, at times, lost footing on that slippery slope. At the same time, the absence of sociocultural theories such as studies of the function of capital and social reproduction by Bourdieu and others afford a tool with which we can better understand culture, diversity and equity. Our mindfulness as researchers, privileged in many ways as generators of knowledge, can help us avoid these pitfalls by including critical and diverse perspectives even in instances when they do not conform to our narrow definitions of what counts as knowledge.

CONCLUSION

The culture of practice that we know as transition education is itself on a journey, one jumpstarted by concerns for equitable postschool outcomes for students with disabilities, but one that needs more fuel to cover the distance in a social context where the space between those with and without privilege and agency, tethered to capital of all kinds, is so great. The recent thrust toward the development of interventions can be seen as a stop along this journey, rather than a destination. Fortunately, the tools for laying those tracks, the strategies for mapping the journey, and the most promising paths along the route are within our reach. Diversity and equity are attainable, provided we are willing to be flexible in our thinking and our efforts to remove systematic barriers.

References

Adler, N. E., & Rehkopf, D. H. (2008). U.S. Disparities in health: Descriptions, causes, and mechanisms. *Annual Review of Public Health, 29*, 235–252. doi:10.1146/annurev.publhealth.29.020907.090852

Alexander, M. (2011). *The new Jim Crow: Mass incarceration in the age of colorblindness.* New York, NY: The New Press.

Algozzine, B., Browder, D., Karvonen, M., Test, D. W., & Wood, W. M. (2001). Effects of interventions to promote self-determination for individuals with disabilities. *Review of Educational Research, 71*, 219–277.

Allen, Q., & White-Smith, K. A. (2014). "Just as bad as prisons": The challenge of dismantling the school-to-prison pipeline through teacher and community education. *Equity & Excellence in Education, 47*, 445–460. doi:10.1080/10665684.2014.958961

Altman, S., O'Connor, S., Anapolsky, E., & Sexton, L. (2014). Federal and state benefits for transition age youth. *Journal of Pediatric Rehabilitation Medicine,* 7(1), 71–77. doi:10.3233/PRM-140270

American Academy of Pediatrics, American Academy of Family Physicians, American College of Physicians, & American Society of Internal Medicine. (2002). A consensus statement on health care transitions for young adults with special health care needs. *Pediatrics, 110* (Supplement 3), 1304–1306.

American Action Fund for Blind Children and Adults. (2016). Summary of the history of the education and rehabilitation of the blind. Retrieved from https://www.actionfund.org/history-blindness

American Educational Research Association. (2006). Standards for reporting on empirical social science research in AERA publications: American Educational Research Association. *Educational Researcher, 35*(6), 33–40.

American Psychological Association. (2010). *Publication manual.* Washington, DC: American Psychological Association.

Anctil, T. M., Ishikawa, M. E., & Tao Scott, A. (2008). Academic identity development through self-determination: Successful college students with learning disabilities. *Career Development for Exceptional Individuals, 31*, 164–174. doi:10.1177/0885728808315331

Annamma, S. A. (2014). Disabling juvenile justice: Engaging the stories of incarcerated young women of color with disabilities. *Remedial and Special Education, 35*, 313–324.

Anyon, J. (2005). *Radical possibilities: Public policy, urban education, and a new social movement.* New York, NY: Routledge.

Arrieta, S. A., & Palladino, J. (2015). A multiple-case study of special education teachers' approaches to LGBT students with emotional-behavior disabilities. *Journal of Ethnographic & Qualitative Research, 10*, 1–12.

Arthur, P. J., & Waugh, R. (2009). Status offenses and the Juvenile Justice and Delinquency Prevention Act: The exception that swallowed the rule. *Seattle Journal for Social Justice,* 7, 555–576.

Artiles, A. J. (2003). Special education's changing identity: Paradoxes and dilemmas in views of culture and space. *Harvard Educational Review, 73*, 164–247.

Artiles, A. J. (2011). Toward an interdisciplinary understanding of educational equity and difference: The case of the racialization of ability. *Educational Researcher, 40*, 431–445.

Artiles, A. J., Bal, A., & Thorius, K. A. K. (2010). Back to the future: A critique of response to intervention's social justice views. *Theory Into Practice, 49*, 250–257. doi:10.1080/00405841.2010.510447

Artiles, A. J., Kozleski, E. B., Trent, S. C., Osher, D., & Ortiz, A. (2010). Justifying and explaining disproportionality, 1968–2008: A critique of underlying views of culture. *Exceptional Children, 76*, 279–299.

Artiles, A. J., Rueda, R., Salazar, J. J., & Higareda, I. (2005). Within-group diversity in minority disproportionate representation: English language learners in urban school districts. *Exceptional Children, 71*, 283–300.

Artiles, A. J., Trent, S., C., & Kuan, L.-A. (1997). Learning disabilities empirical research on ethnic minority students: An analysis of 22 years of studies published in selected refereed journals. *Learning Disabilities Research & Practice, 12*, 82–91.

Arzubiaga, A. E., Artiles, A. J., King, K. A., & Harris-Murri, N. (2008). Beyond research on cultural minorities: Challenges and implications of research as situated cultural practice. *Exceptional Children, 74*, 309–327.

Ashing-Giwa, K. T. (2005). Can a culturally responsive model for research design bring us closer to addressing participation disparities? Lessons learned from cancer survivorship studies. *Ethnicity and Disease, 15*, 130–137.

Aud, S., Wilkinson-Flicker, S., Kristapovich, P., Rathbun, A., Wang, X., & Zhang, J. (2013). *The condition of education 2013* (NCES 2013-037). Washington, DC: National Center for Education Statistics. Retrieved from http://nces.ed.gov/pubsearch

Baer, R. M., Flexer, R. W., Beck, S., Amstutz, N., Hoffman, L., Brothers, J., . . . Zechman, C. (2003). A collaborative followup study on transition service utilization and post-school outcomes. *Career Development for Exceptional Individuals, 26*, 7–25.

Bal, A., & Trainor, A. A. (2016). Culturally responsive research intervention studies: The development of a rubric for paradigm expansion. *Review of Educational Research, 86*, 319–359. doi:10.3102/0034654315585004

Balcazar, F. E., Taylor-Ritzler, T., Dimpfl, S., Portillo-Peña, N., Guzman, A., Schiff, R., & Murvay, M. (2012). Improving the transition outcomes of low-income minority youth with disabilities. *Exceptionality, 20*, 114–132. doi:10.1080/09362835.2012.670599

Baltodano, H. M., Mathur, S. R., & Rutherford, R. B. (2005). Transition of incarcerated youth with disabilities across systems and into adulthood. *Exceptionality, 13*, 103–124. doi:10.1207/s15327035ex1302_4

Blackorby, J., & Wagner, M. (1996). Longitudinal postschool outcomes of youth with disabilities: Findings from the national longitudinal transition study. *Exceptional Children, 62*, 399–413.

Blalock, G., & Patton, J. R. (1996). Transition and students with learning disabilities: Creating sound futures. *Journal of Learning Disabilities, 29*, 7–16.

Blanchett, W. J., Mumford, V., & Beachum, F. (2005). Urban school failure and disproportionality in a post-Brown era. *Remedial & Special Education, 26*, 70–81.

Bon, S. C., Faircloth, S., & LeTendre, G. (2006). The school violence dilemma: Protecting the rights of students with disabilities while maintaining teachers' sense of safety in schools. *Journal of Disability Policy Studies, 17*, 148–157.

Boneshefski, M. J., & Runge, T. J. (2014). Addressing disproportionate discipline practices within a school-wide positive behavioral interventions and supports framework: A practical guide for calculating and using disproportionality rates. *Journal of Positive Behavior Interventions, 16*, 149–158. doi:10.1177/1098300713484064

Bonilla-Silva, E. (2014). *Racism without racists: Color-blind racism and the persistence of racial inequality in America* (4th ed.). Lanham, MD: Rowman & Littlefield Publishers.

Boone, R. S. (1992). Involving culturally diverse parents in transition planning. *Career Development for Exceptional Individuals, 15*, 205–221.

Borman, G. D., Slavin, R. E., Cheung, A. C. K., Chamberlain, A. M., Madden, N. A., & Chambers, B. (2005). The national randomized field trial of success for all: Second-year outcomes. *American Educational Research Journal, 42*, 673–696.

Bourdieu, P. (1974). Cultural reproduction and social reproduction. In R. Brown (Ed.), *Knowledge, education, and cultural change* (pp. 173–184). London, UK: Tavistock Publications.

Bourdieu, P. (1986). The forms of capital. In J. G. Richardson (Ed.), *Handbook of theory and research for the sociology of education* (pp. 241–258). New York, NY: Greenwood Press.

Bourdieu, P. (1990). *The logic of practice* (R. Nice, Trans.). Stanford, CA: Stanford University Press.

Bourdieu, P. (2004). *Science of science and reflexivity* (R. Nice, Trans.). Chicago, IL: Polity Press.

Bourdieu, P., & Wacquant, L. (1992). *An invitation to reflexive sociology*. Chicago, IL: The University of Chicago Press.

Bourdieu, P., & Wacquant, L. (2013). Symbolic capital and social classes. *Journal of Classical Sociology, 13*, 292–302. doi:10.1177/1468795x12468736

Boyd, T. M. (2009). Confronting racial disparity: Legislative responses to the school-to-prison pipeline. *Harvard Civil Rights–Civil Liberties Law Review, 44*, 571–580.

Brault, M. W. (2010, September). Disability among the working age population. Washington, DC: U.S. Census Bureau. Retrieved from https://www.census.gov/prod/2010pubs/acsbr09-12.pdf

Brock, M. E., & Schaefer, J. M. (2015). Location matters: Geographic location and educational placement of students with developmental disabilities. *Research & Practice for Persons with Severe Disabilities, 40*, 154–164. doi:10.1177/1540796915591988

Brolin, D. E. (1983). Career education: Where do we go from here? *Career Development for Exceptional Individuals, 6*, 3–14. doi:10.1177/088572888300600101

Brolin, D. E., & D'Alonzo, B. J. (1979). Critical issues in career education for handicapped students. *Exceptional Children, 45*, 246–253.

Bronfenbrenner, U. (1979). *The ecology of human development: Experiments by nature and design.* Cambridge, MA: Harvard University Press.

Bronfenbrenner, U. (1994). The ecological models of human development. In U. Bronfenbrenner (Ed.), *International Encyclopedia of Education* (2nd ed., Vol. 3). Oxford, England: Elsevier.

Bronfenbrenner, U. (Ed.) (2005). Making human beings human: Biological perspectives on human development. Thousand Oaks, CA: Sage.

Carter, E. W., Austin, D., & Trainor, A. A. (2012). Predictors of post employment outcomes of young adults with severe disabilities. *Journal of Disability Policy Studies, 23*, 50–63. doi:10.1177/1044207311414680

Carter, E. W., Brock, M. E., Bottema-Beutel, K., Bartholomew, A., Boehm, T. L., & Cease-Cook, J. (2013). Methodological trends in secondary education and transition research: Looking backward and moving forward. *Career Development and Transition for Exceptional Individuals, 36*, 15–24.

Carter, E. W., Owens, L., Trainor, A. A., Sun, Y., & Swedeen, B. (2009). Self-Determination skills and opportunities of adolescents with severe intellectual and developmental disabilities. *American Journal on Intellectual & Developmental Disabilities, 114*, 179–192.

Carter, E. W., Trainor, A. A., Ditchman, N., Swedeen, B., & Owens, L. (2011). Community-based summer work experiences of adolescents with high incidence disabilities. *Journal of Special Education, 45*, 89–103. doi: 10.1177/0022466909353204

Cavendish, W. (2016). The role of gender, race/ethnicity, and disability status on the relationship between student perceptions of school and family support self-determination. *Career Development and Transition for Exceptional Individuals*, 1–10. doi:10.1177/2165143416629359

Centers for Disease Control and Prevention. (2012). *Youth violence at a glance*. Retrieved from http://www.cdc.gov/violenceprevention/pdf/yv-datasheet-a.pdf

Centers for Disease Control and Prevention. (2016, May 4). Attention-Deficit/ Hyperactivity disorder (ADHD): Medication and behavior treatment among children ages 4-17 years. Retrieved from https://www.cdc.gov/ncbddd/adhd/data.html

Cervone, B., & Cushman, K. (2015). *Belonging and becoming: The power of social emotional learning in high schools*. Cambridge, MA: Harvard Education Press.

Chan, F., Gelman, J. S., Ditchman, N., Kim, J. H., & Chiu, C. Y. (2009). The World Health Organization ICF model as a conceptual framework of disability. In F. Chan, E. D. S. Cardoso, & J. A. Chronister (Eds.), *Understanding psychosocial adjustment to chronic illness and disability: A handbook for evidence-based practitioners in rehabilitation* (pp. 23–50). New York, NY: Springer Publishing Company.

Cheak-Zamora, N. C., Farmer, J. E., Mayfield, W. A., Clark, M. J., Marvin, A. R., Law, J. K., & Law, P. A. (2014). Health care transition services for youth with autism spectrum disorders. *Rehabilitation Psychology, 59*, 340–348. doi:http://dx.doi.org/10.1037/a0036725

Chiang, H.-M., Cheung, Y., Hickson, L., Xiang, R., & Tsai, L. (2012). Predictive factors of participation in postsecondary education for high school leavers with autism. *Journal of Autism & Developmental Disorders, 42*, 685–696. doi:10.1007/s10803-011-1297-7

Christle, C. A., Jolivette, K., & Nelson, C. M. (2005). Breaking the school to prison pipeline: Identifying school risk and protective factors for youth delinquency. *Exceptionality, 13*(2), 69–88. doi:10.1207/s15327035ex1302_2

Clark, G. M., & Patton, J. R. (1997). *Transition planning inventory*. Austin, TX: PRO-ED.

Clark, H. G., & Mathur, S. R. (2009). Practices in transition for youth in the juvenile justice system. In D. Cheney (Ed.), *Transition of secondary students with emotional or behavioral disorders* (pp. 376–395). Champaign, IL: Research Press.

Clark, H. G., Mathur, S. R., & Helding, B. (2011). Transition services for juvenile detainees with disabilities: Findings on recidivism. *Education & Treatment of Children, 34*, 511–529.

Clark, H. G., & Unruh, D. K. (2010). Transition practices for adjudicated youth with E/BDs and related disabilities. *Behavioral Disorders, 36*, 43–51.

Coalition for Juvenile Justice. (2011). *Deinstitutionalization of status offenders (DSO): Facts and resources*. Washington, DC: Coalition for Juvenile Justice.

Cole, M. (1996). Interacting minds in a life-span perspective: A cultural-historical approach to culture and cognitive development. In P. B. Baltes & U. M. Staudinger (Eds.), *Interactive minds: Life-Span perspectives on the social foundation of cognition* (pp. 59–87). New York, NY: Cambridge University Press.

Cole, M. (2010). What's culture got to do with it? Educational research as a necessarily interdisciplinary enterprise. *Educational Researcher, 39*, 461–470.

Congressional Research Service, Library of Congress, & U.S. Congress. (n.d.-a). Summary: H. R. 2728 114th Congress (2015–2016). *H. R. 2728 - Youth Justice Act of 2015.* Retrieved August 23, 2016, from https://www.congress.gov/bill/114th-congress/house-bill/2728?q=%7B%22search%22%3A%5B%22Youth+Justice+Act%22%5D%7D&resultIndex=1

Congressional Research Service, Library of Congress, & U.S. Congress. (n.d.-b). Summary: S.1169 114th Congress (2015–2016). *S. 1169 - Juvenile Justice and Delinquency Prevention Reauthorization Act of 2015.* Retrieved August 23, 2016, from https://www.congress.gov/bill/114th-congress/senate-bill/1169?q=%7B%22search%22%3A%5B%22Juvenile+Justice+and+Delinquency+Prevention+Reauthorization+Act%22%5D%7D&resultIndex=1

Connor, D. J. (2009). *Urban narratives: Life at the intersections of learning disability, race, and social class.* New York, NY: Peter Lang.

Connor, D. J., Gallagher, D., & Ferri, B. A. (2011). Broadening our horizons: Toward a plurality of methodologies in learning disability research. *Learning Disability Quarterly, 34,* 107–121.

Cook, B. G., Tankersley, M., & Landrum, T. J. (2009). Determining evidence-based practices in special education. *Exceptional Children, 75,* 365–383.

Council for Exceptional Children. (2014). Council for Exceptional Children: Standards for evidence-based practices in special education. *Exceptional Children, 80,* 504–511. doi:10.1177/0014402914531388

Council for Exceptional Children. (2015). *Federal outlook for exceptional children: Fiscal year 2015.* Washington, DC: Council for Exceptional Children.

Cramer, E. D., Gonzalez, L., & Pellegrini-Lafont, C. (2014). From classmates to inmates: An integrated approach to break the school-to-prison pipeline. *Equity & Excellence in Education, 47,* 461–475. doi:10.1080/10665684.2014.958962

Crenshaw, K. W. (1991). Mapping the margins: Intersectionality, identity politics, and violence against women of color. *Stanford Law Review, 43,* 1241–1299.

Davis, M., Green, M., & Hoffman, C. (2009). The service system obstacle course for transition-age youth and young adults. In H. B. Clark & D. K. Unruh (Eds.), *Transition of youth and young adults with emotional or behavioral difficulties* (pp. 25–46). Baltimore, MD: Brookes.

Davis, M., Koroloff, N., & Ellison, M. L. (2012). Between adolescence and adulthood: Rehabilitation research to improve services for youth and young adults. *Psychiatric Rehabilitation Journal, 35,* 167–170. doi:10.2975/35.3.2012.167.170

Davis, M., Koroloff, N., & Johnsen, M. (2012). Social network analysis of child and adult interorganizational connections. *Psychiatric Rehabilitation Journal, 35,* 265–272. doi:10.2975/35.3.2012.265.272

Davis, M., Sheidow, A., & McCart, M. (2015). Reducing recidivism and symptoms in emerging adults with serious mental health conditions and justice system involvement. *Journal of Behavioral Health Services & Research, 42,* 172–190. doi:10.1007/s11414-014-9425-8

de Blasio, B. (2015, July). *Safety with dignity: Policy recommendations from the Mayor's leadership team on school climate and discipline.* Retrieved September 13, 2016, from http://www1.nyc.gov/site/sclt/index.page

Deci, E. L., Vallerand, R. J., Pelletier, L. G., & Ryan, R. M. (1991). Motivation and education: The self-determination perspective. *Educational Psychologist, 26,* 325–346.

Decoteau, J. I. (2014). Trouble at school: Understanding school discipline systems as nets of social control. *Equity & Excellence in Education, 47*, 513–530. doi:10.1080/10665684.2014.958963

DeCuir, J. T., & Dixson, A. D. (2004). "So when it comes out, they aren't that surprised that it is there": Using critical race theory as a tool of analysis of race and racism in education. *Educational Researcher, 33*(5), 26–31.

DeNavas-Walt, C., & Proctor, B. D. (2015, September). Income and poverty in the United States: 2014. Washington, DC: U.S. Census Bureau. Retreived from https://www.census.gov/content/dam/Census/library/publications/2015/demo/p60-252.pdf

Doren, B., & Benz, M. R. (1998). Employment inequality revisited: Predictors of better employment outcomes for young women with disabilities in transition. *Journal of Special Education, 31*, 425–442.

Draper, W., Hawley, C., McMahon, B. T., & Reid, C. A. (2012). Workplace discrimination and the record of disability. *Journal of Vocational Rehabilitation, 36*, 199–206. doi:10.3233/JVR-2012-0594

Dunn, L. (1968). Special education for the mildly retarded–Is much of it justifiable? *Exceptional Children, 35*, 5–22.

Dykes, F., & Thomas, S. (2015). Meeting the needs of the hidden minority: Transition planning tips for LGBTQ youth. *Preventing School Failure, 59*, 179–185. doi:10.1080/1045988X.2014.903462

Edwards, C., & Imrie, R. (2003). Disability and bodies as bearers of value. *Sociology, 32*, 239–256. doi:10.1177/00380385030037002002

Eisenberg, M. E., Gower, A. L., McMorris, B. J., & Bucchianeri, M. M. (2015). Vulnerable bullies: Perpetration of peer harassment among youths across sexual orientation, weight, and disability status. *American Journal of Public Health, 105*, 1784–1791. doi:10.2105/AJPH.2015.302704

Eisenhart, M., & Towne, L. (2003). Contestation and change in national policy on "scientifically-based" education research. *Educational Researcher, 32*(7), 31–38. doi:10.3102/0013189X032007031

Eisenman, L. T. (2001). Conceptualizing the contribution of career-oriented schooling to self-determination. *Career Development for Exceptional Individuals, 24*, 3–17.

Emerson, R. W. (1855). Essay II. *Essays: Second series* (2nd ed., pp. 49–87). Boston: Phillips, Sampson, and Company.

Epstein, R. M., & Street, R. L. (2011). The values and value of patient-centered care. *Annals of Family Medicine, 9*, 100–103. doi:10.1370/afm.1239

Erickson, F., & Gutiérrez, K. (2002). Comment: Culture, rigor, and science in educational research. *Educational Researcher, 31*(8), 21–24. doi:10.2307/3594390

Fairweather, J. S., Stearns, M. S., & Wagner, M. (1989). Resources available in school districts serving secondary special education students: Implications for transition. *The Journal of Special Education, 22*, 419–432.

Farmer, T. W., Lane, K. L., Lee, D. L., Hamm, J. V., & Lambert, K. (2012). The social functions of antisocial behavior: Considerations for school violence prevention strategies for students with disabilities. *Behavioral Disorders, 37*, 149–162.

Feierman, J., Levick, M., & Mody, A. M. I. (2009). The school-to-prison pipeline . . . and back: Obstacles and remedies for the re-enrollment of adjudicated youth. *New York Law School Law Review, 54*, 1115–1129.

Ferri, B. A., & Connor, D. J. (2005). Tools of exclusion: Race, disability, and (re)segregated education. *The Voice of Scholarship in Education, 7*(28), 1–13.

Field, S., & Hoffman, A. (1996). *Steps to Self-Determination: A curriculum to help adolescents learn to achieve their goals*. Austin, TX: PRO-ED.

Field, S., & Hoffman, A. (2002). Lessons learned from implementing the *Steps to Self-Determination* curriculum. *Remedial and Special Education, 23*, 90–98.

Field, S., Martin, J., Miller, R., Ward, M., & Wehmeyer, M. L. (1998). Self-determination for persons with disabilities: A position statement of the division on career development and transition. *Career Development for Exceptional Individuals, 21*, 113–128.

Fierros, E. G., & Conroy, J. W. (2002). Double jeopardy: An exploration of restrictiveness and race in special education. In D. J. Losen & G. Orfield (Eds.), *Racial Inequity in Special Education* (pp. 39–70). Cambridge, MA: Harvard Educational Press.

Finkelhor, D., Turner, H., Ormrod, R., & Hamby, S. L. (2009). Violence, abuse, and crime exposure in a national sample of children and youth. *Pediatrics, 124*, 1411–1423. doi:10.1542/peds.2009-0467

Fleming, A. R., & Fairweather, J. S. (2012). The role of postsecondary education in the path from high school to work for youth with disabilities. *Rehabilitation Counseling Bulletin, 55*(2), 71–81. doi:10.1177/0034355211423303

Flore, P. C., & Wicherts, J. M. (2015). Does stereotype threat influence performance of girls in stereotyped domains? A meta-analysis. *Journal of School Psychology, 53*(1), 25–44. doi:10.1016/j.jsp.2014.10.002

Forness, S. R. (1988). Planning for the needs of children with serious emotional disturbance: The national special education and mental health coalition. *Behavioral Disorders, 13*, 127–133.

Fraker, T. M., Luecking, R. G., Mamun, A. A., Martinez, J. M., Reed, D. S., & Wittenburg, D. C. (2016). An analysis of 1-year impacts of youth transition demonstration projects. *Career Development and Transition for Exceptional Individuals, 39*, 34–46.

Fuchs, L. S., Fuchs, D., Compton, D. L., Wehby, J., Schumacher, R. F., Gersten, R., & Jordan, N. C. (2015). Inclusion versus specialized intervention for very-low-performing students: What does access mean in an era of academic challenge? *Exceptional Children, 81*, 134–157. doi:10.1177/0014402914551743

Furdella, J., & Puzzanchera, C. (Eds.). (2015, October). *Delinquency cases in juvenile court, 2013*. Washington, DC: U.S. Department of Justice and Office of Juvenile Justice and Delinquency Prevention.

Gagnon, J. C., & Barber, B. (2010). Characteristics of and services provided to youth in secure care facilities. *Behavioral Disorders, 36*, 7–19.

Gagnon, J. C., Houchins, D. E., & Murphy, K. M. (2012). Current juvenile corrections professional development practices and future directions. *Teacher Education and Special Education, 35*, 333–344. doi:10.1177/0888406411434602

García, S. B. (2002). Parent-professional collaboration in culturally sensitive assessment. In A. J. Artiles & A. A. Ortiz (Eds.), *English language learners with special needs: Identification, assessment, and instruction* (pp. 87–106). Washington, D.C.: Center for Applied Linguistics.

García, S. B., & Ortiz, A. A. (2013). Intersectionality as a framework for transformative research in special education. *Multiple Voices for Ethnically Diverse Exceptional Learners, 13*(2), 32–47.

García, S. B., Perez, A. M., & Ortiz, A. A. (2000). Interpreting Mexican-American mothers' beliefs about language disabilities from a sociocultural perspective. *Remedial & Special Education, 21*, 90–120.

Gee, G. C., Walsemann, K. M., & Brondolo, E. (2012). A life course perspective on how racism may be related to health and inequities. *American Journal of Public Health, 102*, 967–974.

Gibson, P. A., & Haight, W. (2013). Caregivers' moral narratives of their African American children's out-of-school suspensions: Implications for effective family-school collaborations. *Social Work, 58*, 263–272. doi:10.1093/sw/swt017

Gil-Kashiwabara, E., Hogansen, J. M., Geenen, S., Powers, K., & Powers, L. E. (2007). Improving transition outcomes for marginalized youth. *Career Development for Exceptional Individuals, 30*, 80–91. doi:10.1177/08857288070300020501

Gonsoulin, S., Zablocki, M., & Leone, P. E. (2012). Safe schools, staff development, and the school-to-prison pipeline. *Teacher Education and Special Education, 35*, 309–319. doi:10.1177/0888406412453470

Grandin, T., & Panek, R. (2013). *The autistic brain: Thinking across the spectrum.* New York, NY: Houghton Mifflin Harcourt.

Gray, L., & Lewis, L. (2015, May). *Public school safety and discipline report 2013–14.* Washington, DC: National Center for Education Statistics. Retrieved from http://nces.ed.gov/pubsearch

Greenan, J. P., & Phelps, L. A. (1982). Policy issues and action strategies related to handicapped learners in vocational education. *Career Development for Exceptional Individuals, 5*, 38–47.

Greenberg, E., Dunleavy, E., & Kutner, M. (2007, May). *Literacy behind bars: Results for the 2003 National assesment of adult literacy prison survey.* Washington, DC: U.S. Department of Education and Institute of Education Sciences.

Griffin, M. M. (2011). Promoting IEP participation: Effects of interventions, considerations for CLD students. *Career Development and Exceptional Individuals, 34*, 153–164. doi:10.1177/0885728811410561

Grusky, D. B., Mattingly, M. J., & Varner, C. (Eds.) (2015). State of the states: The poverty and inequality report [Special issue 2015]. *Pathways*, 1–60.

Gudykunst, W. B., & Kim, Y. Y. (1997). *Communicating with strangers: An approach to intercultural communication* (2nd ed.). New York, NY: McGraw-Hill.

Gutiérrez, K. D., & Penuel, W. R. (2014). Relevance to practice as a criterion for rigor. *Educational Researcher, 43*(1), 19–23. doi:10.3102/0013189x13520289

Gutiérrez, K. D., & Rogoff, B. (2003). Cultural ways of learning: Individual traits or repertoires of practice. *Educational Researcher, 32*(5), 19–25.

Haber, M. G., Mazzotti, V. L., Rowe, D. A., Bartholomew, A., Test, D. W., & Fowler, C. H. (2016). What works, when, for whom, and with whom: A meta-analytic review of predictors of postsecondary success for students with disabilities. *Review of Educational Research, 86*, 123–162.

Haight, W., Gibson, P. A., Kayama, M., Marshall, J. M., & Wilson, R. (2014). An ecological-systems inquiry into racial disproportionalities in out-of-school suspensions from youth, caregiver and educator perspectives. *Children & Youth Services Review, 46*, 128–138. doi:10.1016/j.childyouth.2014.08.003

Halpern, A. S. (1985). Transition: A look at the foundations. *Exceptional Children, 51*, 479–486.

Halpern, A. S., Yovanoff, P., Doren, B., & Benz, M. R. (1995). Predicting participation in postsecondary education for school leavers with disabilities. *Exceptional Children, 62*, 151–164.

Hanley-Maxwell, C., Whitney-Thomas, J., & Pogoloff, S. M. (1995). The second shock: A qualitative study of parents' perspectives and needs during their child's transition from school to adult life. *The Association for Persons with Severe Handicaps, 20*(1), 3–15.

Hardman, M., & McDonnell, J. (1987). Implementing federal transition initiatives for youths with severe handicaps: The Utah community-based transition project. *Exceptional Children, 53*, 493–498.

Harry, B. (1992a). Making sense of disability: Low-income, Puerto Rican parents' theories of the problem. *Exceptional Children, 59*, 27–40.

Harry, B. (1992b). Restructuring the participation of African-American parents in special education. *Exceptional Children, 59*, 123–131.

Harry, B. (1996). These families, those families: The impact of researcher identities on the research act. *Exceptional Children, 62*, 292–300.

Harry, B., Allen, N., & McLaughlin, M. J. (1995). Communication versus compliance: African American parents' involvement in special education. *Exceptional Children, 61*, 364–377.

Harry, B., Kalyanpur, M., & Day, M. (1999). *Building cultural reciprocity with families.* Baltimore, MD: Paul H. Brookes.

Harry, B., & Klingner, J. K. (2006). *Why are so many minority students in special education?* New York, NY: Teachers College Press.

Hasazi, S. B., Gordon, L. R., & Roe, C. A. (1985). Factors associated with the employment status of handicapped youth exiting high school from 1979 to 1983. *Exceptional Children, 51*, 455–477.

Heal, L. W., & Khoju, M. (1997). Predicting quality of life of youths after they leave special education high school programs. *Journal of Special Education, 31*, 279–299.

Heal, L. W., & Rusch, F. R. (1995). Predicting employment for students who leave special education high school programs. *Exceptional Children, 61*, 472–487.

Heller, T. (2014). Mandatory school-based mental health services and the prevention of school violence. *Health Matrix: Journal of Law-Medicine, 24*, 279–316.

Higgins, E. L., Raskind, M. H., Goldberg, R. J., & Herman, K. L. (2002). Stage of acceptance of a learning disability: The impact of labeling. *Learning Disability Quarterly, 25*(4), 3–18.

Hockenberry, S., & Puzzanchera, C. (2015). *Juvenile court statistics 2013.* Pittsburgh, PA: National Center for Juvenile Justice.

Holler, B., & Gugerty, J. (1984). Reflections about on-the-job training for high school special education students. *Career Development for Exceptional Individuals,* 7(2), 87–92. doi:10.1177/088572888400700205

Horner, R. H., Carr, E. G., Halle, J. W., McGee, G., Odom, S. L., & Wolery, M. (2005). The use of single-subject research to identify evidence-based practices in special education. *Exceptional Children, 71*, 165–179.

Horvat, E. M., Weininger, E. B., & Lareau, A. (2003). From social ties to social capital: Class differences in the relations between schools and parent networks. *American Educational Research Journal, 40*, 319–351.

Houchins, D. E., Jolivette, K., Wessendorf, S., McGlynn, M., & Nelson, C. M. (2005). Stakeholders' view of implementing positive behavioral support in a juvenile justice setting. *Education & Treatment of Children, 28*, 380–399.

Hughes, C. (2013). Poverty and disability: Addressing the challenge of inequality. *Career Development and Transition for Exceptional Individuals, 36*, 37–42. doi:10.1177/2165143413476735

Jahoda, A., Kemp, J., Riddell, S., & Banks, P. (2008). Feelings about work: A review of the socio-emotional impact of supported employment on people with intellectual disabilities. *Journal of Applied Research in Intellectual Disabilities, 21*, 1–18. doi:10.1111/j.1468-3148.2007.00365.x

Jolivette, K., & Nelson, C. M. (2010). Adapting positive behavioral interventions and supports for secure juvenile justice settings: Improving facility-wide behavior. *Behavioral Disorders, 36*, 28–42.

Kagitcibasi, C. (2013). Adolescent autonomy-relatedness and the family in cultural context: What is optimal? *Journal of Research on Adolescence, 23*, 223–235. doi:10.1111/jora.12041

Kalyanpur, M., & Harry, B. (1999). *Culture in special education: Building reciprocal family-professional relationships.* Baltimore, MD: Brookes.

Karpur, A., Clark, H. B., Caproni, P., & Sterner, H. (2005). Transition to adult roles for students with emotional/behavioral disturbances. *Career Development for Exceptional Individuals, 28*, 36–46. doi:10.1177/08857288050280010601

Karpur, A., Nazarov, Z., Brewer, D. R., & Bruyère, S. M. (2014). Impact of parental welfare participation: Transition to postsecondary education for youth with and without disabilities. *Career Development and Transition for Exceptional Individuals, 37*, 18–28. doi:10.1177/2165143414522093

Katsiyannis, A., & Ward, T. J. (1992). Parent participation in special education: Compliance issues as reported by parent surveys and state compliance reports. *Remedial and Special Education, 13*, 50–55.

Kayama, M., Haight, W., Gibson, P. A., & Wilson, R. (2015). Use of criminal justice language in personal narratives of out-of-school suspensions: Black students, caregivers, and educators. *Children & Youth Services Review, 51*, 26–35. doi:10.1016/j.childyouth.2015.01.020

Kena, G., Musu-Gillette, L., Robinson, J., Wang, X., Rathbun, A., Zhang, J., . . . Dunlop Valez, E. (2015). *The condition of education 2015* (NCES 2015-144). Washington, DC: National Center for Education Statistics. Retrieved from http://nces.ed.gov/pubsearch

Kim, K.-N. (2013). Career trajectory in high school dropouts. *Social Science Journal, 50*, 306–312. doi:10.1016/j.soscij.2013.03.005

Kim, Y. Y. (2003). Adapting to an unfamiliar culture: An interdisciplinary overview. In W. B. Gudykunst (Ed.), *Cross-cultural and intercultural communication* (pp. 243–258). Thousand Oaks, CA: Sage.

Kirk, D. S., & Sampson, R. J. (2013). Juvenile arrest and collateral educational damage in the transition to adulthood. *Sociology of Education, 86*, 36–62. doi:10.1177/0038040712448862

Kirkland, D. (2013). *A search past silence: The literacy of young Black men.* New York, NY: Teachers College Press.

Klodnick, V. V., Sabella, K., Brenner, C. J., Krzos, I. M., Ellison, M. L., Kaiser, S. M., . . . Fagan, M. A. (2015). Perspectives of young emerging adults with serious mental health conditions on vocational peer mentors. *Journal of Emotional & Behavioral Disorders, 23*, 226–237. doi:10.1177/1063426614565052

Knowlton, H. E., & Clark, G. M. (1987). Transition issues for the 1990s. *Exceptional Children, 53*, 562–563. doi:10.1177/001440298705300611

Kohler, P. D. (1993). Best practices in transition: Substantiated or implied? *Career Development for Exceptional Individuals, 16*, 107–121.

Kohler, P. D. (1996). *Taxonomy for transition programming: A model for planning, organizing, and evaluating transition education, services, and programs*. Champaign-Urbana, IL: University of Illinois.

Kohler, P. D., Destefano, L., Wermuth, T. R., Grayson, T. E., & McGinty, S. (1994). An analysis of exemplary transition programs: How and why are they selected? *Career Development for Exceptional Individuals, 17*, 187–201.

Kohler, P. D., & Field, S. (2003). Transition-Focused Education: Foundation for the Future. *Journal of Special Education, 37*, 174–183.

Kohler, P. D., Gothberg, J. E., Fowler, C. H., & Coyle, J. (2016). Taxonomy for transition programming 2.0: A model for planning, organizing, and evaluating transition education, services, and programs. Kalamazoo, MI: Western Michigan University. Retrieved from http://www.transitionta.org/sites/default/files/Tax_Trans_Prog_0.pdf

Krezmien, M. P., Leone, P. E., & Achilles, G. M. (2006). Suspension, race, and disability: Analysis of statewide practices and reporting. *Journal of Emotional and Behavioral Disorders, 14*, 217–226.

Krezmien, M. P., Leone, P. E., Zablocki, M. S., & Wells, C. S. (2010). Juvenile court referrals and the public schools: Nature and extent of the practice in five states. *Journal of Contemporary Criminal Justice, 26*, 273–293.

Kupchik, A., & Catlaw, T. J. (2015). Discipline and participation: The long-term effects of suspension and school security on the political and civic engagement of youth. *Youth & Society, 47*(1), 95–124. doi:10.1177/0044118X14544675

Kurth, J. A., Morningstar, M. E., & Kozleski, E. B. (2014). The persistence of highly restrictive special education placements for students with low-incidence disabilities. *Research & Practice for Persons with Severe Disabilities, 39*, 227–239. doi:10.1177/1540796914555580

Ladson-Billings, G. (2006). From the achievement gap to the education debt: Understanding achievement in the U.S. schools. *Educational Researcher, 35*, 3–12. doi:10.3102/0013189X035007003

Lane, K. L., & Carter, E. W. (2006). Supporting transition-age youth with and at risk for emotional and behavioral disorders at the secondary level. *Journal of Emotional and Behavioral Disorders, 14*, 66–70. doi:10.1177/10634266060140020301

Lareau, A. (1989). *Home advantage: Social class and parental intervention in elementary education*. London, UK: The Falmer Press.

Lareau, A., & Horvat, E. M. (1999). Moments of social inclusion and exclusion race, class, and cultural capital in family-school relationships. *Sociology of Education, 72*, 37–53.

Lather, P. (2006). Paradigm proliferation as a good thing to think with: Teaching research in education as a wild profusion. *International Journal of Qualitative Studies in Education, 19*, 35–57. doi:10.1080/09518390500450144

Lee, S.-H., Wehmeyer, M. L., Palmer, S. B., Soukup, J. H., & Little, T. D. (2008). Self-determination and access to the general education curriculum. *Journal of Special Education, 42*, 91–107.

Lee, T., Cornell, D., Gregory, A., & Xitao, F. (2011). High suspension schools and dropout rates for Black and White students. *Education & Treatment of Children, 34*, 167–192.

Leonardo, Z., & Broderick, A. A. (2011). Smartness as property: A critical exploration of intersections between whiteness and disability studies. *Teachers College Record, 113*, 2206–2232.

Leone, P. E., Krezmien, M., Mason, L., & Meisel, S. M. (2005). Organizing and delivering empirically based literacy instruction to incarcerated youth. *Exceptionality, 13*(2), 89–102. doi:10.1207/s15327035ex1302_3

Levesque, K., Premo, M., Vergun, R., Emanuel, D., Klein, S., Henke, R., & Kegahiro,

S. (1995). *Vocational education in the United States: The early 1990s.* Washington, DC: National Center for Educational Statistics.

Levine, P., & Edgar, E. (1994). An analysis by gender of long-term postschool outcomes for youth with and without disabilities. *Exceptional Children, 61*, 282–300.

Lewis, T., & Cheng, S. Y. (2006). Tracking, expectations, and the transformation of vocational education. *American Journal of Education, 113*(1), 67–99. doi:10.1086/506494

Lindstrom, L., Hirano, K. A., McCarthy, C., & Alverson, C. Y. (2014). "Just having a job": Career advancement for low-wage workers with intellectual and developmental disabilities. *Career Development and Transition for Exceptional Individuals, 37*, 40–49. doi:10.1177/2165143414522092

Livsey, S., Sickmund, M., & Sladky, A. (2009, January). *Juvenile residential facility census, 2004: Selected findings.* Washington, DC: U.S. Department of Justice.

Lochman, J. E., Boxmeyer, C. L., Powell, N. P., Lixin, Q., Wells, K., & Windle, M. (2012). Coping power dissemination study: Intervention and special education effects on academic outcomes. *Behavioral Disorders, 37*, 192–205.

Loeber, R., Farrington, D. P., & Petechuk, D. (2013, July). *Bulletin 1: From juvenile delinquency to young adult offending.* Washington, DC: U.S. Department of Justice.

Lollar, D. (2010). *Launching into adulthood: An integrated response to support transition of youth with chronic health conditions and disabilities.* Baltimore, MD: Brookes.

Losen, D. J., & Orfield, G. (2002). *Racial inequity in special education.* Cambridge, MA: Harvard Education Press.

Lotstein, D. S., Kuo, A. A., Strickland, B., & Tait, F. (2010). The transition to adult health care for youth with special health care needs: Do racial and ethnic disparities exist? *Pediatrics, 126*, S129–S136. doi:10.1542/peds.2010-1466F

Lotstein, D. S., McPherson, M., Strickland, B., & Newacheck, P. W. (2005). Transition planning for youth with special health care needs: Results from the national survey of children with special health care needs. *Pediatrics, 115*, 1562–1568. doi:10.1542/peds.2004-1262

Madaus, J. W., Dukes, L. L., & Carter, E. W. (2013). Introduction to the special issue: Reflecting on the past, present, and future of CDTEI. *Career Development and Transition for Exceptional Individuals, 36*, 4–5.

Madaus, J. W., Grigal, M., & Hughes, C. (2014). Promoting access to postsecondary education for low-income students with disabilities. *Career Development and Transition for Exceptional Individuals, 37*, 50–59. doi:10.1177/2165143414525037

Madrigal-Garcia, Y. I., & Acevedo-Gil, N. (2016). The new Juan Crow in education: Revealing panoptic measures and inequitable resources that hinder Latina/o postsecondary pathways. *Journal of Hispanic Higher Education, 15*, 154–181.

Mallett, C. A. (2014). The "learning disabilities to juvenile detention" pipeline: A case study. *Children & Schools, 36*, 147–154. doi:10.1093/cs/cdu010

Manning, J. P., & Gaudelli, W. (2006). What teacher educators should know about poverty and special education. *Teacher Education and Special Education, 29*, 236–243.

Martin, J. E., Van Dycke, J. L., Greene, B. A., Gardner, J. E., Christensen, W. R., Woods, L. L., & Lovett, D. L. (2006). Direct observation of teacher-directed secondary IEP meetings: Establishing the need for student IEP meeting instruction. *Exceptional Children, 72*, 187–200.

Mathur, S. R., & Griller Clark, H. (2014). Community engagement for reentry success of youth from juvenile justice: Challenges and opportunities. *Education & Treatment of Children, 37*, 713–734.

Mathur, S. R., & Schoenfeld, N. (2010). Effective instructional practices in juvenile justice facilities. *Behavioral Disorders, 36*, 20–27.

Maxwell, L. A. (2014, August 19). U.S. school enrollment hits majority-minority milestone. *Education Week*. Retrieved from http://www.edweek.org/ew/articles/2014/08/20/01demographics.h34.html

Maynard, B., Salas-Wright, C., & Vaughn, M. (2015). High school dropouts in emerging adulthood: Substance use, mental health problems, and crime. *Community Mental Health Journal, 51*, 289–299. doi:10.1007/s10597-014-9760-5

Mazzotti, V. L., Rowe, D. A., Sinclair, J., Poppen, M., Woods, W. E., & Shearer, M. L. (2015). Predictors of post-school success: A systematic review of NLTS2 secondary analyses. *Career Development and Transition for Exceptional Individuals, 36*, 140–151. doi:10.1177/2165143415588047

McDaniel, S. C., Jolivette, K., & Ennis, R. P. (2014). Barriers and facilitators to integrating SWPBIS in alternative education settings with existing behavior management systems. *Journal of Disability Policy Studies, 24*, 247–256.

McDermott, R., Goldman, S., & Varenne, H. (2006). The cultural work of learning disabilities. *Educational Researcher, 35*(6), 12–17.

McDermott, M., & Samson, F. L. (2005). White racial and ethnic identity in the United States. *Annual Review of Sociology, 31*, 245–261.

McDermott, R., & Varenne, H. (1999). Adam, Adam, Adam, and Adam: The cultural construction of a learning disability. In H. Varenne & R. McDermott (Eds.), *Successful failure: The school America builds*. Boulder, CO: Westview Press.

McMahon, B. T., & Shaw, L. R. (2005). Workplace discrimination and disability. *Journal of Vocational Rehabilitation, 23*, 137–143.

McManus, M. A., Pollack, L. R., Cooley, W. C., McAllister, J. W., Lotstein, D. S., Strickland, B., & Mann, M. Y. (2013). Current status of transition preparation among youth with special needs in the United States. *Pediatrics, 131*, 1090–1097. doi:10.1542/peds.2012-3050

Meehl, P. E. (1971). High school yearbooks: A reply to Schwarz. *Journal of Abnormal Psychology, 77*, 143–148. doi:10.1037/h0030750

Milliman. (n.d.). *Understanding healthcare costs: The employer-sponsored insurance system* [Video]. Retrieved July 29, 2016, from http://us.milliman.com/insight/videos/Understanding-healthcare-costs-The-employer-sponsored-insurance-system/

Mithaug, D. E., Horiuchi, C., N, & Fanning, P., N. (1985). A report on the Colorado statewide follow-up survey of special education students. Exceptional Children, 5, 397–404.

Mlawer, M. A. (1993). Who should fight? Parents and the advocacy expectation. *Journal of Disabiltiy Policy Studies, 4*, 105–116.

Morningstar, M. E., Frey, B. B., Noonan, P. M., Ng, J., Clavenna-Deane, B., Graves, P., . . . Williams-Diehm, K. (2010). A preliminary investigation of the relationship of transition preparation and self-determination for students with disabilities in postsecondary educational settings. *Career Development for Exceptional Individuals, 33*, 80–94. doi:10.1177/0885728809356568

Morris, E. W., & Perry, B. L. (2016). The punishment gap: School suspension and racial disparities in achievement. *Social Problems, 63*(1), 68–86. doi:10.1093/socpro/spv026

National Academy of Sciences, Engineering, and Medicine. (2015). *The growing gap in life expectancy by income: Implications for federal programs and policy responses*. Washington, DC: National Academy of Sciences, Engineering, and Medicine.

National Longitudinal Transition Study-2 (NLTS2). (2004, November). A profile of students with ADHD who receive special education services: Facts from OSEP's National Longitudinal Studies. Menlo Park, CA: SRI International. Retreived from http://nlts2.org/fact_sheets/nlts2_fact_sheet_2004_11.pdf.

National Longitudinal Transition Study-2 (NLTS2). (2005, November). *High school completion by youth with disabilities.* Facts from the National Longitudinal Transition Study-2. Menlo Park, CA: SRI International. Retrieved from https://ies.ed.gov/ncser/pdf/NLTS2_selfdeterm_11_23_05.pdf

National Longitudinal Transition Study-2 (NLTS2). (2006). School behavior and disciplinary experiences of youth with disabilities. Facts from the National Longitudinal Transition Study-2 (NLTS2). Retrieved from http://ezproxy.library.wisc.edu/login?url=http://search.ebscohost.com/login.aspx?direct=true&db=eric&AN=ED492093&site=ehost-live

National Research Council. (2002a). *Minority students in special and gifted education.* Washington, DC: National Academy Press.

National Research Council. (2002b). *Scientific research in education.* Washington, DC: National Academy Press.

National Research Council. (2005). *Advancing scientific research in education.* Washington, DC: National Research Council.

Neiman, S., & Hill, M. R. (2011, May). *Crime, violence, discipline, and safety in US public schools: Findings from the school survey on crime and safety: 2009–2010.* Washington, DC: U.S. Department of Education, Institute of Education Sciences.

Nelson, C. M., Jolivette, K., Leone, P. E., & Mathur, S. R. (2010). Meeting the needs of at-risk and adjudicated youth with behavioral challenges: The promise of juvenile justice. *Behavioral Disorders, 36*, 70–80.

Nelson, J. R., Smith, D. J., & Dodd, J. M. (1994). The effects of learning strategy instruction on the completion of job applications by students with learning disabilities. *Journal of Learning Disabilities, 27*, 104–110.

New York Civil Liberties Union. (2015, July 23). *NYC report a monumental step toward safe and nurturing schools* [Press release]. Retrieved from http://www.nyclu.org/news/nyc-report-monumental-step-toward-safe-nurturing-schools

Newman, L., & Madaus, J. W. (2015). An analysis of factors related to receipt of accommodations and services by postsecondary students with disabilities. *Remedial & Special Education, 36*, 208–219. doi:10.1177/0741932515572912

Newman, L., Wagner, M., Cameto, R., & Knokey, A.-M. (2009). *The post–high school outcomes of youth with disabilities up to 4 years after high school: A report from the National Longitudinal Transition Study-2 (NLTS2).* Menlo Park, CA: SRI International.

Newman, L., Wagner, M., Huang, T., Shaver, D., Knokey, A.-M., Yu, J., . . . Cameto, R. (2011). *Secondary school programs and performance of students with disabilities. A special topic report of findings from the National Longitudinal Transition Study-2 (NLTS2)* (NCSER 2012 –3000). Menlo Park, CA: SRI International. Retrieved from http://ezproxy.library.wisc.edu/login?url=http://search.ebscohost.com/login.aspx?direct=true&db=eric&AN=ED526242&site=ehost-live

Newman, L., Wagner, M., Knokey, A.-M., Marder, C., Nagle, K., Shaver, D., & Wei, X. (2011). *The post–high school outcomes of young adults with disabilities up to 8 years after high school: A report from the National Longitudinal Transition Study-2 (NLTS2).* Menlo Park, CA: SRI International.

Nietupski, J. A., Hamre-Nietupski, S., Welch, J., & Anderson, R. J. (1983). Establishing and maintaining vocational training sites for moderately and severely handicapped students: Strategies for community/vocational trainers. *Education and Training of the Mentally Retarded, 18*, 169–175.

Noltemeyer, A., & McLoughlin, C. (2010). Patterns of exclusionary discipline by school typology, ethnicity, and their interaction. *Perspectives on Urban Interaction,* 7(1), 27–40.

Noltemeyer, A. L., Ward, M. R., & McLoughlin, C. (2015). Relationship between school suspension and student outcomes: A meta-analysis. *School Psychology Review, 44*, 224–240.

Odom, S. L., Brantlinger, E., Gersten, R., Horner, R. H., Thompson, B., & Harris, K. (2005). Research in special education: Scientific methods and evidence-based practices. *Exceptional Children, 71*, 137–148.

Osher, D., Coggshall, J., Colombi, G., Woodruff, D., Francois, S., & Osher, T. (2012). Building school and teacher capacity to eliminate the school-to-prison pipeline. *Teacher Education and Special Education, 35*, 284–295. doi:10.1177/0888406412453930

Oswald, D. P., & Coutinho, M. J. (1996). Leaving school: The impact of state economic and demographic factors for students with serious. *Journal of Emotional & Behavioral Disorders, 4*(2), 1–14.

O'Toole, G. (2012, August). Life is a journey not a destination. Retreived from http://quoteinvestigator.com/2012/08/31/life-journey/

Ottley, A. H. (2014). Empty promise: Black American veterans and the new GI Bill. *New Directions for Adult & Continuing Education, 2014,* 144, 79–88. doi:10.1002/ace.20116

Ougaard, M. (2013). What is theory in political science? In H. Corvellec (Ed.), *What is theory? Answers from the social and cultural sciences.* Copenhagen, Denmark: CBS Press.

Palmer, S. B., Wehmeyer, M. L., Shogren, K. A., Williams-Diehm, K. L., & Soukup, J. H. (2012). An evaluation of the Beyond High School model on the self-determination of students with intellectual disability. *Career Development and Transition for Exceptional Individuals, 35*, 76–84. doi:10.1177/0885728811432165

Parker-McGowan, Q., Mo, C., Reichle, J., Pandit, S., Johnson, L., Kreibich, S., . . . Jackson, C. (2014). Describing treatment intensity in milieu teaching interventions for children with developmental disabilities: A review. *Language, Speech & Hearing Services in Schools, 45*, 351–364. doi:10.1044/2014_LSHSS-13-0087

Patton, J. R., & Dunn, C. (1998). *Transition from school to young adulthood.* Austin, TX: PRO-ED.

Phillips, B. N., Robison, L. J., & Kosciulek, J. F. (2014). The influence of social capital on starting wage for people with and without disabilities. *Rehabilitation Counseling Bulletin, 58*(1), 37–45. doi:10.1177/0034355214524834

Povenmire-Kirk, T. C., Lindstrom, L., & Bullis, M. (2010). De escuela a la vida adulta/From school to adult life: Transition needs for Latino youth with disabilities and their families. *Career Development for Exceptional Individuals, 33*, 41–51. doi:10.1177/0885728809359004

Powers, L. E., Geenen, S., Powers, J., Pommier-Satya, S., Turner, A., Dalton, L. D., . . . Swank, P. (2012). My Life: Effects of a longitudinal, randomized study of self-determination enhancement on the transition outcomes of youth in foster care and special education. *Children & Youth Services Review, 34*, 2179–2187. doi:10.1016/j.childyouth.2012.07.018

Pyscher, T., & Lozenski, B. J. (2014). Throwaway youth: The sociocultural location of resistance to schooling. *Equity & Excellence in Education, 47*, 531–545. doi:10.1080/10665684.2014.958964

Quinn, M. M., Poirier, J. M., & Garfinkel, L. (2005). Girls with mental health needs in the juvenile justice system: Challenges and inequities confronting a vulnerable population. *Exceptionality, 13*, 125–139. doi:10.1207/s15327035ex1302_5

Rabren, K., Carpenter, J., Dunn, C., & Carney, J. S. (2014). Actions against poverty: The impact of career technical education. *Career Development and Transition for Exceptional Individuals, 37*, 29–39. doi:10.1177/2165143414522091

Razeghi, J. A., & Davis, S. (1979). Federal mandates for the handicapped: vocational education opportunity and employment. *Exceptional Children, 45*, 353–359.

Reay, D. (1998). Bourdieu and education: Acts of practical theory. In M. Grenfell & D. James (Eds.), *Bourdieu and education: Acts of practical theory* (pp. 55–71). London, UK: Falmer Press.

Reid, D. K., & Knight, M. G. (2006). Disability justifies exclusion of minority students: A critical history grounded in disability studies. *Educational Researcher, 35*(6), 18–23.

Reid, K., & Valle, J. W. (2004). The discursive practice of learning disability: Implications for instruction and parent-school relations. *Journal of Learning Disabilities, 37*, 466–481.

Repetto, J. B., Jaress, J., Lindsey, J., & Bae, J. (2016). Investigation of health care components in transition IEPs. *Career Development and Transition for Exceptional Individuals, 39*, 4–11.

Rimmerman, A., Botuck, S., Levy, J. M., & Royce, J. M. (1996). Job placement of urban youth with developmental disabilities: Research and implications. *Journal of Rehabilitation, 62*(1), 56–64.

Rivas-Drake, D., Seaton, E. K., Markstrom, C., Quintana, S., Syed, M., Lee, R. M., . . . Yip, T. (2014). Ethnic and racial identity in adolescence: Implications for psychosocial, academic, and health outcomes. *Child Development, 85*(1), 40–57. doi:10.1111/cdev.12200

Rivkin, D. H. (2009). Decriminalizing students with disabilities. *New York Law School Law Review, 54*, 909–952.

Robinson, J. H., Callister, L. C., Berry, J. A., & Dearing, K. A. (2008). Patient-centered care and adherence: Definitions and applications to improve outcomes. *Journal of American Academy of Nurse Practitioners, 20*, 600–607. doi:10.1111/j.1745-7599.2008.00360.x

Rogoff, B. (2003). *The cultural nature of human development.* New York, NY: Oxford University Press.

Rojewski, J. W. (1999). Occupational and educational aspirations and attainment of young adults with and without LD. *Journal of Learning Disabilities, 32*, 533–552.

Rojewski, J. W., Lee, I. H., & Gregg, N. (2015). Causal effects of inclusion on postsecondary education outcomes of individuals with high-incidence disabilities. *Journal of Disability Policy Studies, 25*, 210–219. doi:10.1177/1044207313505648

Rose, C. A., & Espelage, D. L. (2012). Risk and protective factors associated with the bullying involvement of students with emotional and behavioral disorders. *Behavioral Disorders, 37*, 133–148.

Rueda, R., Monzo, L., Shapiro, J., Gomez, J., & Blacher, J. (2005). Cultural models of transition: Latina mothers of young adults with developmental disabilities. *Exceptional Children, 71*, 401–414.

Rusch, F. R., Kohler, P. D., & Hughes, C. (1992). An analysis of OSERS-sponsored secondary special education and transitional services research. *Career Development for Exceptional Individuals, 15*, 121–143.

Russinova, Z., Griffin, S., Bloch, P., Wewiorski, N. J., & Rosoklija, I. (2011). Workplace prejudice and discrimination toward individuals with mental illnesses. *Journal of Vocational Rehabilitation, 35*, 227–241. doi:10.3233/JVR-2011-0574

Russo Jameson, D. (2007). Self-determination and success outcomes of two-year college students with disabilities. *Journal of College Reading and Learning, 37*(2), 26–46.

Rutherford, R. B., & Nelson, C. M. (2005). Disability and involvement with the juvenile delinquency system: Knowing versus doing. *Exceptionality, 13*, 65–67. doi:10.1207/s15327035ex1302_1

Ryan, J. B., Katsiyannis, A., Peterson, R., & Chmelar, R. (2007). IDEA 2004 and disciplining students with disabilities. *NASSP Bulletin, 91*, 130–140.

Ryan, R. M., & Deci, E. L. (2000). Self-determination theory and the facilitation of intrinsic motivation, social development, and well-being. *American Psychologist, 55*(1), 68–78.

Rylance, B. J. (1998). Predictors of post–high school employment for youth identified as severely emotionally disturbed. *Journal of Special Education, 32*, 184–192.

Ryndak, D. L., Moor, M. A., Orlando, A.-M., & Delano, M. (2009). Access to the general curriculum: The mandate and role of context in research-based practice for students with extensive support needs. *Research & Practice for Persons with Severe Disabilities, 33*, 199–213.

Sacco, F. C., & Twemlow, S. W. (2014). Behavioral health homes: A model for implementation of the Affordable Care Act. *International Journal of Applied Psychoanalytic Studies, 11*, 172–183. doi:10.1002/aps.1407

Sanford, C., Newman, L., Wagner, M., Knokey, A.-M., & Shaver, D. (2011). *The post-high school outcomes of young adults with disabilities up to 6 years after high school.* Menlo Park, CA: SRI International.

Schnoes, C., Reid, R., Wagner, M., & Marder, C. (2006). ADHD among students receiving special education services: A national survey. *Exceptional Children, 72*, 483–496.

Schuh, M. C., Sundar, V., & Hagner, D. C. (2015). Friendship is the ocean: Importance of friendship, acceptance, and leadership in the transition to adulthood. *Career Development and Transition for Exceptional Individuals, 38*, 152–161.

Schwandt, T. A. (2005). A diagnostic reading of scientifically based research for education. *Educational Theory, 55*, 284–305. doi:10.1111/j.1741-5446.2005.00004.x

Schwandt, T. A. (2012). Valuing methodological diversity. *Qualitative Social Work, 11*, 125–129. doi:10.1177/1473325011433928a

Shattuck, P. T., Narendorf, S. C., Cooper, B., Sterzing, P. R., Wagner, M., & Taylor, J. L. (2012). Postsecondary education and employment among youth with an autism spectrum disorder. *Pediatrics, 129*, 1042–1049. doi:10.1542/peds.2011-2864

Shippen, M. E., Patterson, D., Green, K. L., & Smitherman, T. (2012). Community and school practices to reduce delinquent behavior: Intervening on the school-to-prison pipeline. *Teacher Education and Special Education, 35*, 296–308. doi:10.1177/0888406412445930

Shogren, K. A., Wehmeyer, M. L., Palmer, S. B., Soukup, J. H., Little, T. D., Garner, N., & Lawrence, M. (2007). Examining individual and ecological predictors of the self-determination of students with disabilities. *Exceptional Children, 73*, 488–509.

Shroka, J. S., & Schwartz, S. E. (1982). Job placement of handicapped persons: A positive approach. *Career Development for Exceptional Individuals, 5*, 116–121. doi:10.1177/088572888200500205

Sickmund, M., & Puzzanchera, C. (Eds.). (2014). *Juvenile offenders and victims: 2014 national report.* Pittsburgh, PA: National Center for Juvenile Justice.

Sileo, T. W., Sileo, A. P., & Prater, M. A. (1996). Parent and professional partnerships in special education: Multicultural considerations. *Intervention in School and Clinic, 31*, 145–153.

Sitlington, P. L., & Frank, A. R. (1993). Success as an adult–Does gender make a difference for graduates with mental disabilities? *Career Development for Exceptional Individuals, 16*, 171–182.

Skiba, R. J., Arredondo, M. I., & Williams, N. T. (2014). More than a metaphor: The contribution of exclusionary discipline to a school-to-prison pipeline. *Equity & Excellence in Education, 47*, 546–564. doi:10.1080/10665684.2014.958965

Skiba, R. J., Horner, R. H., Choong-Geun, C., Rausch, M. K., May, S. L., & Tobin, T. (2011). Race is not neutral: A national investigation of African American and Latino disproportionality in school discipline. *School Psychology Review, 40*(1), 85–107.

Skiba, R. J., Michael, R., Nardo, A., & Peterson, R. (2002). The color of discipline: Sources of racial and gender disproportionality in school punishment. *The Urban Review, 34*, 317–342. doi:10.1023/a:1021320817372

Skiba, R. J., & Peterson, R. L. (2000). School discipline at a crossroads: From zero tolerance to early response. *Exceptional Children, 66*, 335–347.

Skloot, R. (2010). *The immortal life of Henrietta Lacks.* New York, NY: Crown.

Slavin, R. E. (2002). Evidence-based education policies: Transforming educational practice and research. *Educational Researcher, 31*(7), 15–21. doi:10.3102/0013189X031007015

Slavin, R. E. (2003). A reader's guide to scientifically based research. *Educational Leadership, 60*(5), 12–16.

Smith, A., & Kozleski, E. B. (2005). Witnessing Brown: Pursuit of an equity agenda in American education. *Remedial & Special Education, 26*, 270–280.

Smith, C. D. (2009). Deconstructing the pipeline: Evaluating school-to-prison pipeline equal protection cases through a structural racism framework. *Fordham Urban Law Journal, 36*, 1009–1049.

Smith-Osborne, A. (2009). Does the GI Bill support educational attainment for veterans with disabilities? Implications for current veterans in resuming civilian life. *Journal of Sociology & Social Welfare, 36*, 111–125.

Snapp, S. D., Hoenig, J. M., Fields, A., & Russell, S. T. (2015). Messy, butch, and queer: LGBTQ youth and the school-to-prison pipeline. *Journal of Adolescent Research, 30*, 57–82. doi:10.1177/0743558414557625

Solari, E. J., & Gerber, M. M. (2008). Early comprehension instruction for Spanish-speaking English language learners: Teaching text-level reading skills while maintaining effects on word-level skills. *Learning Disabilities Research & Practice, 23*, 155–168. doi:10.1111/j.1540-5826.2008.00273.x

Stanton-Salazar, R. D. (2001). *Manufacturing hope and despair: The school and kin support networks of U.S.-Mexican youth.* New York, NY: Teachers College Press.

Stanton-Salazar, R. D., & Dornbusch, S. M. (1995). Social capital and the reproduction of inequality: Information networks among Mexican-origin high school students. *Sociology of Education, 68*, 116–135.

Stein, K. F. (2012). Experiences of selected emerging adults with emotional or behavioral difficulties in higher education. *Career Development and Transition for Exceptional Individuals, 35*, 168–179.

Steinberg, L. (2008). A social neuroscience perspective on adolescent risk-taking. *Developmental Review, 28*, 78–106. doi:10.1016/j.dr.2007.08.002

Stewart, M., Brown, J. B., Donner, A., McWhinney, I. R., Oates, J., Weston, W. W., & Jordan, J. (2000). The impact of patient-centered care on outcomes. *The Journal of Family Practice, 49*, 796–804.

Stonebrook, M. S. (2016, April 19). Title II of the Americans with Disabilities Act: The potential for police liability and ways to avoid it. *The Police Chief Magazine.*

Sullivan, A. L., & Artiles, A. J. (2011). Theorizing racial inequity in special education: Applying structural inequity theory to disproportionality. *Urban Education, 46*, 1526–1552. doi:10.1177/0042085911416014

Sullivan, A. L., & Bal, A. (2013). Disproportionality in special education: Effects of individual and school variables on disability risk. *Exceptional Children, 79*, 475–494.

Sullivan, A. L., Klingbeil, D. A., & Van Norman, E. R. (2013). Beyond behavior: Multilevel analysis of the influence of sociodemographics and school characteristics on students' risk of suspension. *School Psychology Review, 42*, 99–114.

Sullivan, A. L., Van Norman, E. R., & Klingbeil, D. A. (2014). Exclusionary discipline of students with disabilities: Student and school characteristics predicting suspension. *Remedial & Special Education, 35*, 199–210. doi:10.1177/0741932513519825

Swartz, D. (1997). *Culture and power: The sociology of Pierre Bourdieu.* Chicago, IL: University of Chicago Press.

Szymanski, E., King, J. D., & Parker, R. M. (1989). The state-federal rehabilitation program: Interface with special education. *Exceptional Children, 56*, 70–77.

Targett, P., Wehman, P., West, M., Dillard, C., & Cifu, G. (2013). Promoting transition to adulthood for youth with physical disabilities and health impairments. *Journal of Vocational Rehabilitation, 39*, 229–239. doi:10.3233/JVR-130653

Taylor, J. A., & Baker, R. A. (2001). Discipline and the special education student. *Educational Leadership, 59*(4), 28–30.

Test, D. W., Fowler, C. H., Richter, S. M., White, J., Mazzotti, V., Walker, A. R., . . . Kortering, L. (2009). Evidence-based practices in secondary transition. *Career Development for Exceptional Individuals, 32*, 115–128. doi:10.1177/0885728809336859

Test, D. W., Mazzotti, V. L., Mustian, A. L., Fowler, C. H., Kortering, L., & Kohler, P. D. (2009). Evidence-based secondary transition predictors for improving postschool outcomes for students with disabilities. *Career Development for Exceptional Individuals, 32*, 160–181. doi:10.1177/0885728809346960

Thurau, L. H., & Wald, J. (2009). Controlling partners: When law enforcement meets discipline in public schools. *New York Law School Law Review, 54*, 977–1020.

Townsend Walker, B. L. (2012). Teacher education and African American males: Deconstructing pathways from the schoolhouse to the "big house." *Teacher Education and Special Education, 35*, 320–332. doi:10.1177/0888406412461158

Trainor, A. A. (2002). Self-determination for students with learning disabilities: Is it a universal value? *International Journal of Qualitative Studies in Education, 15*, 711–725.

Trainor, A. A. (2003). *Self-determination and postsecondary transition planning for culturally and lingustically diverse students with learning disabilities* (Unpublished doctoral dissertation). University of Texas, Austin.

Trainor, A. A. (2005). Self-determination perceptions and behaviors of diverse students with LD during the transition planning process. *Journal of Learning Disabilities, 38*, 233–249.

Trainor, A. A. (2007). Perceptions of adolescent girls with LD regarding self-determination and postsecondary transition planning. *Learning Disability Quarterly, 30*, 31–45.

Trainor, A. A. (2010a). Diverse approaches to parent advocacy during special education home-school interactions: Identification and use of cultural and social capital. *Remedial and Special Education, 31*, 34–47. doi:10.1177/0741932508324401

Trainor, A. A. (2010b). Educators' expectations of parent participation: The role of cultural and social capital. *Multiple Voices for Ethnically Diverse Exceptional Learners, 12*(2), 33–50.

Trainor, A. A. (2010c). Reexamining the promise of parent participation in special education: An analysis of cultural and social capital. *Anthropology & Education Quarterly, 41*, 245–263.

Trainor, A. A., & Bal, A. (2014). Development and preliminary analysis of a rubric for culturally responsive research. *Journal of Special Education, 47*, 203–216. doi:10.1177/0022466912436397

Trainor, A. A., Carter, E. W., Swedeen, B., Cole, O., & Smith, S. A. (2011). Perspectives of adolescents with disabilities on summer employment and community experiences. *Journal of Special Education, 45*, 157–170.

Trainor, A. A., & Leko, M. M. (2014). Qualitative special education research: Purpose, rigor, and contribution. *Remedial and Special Education, 35*, 263–266. doi:10.1177/0741932514536996

Trainor, A. A., Lindstrom, L., Simon-Burroughs, M., Martin, J. E., & Sorrells, A. (2008). From marginalized to maximized opportunities for diverse youth with disabilities: A position paper of the Division on Career Development and Transition. *Career Development for Exceptional Individuals, 31*, 56–64.

Trainor, A. A., Murray, A., & Kim, H. (2016). English learners with disabilities in high school: Population characteristics, transition programs, and postschool outcomes. *Remedial and Special Education, 37*, 146–158. doi:10.1177/0741932515626797

Turnbull, A. P., & Turnbull, H. R. (1982). Parent involvement in the education of handicapped children: A critique. *Mental Retardation, 20*, 115–122.

U.S. Census Bureau. (2012). *Employment status: 2009-2013 American Community Survey 5-year estimates.* Retrieved from https://factfinder.census.gov/faces/tableservices/jsf/pages/productview.xhtml?src=bkmk

U.S. Department of Education. (1995). *Seventeenth annual report to Congress on the implementation of the Individuals with Disabilities Education Act.* Retrieved from http://www2.ed.gov/pubs/OSEP95AnlRpt/index.html

U.S. Department of Education. (1999, March). *Children with ADHD: Topic brief* (Press Release). Retrieved from http://www2.ed.gov/policy/speced/leg/idea/brief6.html

U.S. Department of Education. (2011). *Supportive school discipline initiative* (Press Release). Retrieved from http://www2.ed.gov/policy/gen/guid/school-discipline/index.html

U.S. Department of Education & Office for Civil Rights. (2012). *Helping to ensure equal access to education: Report to the President and Secretary of Education.* Washington, DC: U.S. Department of Education. Retreived from https://www2.ed.gov/about/reports/annual/ocr/report-to-president-2009-12.pdf

U.S. Department of Education & Office for Civil Rights. (2014, March). *Data snapshot: School discipline.* Retrieved from http://www2.ed.gov/about/offices/list/ocr/docs/crdc-discipline-snapshot.pdf

U.S. Department of Education & Office of Planning, Evaluation and Policy Development. (2010, March). *A blueprint for reform: The reauthorization of the Elemenatary and Secondary Education Act.* Washington, DC: U.S. Department of Education. Retreived from https://www2.ed.gov/policy/elsec/leg/blueprint/blueprint.pdf

U.S. Department of Education & U.S. Office of Special Education and Rehabilitative Services. (2014, December). *Thirtysixth Annual Report to Congress on the Implementation of the Individuals with Disabilities Education Act, 2014.* Washington, DC: U.S. Department of Education. Retrieved from https://www2.ed.gov/about/reports/annual/osep/2014/parts-b-c/index.html#download

U.S. Department of Education & U.S. Office of Special Education and Rehabilitative Services. (2015). *Thirtyseventh Annual Report to Congress on the Implementation of the Individuals with Disabilities Education Act, 2015.* Retrieved from https://www2.ed.gov/about/reports/annual/osep/2015/parts-b-c/37th-arc-for-idea.pdf

U.S. Department of Health and Human Services & Office of Disease Prevention and Health Promotion. (2008). *Phase 1 report: Recommendations for the framework and format of Healthy People 2020.* Retrieved from https://www.healthypeople.gov/sites/default/files/PhaseI_0.pdf

U.S. Department of Labor & Office of Disability Employment Policy. (n.d.). *Skills to pay the bills: Mastering soft skills for workplace success.* Washington, DC: Author.

U.S. Government Accountability Office. (2008, June). *Young adults with serious mental illness: Some states and federal agencies are taking steps to address their transition challenges.* Washington, DC: Author.

U.S. Office of Special Education Programs. (2003). *Identifying and treating Attention Deficit and Hyperactivity Disorder: A resource for school and home.* Washington, DC: U.S. Department of Education.

Umaña-Taylor, A. J., Quintana, S. M., Lee, R. M., Cross, W. E., Rivas-Drake, D., Schwartz, S. J., . . . Seaton, E. (2014). Ethnic and racial identity during adolescence and into young adulthood: An integrated conceptualization. *Child Development, 85*(1), 21–39. doi:10.1111/cdev.12196

Unruh, D. K., & Bullis, M. (2005). Female and male juvenile offenders with disabilities: Differences in the barriers to their transition to the community. *Behavioral Disorders, 30*, 105–117.

Unruh, D. K., Waintrup, M., & Canter, T. (2010). Project STAY OUT: A facility-to-community transition intervention targeting incarcerated adolescent offenders. In D. Cheney (Ed.), *Transition of secondary students with emotional or behavioral disorders* (pp. 347–374). Champaign, IL: Research Press.

Unruh, D. K., Waintrup, M., Canter, T., & Smith, S. (2009). Improving the transition outcomes of adolescent young offenders. In H. B. Clark & D. Unruh (Eds.), *Transition of youth and young adults with emotional or behavioral difficulties.* Baltimore, MD: Brookes.

Valencia, R. R. (1997). *The evolution of deficit thinking: Educational thought and practice.* London, UK; Washington, D.C.: Falmer Press.

Valenzuela, A. (1999). *Subtractive schooling: U.S.-Mexican youth and the politics of caring.* Albany, NY: State University of New York Press.

Van Cleve, J. V. (2007). The academic integration of deaf children: A historical perspective. In J. V. Van Cleve (Ed.), *The deaf history reader* (pp. 116-135). Washington, DC: Gallaudet University Press.

Vincent, C. G., Randall, C., Cartledge, G., Tobin, T. J., & Swain-Bradway, J. (2014). Toward a conceptual integration of cultural responsiveness and schoolwide positive behavior support. *Journal of Positive Behavior Interventions, 13*, 219–229. doi:10.1177/1098300711399765

Visser, S. N., Danielson, M. L., Bitsko, R. H., Holbrook, J. R., Kogna, M. D., Ghandour, R. M., . . . Blumberg, S. J. (2014). Trends in the parent-report of health care provider–diagnosed and medicated attention-deficit/hyperactivity disorder: United States, 2003–2011. *Journal of the American Academy of Child & Adolescent Psychiatry, 53*, 34–46. doi:10.1016/j.jaac.2013.09.001

Voltz, D. L. (1994). Developing collaborative parent-teacher relationships with culturally diverse parents. *Intervention in School and Clinic, 29*, 288–291.

Vorhies, V., Davis, K., Frounfelker, R., & Kaiser, S. (2012). Applying social and cultural capital frameworks: Understanding employment perspectives of transition age youth with serious mental health conditions. *Journal of Behavioral Health Services & Research, 39*, 257–270. doi:10.1007/s11414-012-9274-2

Wagner, M., Blackorby, J., Cameto, R., & Newman, L. (1993). *What makes a difference? Influences on postschool outcomes of youth with disabilities.* Menlo Park, CA: SRI International.

Wagner, M., Blackorby, J., & Hebbeler, K. (1993). Beyond the report card: The multiple dimensions of secondary school performance of students with disabilities. Menlo Park, CA: SRI International.

Wagner, M., Cameto, R., & Newman, L. (2003). *Youth with disabilities: A changing population.* Menlo Park, CA: SRI International.

Wagner, M., Kutash, K., Duschnowski, A. J., & Epstein, M. H. (2005). The special education elementary longitudinal study and the national longitudinal transition study: Study designs and implications for children and youth with emotional disturbance. *Journal of Emotional & Behavior Disorders, 13*, 25–41.

Wagner, M., Newman, L., Cameto, R., Garza, N., & Levine, P. (2005). *After high school: A first look at the postschool experiences of youth with disabilities.* Menlo Park, CA: SRI International.

Wagner, M., Newman, L., Cameto, R., & Levine, P. (2005). *Changes over time in the early postschool outcomes of youth with disabilities.* Menlo Park, CA: SRI International.

Wagner, M., Newman, L., Cameto, R., Levine, P., & Marder, C. (2003). *Going to school: Instructional contexts, programs, and participation of secondary school students with disabilities. A report from the National Longitudinal Transition Study-2 (NLTS2).* Menlo Park, CA: SRI International.

Wagner, M., Newman, L., D'Amico, R., Jay, E. D., Butler-Nalin, P., Marder, C., & Cox, R. (1991). *Youth with disabilities: How are they doing? The first comprehensive report from the National Longitudinal Transition Study of special education students.* Menlo Park, CA: SRI International.

Wagner, M., Newman, L., & Javitz, H. (2014). The influence of family socioeconomic status on the post–high school outcomes of youth with disabilities. *Career Development and Transition for Exceptional Individuals, 37*(1), 5–17. doi:10.1177/2165143414523980

Waintrup, M. G., & Unruh, D. K. (2008). Career development programming strategies for transitioning incarcerated adolescents to the world of work. *Journal of Correctional Education, 59*, 127–144.

Waller, K. S., Houchins, D. E., & Nomvete, P. T. (2010). Establishing a school-based mentoring program for youth who are transitioning from a secure facility. *Beyond Behavior, 19*(3), 30–35.

Washburn, J. J., Teplin, L. A., Voss, L. S., Simon, C. D., Abram, K. M., McClelland, G. M., & Olson, N. D. (2015, September). *Detained youth processed in juvenile and adult court: Psychiatric disorders and mental health needs.* Washington, DC: U.S. Department of Justice.

Wasserberg, M. J. (2014). Stereotype threat effects on African American children in an urban elementary school. *Journal of Experimental Education, 82*, 502–517. doi:10.1080/00220973.2013.876224

Webb, J., Schirato, T., & Danaher, G. (2002). *Understanding Bourdieu.* London, UK: SAGE Publications, Inc.

Wehman, P., Chen, C.-C., West, M., & Cifu, G. (2014). Transition planning for youth with traumatic brain injury: Findings from the National Longitudinal Transition Survey-2. *NeuroRehabilitation, 34*, 365–372. doi:10.3233/NRE-131029

Wehman, P., & Hill, J. W. (1981). Competitive employment for moderately and severely handicapped individuals. *Exceptional Children, 47*, 338-345.

Wehman, P., Kregel, J., & Barcus, J. M. (1985). From school to work: A vocational transition model for handicapped students. *Exceptional Children, 52*, 25-37.

Wehmeyer, M. L. (1992). Self-determination and the education of students with mental retardation. *Education & Training in Mental Retardation, 27*, 302–314.

Wehmeyer, M. L. (2002). The confluence of person-centered planning and self-determination. In S. Holburn & P. Vietze (Eds.), *Person-centered planning: Research, practice, and future directions.* Baltimore, MD: Paul H. Brookes.

Wehmeyer, M. L. (2013). *The story of intellectual disability*. Baltimore, MD: Brookes.

Wehmeyer, M. L., Abery, B. H., Mithaug, D. E., & Stanciffe, R. J. (Eds.). (2003). *Theory in self-determination: Foundations for educational practice.* Springfield, IL: Charles C. Thomas.

Wehmeyer, M. L., Lawrence, M., Garner, N., Soukup, J. H., & Palmer, S. (2004). *Whose future is it anyway? A student directed transition planning process* (2nd ed.). Lawrence, KS: Beach Center on Disability, University of Kansas.

Wehmeyer, M. L., Palmer, S. B., Shogren, K. A., Williams-Diehm, K., & Soukup, J. H. (2013). Establishing a causal relationship between intervention to promote self-determination and enhanced student self-determination. *Journal of Special Education, 46*, 195–210. doi:10.1177/0022466910392377

Wei, X., Yu, J. W., & Shaver, D. (2014). Longitudinal effects of ADHD in children with learning disabilities or emotional disturbances. *Exceptional Children, 80*, 205–219.

Weicker, L. P. (1987). A look at policy and its effect on special education and vocational rehabilitation services. *Career Development for Exceptional Individuals, 10*(1), 6–9. doi:10.1177/088572888701000103

Wilcox, B. L., Turnbull, H. R., & Turnbull, A. P. (2000). Behavioral issues and IDEA: Positive behavioral interventions and supports and the functional behavioral assessment in the disciplinary context. *Exceptionality, 8*, 173–187.

Wilkerson, K., Gagnon, J. C., Mason-Williams, L., & Lane, H. B. (2012). Reading instruction for students with high-incidence disabilities in juvenile corrections. *Preventing School Failure, 56*, 219–231. doi:10.1080/1045988X.2011.652698

Will, M. C. (1983). *OSERS programming for the transition of youth with disabilities: Bridges from school to working life.* Washington, DC: Office of Special Education and Rehabilitative Services.

Will, M. C. (1984). *Bridges from school to working life*. Programs for the Handicapped: Clearinghouse on the Handicapped, No. 2, Washington, DC: Department of Education and Office of Special Education and Rehabilitative Services.

Williams, B., & Le Menestrel, S. M. (2013). Social capital and vulnerability from the family, neighborhood, school, and community perspectives. *New Directions for Youth Development, 138*, 97–107. doi:10.1002/yd.20060

Williams, J. L., Tolan, P. H., Durkee, M. I., Francois, A. G., & Anderson, R. E. (2012). Integrating racial and ethnic identity research into developmental understanding of adolescents. *Child Development Perspectives, 6*, 304–311. doi:10.1111/j.1750-8606.2012.00235.x

Wilson, H. (2014). Turning off the school-to-prison pipeline. *Reclaiming Children & Youth, 23*(1), 49–53.

Winch, C. (2000). *Education, work and social capital: Towards a new conception of vocational education*. London, UK: Routledge.

Winkle-Wagner, R. (2010). Foundations of educational inequality: Cultural capital and social reproduction. *ASHE Higher Education Report, 36*(1), 1–128. doi:10.1002/aehe.3601

Winn, M. T., & Behizadeh, N. (2011). The right to be literate: Literacy, education, and the school-to-prison pipeline. *Review of Research in Education, 35*, 147–173.

Yosso, T. J. (2005). Whose culture has capital? A critical race theory discussion of community cultural wealth. *Race, Ethnicity & Education, 8*(1), 69–91. doi:10.1080/1361332052000341006

Yosso, T. J., & García, D. G. (2007). "This is no slum!" *Aztlan, 32*, 145–179.

Youngstrom, E. A., Freeman, A., & McKeown Jenkins, M. (2009). The assessment of children and adolescents with bipolar disorder. *Child and Adolescent Psychiatric Clinics of North America, 18*, 353–390. doi:10.1016/j.chc.2008.12.002

Zablocki, M., & Krezmian, M. (2013). Drop-out predictors among students with high-incidence disabilities: A national longitudinal and transitional study analysis. *Journal of Disability Policy Studies, 21*(1), 53–64. doi:10.1177/1044207311427726

Zionts, L. T., Zionts, P., Harrison, S., & Bellinger, O. (2003). Urban African American families' perceptions of cultural sensitivity within the special education system. *Focus on Autism & Other Developmental Disabilities, 18*(1), 41–50.

Zirkel, P. A. (2010). Manifestation determinations under the new Individuals with Disabilities Education Act: An update. *Remedial and Special Education, 31*, 378–384.

Index

About the Author

Audrey A. Trainor, PhD, is an associate professor of special education in the Department of Teaching and Learning at New York University. The focus of Audrey's work is equitable postschool outcomes for students identified with disabilities, including transitions to postsecondary education, employment, and community engagement for students with learning and socio-emotional difficulties and behavioral challenges. She has conducted numerous qualitative studies with adolescents with disabilities and their families, most often employing grounded theory and ethnographic approaches to interviewing. She has also been a member of research teams for employing mixed research methods including the secondary analyses of nationally representative, longitudinal data and randomized experiments designed to increase transition opportunities for students identified with intellectual and other disabilities.

Audrey also studies the role of research in shaping equitable education opportunities for all students. She uses critical theories to conduct research, examining issues of cultural and linguistic diversity and the culture of special education processes. In her role as university faculty, she teaches courses in teacher preparation and leads her departmental programs in special education. She has also taught graduate courses in qualitative research and data analysis. Audrey received the 2015 Patricia L. Sitlington Research in Transition Award from the Council for Exceptional Children's Division of Career Development and Transition (DCDT). In 2014, she was named the Gershman/Ahler Distinguished Lecturer on Qualitative Research. She served as the 2012–2013 DCDT president. Audrey has authored more than 60 publications, including research articles, books, and chapters. She is a member of the associate editorial boards for the *Journal of Special Education* and *Remedial and Special Education.*

Prior to beginning her career in higher education at the University of Wisconsin, where she researched and taught from 2004–2015. She earned her PhD from the University of Texas at Austin. Audrey was a high school special educator in the state of North Carolina for nearly a decade. Her first teaching position was in Osaka, Japan, as part of the Japan Exchange Teaching Program.